The Politics of Paul Robeson's Othello

The Politics of Paul Robeson's
OTHELLO

❖ ❖ ❖

Lindsey R. Swindall

University Press of Mississippi / *Jackson*

Margaret Walker Alexander Series
in African American Studies

www.upress.state.ms.us

The University Press of Mississippi is a member of
the Association of American University Presses.

Copyright © 2011 by University Press of Mississippi
All rights reserved
Manufactured in the United States of America

First printing 2011

∞

Library of Congress Cataloging-in-Publication Data

Swindall, Lindsey R., 1977–
The politics of Paul Robeson's Othello / Lindsey R. Swindall.
p. cm. — (Margaret Walker Alexander Series in African American Studies)
Includes bibliographical references and index.
ISBN 978-1-60473-824-7 (cloth : alk. paper) —
ISBN 978-1-60473-825-4 (ebook) 1. Robeson, Paul, 1898–1976—Political and social views. 2. African Americans—Biography. 3. Shakespeare, William, 1564–1616. Othello. 4. Shakespeare, William, 1564–1616—Stage history. 5. Othello (Fictitious character) 6. Acting—Political aspects. 7. African American actors. 8. Theater—Political aspects. I. Title.
E185.97.R63S95 2010
782'.0092—dc22

[B]   2010022783

British Library Cataloging-in-Publication Data available

CONTENTS

Acknowledgments vii

Introduction 3

CHAPTER ONE
An Introduction to Shakespeare's *Othello*
11

CHAPTER TWO
Robeson's Professional Debut as Othello
26

CHAPTER THREE
A Burgeoning Political Consciousness: Robeson in the 1930s
50

CHAPTER FOUR
Robeson's Othello on Broadway
69

CHAPTER FIVE
"I Give of My Talents to the People": Robeson's Politics in the 1940s
108

CHAPTER SIX
Robeson, *Othello*, and the Politics of the Cold War
135

CHAPTER SEVEN
Robeson at Stratford
167

Conclusion 190

Notes 195

Sources 219

Index 229

ACKNOWLEDGMENTS

First, I must offer thanks to those supporters who have witnessed this project take shape since its inception: John H. Bracey, Jr., Ernest Allen, Jr., James Smethurst, and Harley Erdman. I hope I have made them proud. Thanks also to Robert Paul Wolff, former director of the Graduate Program in Afro-American Studies at the University of Massachusetts, Amherst, who is always available to answer questions large or small. I am grateful to Arthur Kinney, Carl Nightingale, and Aldon Neilson, who offered input on my work at various stages. I would like to acknowledge the Gilder Lehrman Institute of American History for their research grant which enabled me to delve into several collections in New York City as I began this project. Thanks also to Randall Burkett and the helpful staff in the Special Collections at Emory University's Woodruff Library who awarded me a grant to pursue research in their valuable collections. I appreciated the assistance I received from Joellen Elbashir at the Moorland-Spingarn Research Center at Howard University. Many thanks need to go to the librarians at the Shakespeare Centre in Stratford-upon-Avon who were very prompt in sending materials from the U.K. I'm also appreciative to staff at the Interlibrary Loan office in the W. E. B. Du Bois Library at the University of Massachusetts, Amherst, and the Hamilton Library at Franklin College for ordering materials so efficiently.

I would like to thank my friends and colleagues at Franklin College in Franklin, Indiana, for their encouragement and support as I revised the book manuscript, especially Carolyn Owens, Ralph Guentzel, Simone Pilon, Johanna Moya-Fabregas, Richard Gawthrop, and Kristin Flora. I owe a sincere debt of gratitude to the colleague who read the manuscript for the University Press of Mississippi and offered many insightful critiques. The book is definitely stronger because of her input. Walter Biggins, my editor at University Press, has been extremely helpful through the process of publishing my first book. I would also like to thank Seetha Srinivasan, director emerita of the University Press of Mississippi, with whom I first discussed publishing this project. A special note of thanks is due to two teachers who prodded my writing in its very formative stages: Sandra Pell and Terry Blankenship. Many thanks to friends and family who have provided listening ears, helpful feedback, shoulders upon which to sigh, couches upon which to sleep, as well as much-needed happy hour breaks: Marshall and Lisa Swindall, Lizabeth Foster, H. Edward Foster, Seth Foster, Jennifer Jensen Wallach, Jessica Overstreet, James Buckwalter, David Austin, Katja Meinke, Margaret Burggren, Sarah C. Baron, Alicia and Robb Contreras, and David Ritter. Bright moments to W. S. Tkweme who quite presciently handed me a biography of Paul Robeson some years ago and suggested that I might find this man's life to be of interest.

On a final personal note, I feel, if but in a small way, connected to Paul Robeson's legacy as Othello. As an undergraduate exchange student studying in Warwick, England, for the 1999–2000 school year, I went to just about every Shakespeare production I could afford in Stratford and London. One weekend, a friend and I saw Ray Fearon's portrayal of the Moor of Venice with the Royal Shakespeare Company at the Barbican Theatre. Despite our seats being about as far from the action of the play as possible and the resonating snore of my companion, I was enraptured. Having studied the play in high school and college, I went into the production with a pretty solid idea of what to expect. Yet, the pathos of this revival left me dazed. I vividly recall leaning on the back of the empty seat in front of me trying unsuccessfully to conceal the stream of tears that could not be contained during the cathartic final act of the play. The weight of the tragedy had, for the first time, rendered me emotionally devastated. Afterward, with a tear-smudged face, I staggered to the tube station and felt privileged to have taken part in, what was for me, such a profound artistic encounter.

At that moment, I was clueless that I would spend several years of my life pondering this play, but the seed was sown inside of me as to the magic that can occur on the Shakespearean stage. When I was researching this project, I discovered that Ray Fearon was only the second actor of African descent to play Othello for the Royal Shakespeare Company since Paul Robeson had forty years earlier. Learning this was an epiphany for me since I had been so moved by Fearon's performance. As Paul Robeson was the inheritor of Ira Aldridge's foundational legacy, Fearon was an heir of Robeson. This narrative is all I have to offer as progeny to their gifted artistry. I do so humbly.

The Politics of Paul Robeson's Othello

INTRODUCTION

May 1944 was a tense month in the struggle against fascism. The Allied bombing of Germany continued unabated while clandestine operations for an invasion of France coalesced on the coast of England. As soldiers dutifully followed orders in the European theater of war, artists back in the United States waged a battle of their own. That month, the Entertainment Industry Emergency Committee sponsored a radio program in New York City which was broadcast over the Blue Network. For this half hour, African American tenants of apartments in Harlem and brownstones in Brooklyn could visualize the impact their brothers, sons, and nephews were having in the war effort. Listeners could also conceptualize the importance of conveying that antifascist spirit from the war front back to the home front as they heard artists like Teddy Wilson, Helen Hayes, and Canada Lee assert that "the problem of racial discrimination," like the issue of Hitler's menacing empire building and Hirohito's blatant attack on Hawaii, "is one which we must face and solve." Perhaps the best-known voice on that program was the unmistakable baritone of Paul Robeson. In a dramatic reading the narrator queried Robeson, "And if the Negro pilots of the [Ninety-ninth] Squadron could send a greeting to Abe [Lincoln] what do you think they'd say . . . ?" To which Robeson responded, "You set us marching toward freedom and we're marching with the world." His reply highlighted the vital contribution of African American troops in the war effort. Robeson also pointed out that Hitler did not care much for this squadron because "it upsets his race theories and it upsets a lot of Nazi planes, too."[1]

Robeson's presence at a politically motivated entertainment event was in itself wholly unremarkable. The aims of the committee to counteract "the evil of race antagonism" and ensure "that this war has not been fought in vain" cohered well with his antifascist principles. What was notable about this occasion was that Robeson had rushed so quickly from the Shubert

Theatre, where he was performing nightly in Shakespeare's *Othello*, to the radio studio that he had no time to change out of the flowing robes worn by the Moorish general. Fredi Washington noted in her enthusiastic article in the *People's Voice* newspaper that Robeson's fashion faux pas occurred "much to his embarrassment." What transpired as a minor inconvenience and was probably soon forgotten represented, in retrospect, a potent symbol of the unique fusion between Robeson's artistic career and his political activism. He was, at this time, one of the most recognizable celebrities on the U.S. as well as the world stage. The production of *Othello* in which he was starring got rave reviews and was in the process of playing a record number of shows on Broadway. Robeson's solo vocal concerts were also well known and highly acclaimed.

Significantly, audiences were equally familiar with his stature as a politically engaged artist. Over the course of the war, Robeson helped raise money for war bonds, encouraged support for refugee relief, trumpeted the cause of friendship with the Soviets, and emphasized the need for victory over manifestations of domestic fascism as well as fascism overseas in speeches and appearances across the country. His interpretation of Shakespeare's Moor broke the barrier against African Americans performing that role on Broadway. His noble personification of the character embodied the dignity of the African American community and implicitly argued against the history of discrimination against this minority group. Yet, the visceral merging of Robeson the actor and Robeson the political advocate was never more apparent than at this broadcast when he promoted the cause of racial justice quite literally as Othello. At this moment, more than perhaps any other, the artist and the activist were indistinguishable.

"To Be an Artist Was an Element of the Struggle"

Born in New Jersey in 1898, just two years after the notorious *Plessy v. Ferguson* Supreme Court decision gave legal sanction to segregation, Paul Robeson came of age at a time when the fury of racial discrimination was largely unfettered by federal oversight. As he later reminded audiences at his speeches and readers of his columns, Robeson's father had escaped enslavement in North Carolina, making Paul Robeson just one generation removed from the insidious history of unpaid, forced labor which laid the economic foundation of the United States. Sensing the legal underpinnings of race discrimination at a young age, Robeson astutely observed in his senior thesis at Rutgers University that citizenship protection for African Americans should have been enshrined in the Fourteenth Amendment to the Constitution. However, enforcement of this law had by and large been ignored since the collapse of Reconstruction. He completed a law degree at Columbia University but was thwarted by bigotry in his pursuit of a career in that field.

It was in the 1920s, when the art scene in New York's Harlem was blossoming, that Robeson began taking small stage roles and performed his first recital of African American spirituals. Robeson possessed a distinctive, sonorous baritone, along with a strong background in oratory that was buttressed during his formative years by his father's preaching in the A.M.E. Zion church. Fortified with these natural talents, Robeson, the promising new artist, became a familiar face in the New York cultural scene. By 1930, his career as an actor and vocalist was solidified by roles in plays such as *All God's Chillun Got Wings*, *The Emperor Jones*, and *Show Boat* and by numerous accolades for his concerts. It was via this, somewhat indirect, path that Robeson the Phi Beta Kappa scholar and aspiring attorney came to pursue a successful livelihood in the arts. The acute mind and political insights developed during his education were not abandoned even though he ultimately did not practice law. Rather, as Robeson became increasingly politically active in the 1930s, his activism influenced his art and enriched his stage performances. Similarly, as his stagecraft was honed, the diction and comportment of the artist imparted a singularly performative element to his political appearances.

Intrinsic to Robeson's political principles was the constant struggle to obtain justice and human dignity for African Americans and oppressed people worldwide. The marriage of these principles to Robeson's art was represented, for example, by his conscious decision to concentrate on African American spirituals and folk music from many countries in his vocal programs. Conveying the dignity of people of African descent became central to his theatrical interpretations. Reviews of Robeson, especially from the middle 1940s to the late 1950s, were replete with references to his dignified portrayals. Robeson explained his identification with this cause in an interview in 1958 when his outspoken politics were unwelcomed by cold war reactionaries: "They can shut me up, I'll gladly shut up tomorrow if the poor colored worker is freed of discrimination and can stand up with dignity and be a man."[2] Benjamin Davis, a councilman in New York and friend of Robeson's, connected the cause of dignity directly to Robeson's art that same year: "Mr. Robeson is one of the great artists of our generation

... because he has represented and suffered for a cause which should be dear to all of us—the cause of human dignity."[3] More recently, fellow actor and friend of Robeson's, Ossie Davis, summarized poetically the conflation of Robeson's art and political advocacy: "Paul was an artist and an activist because he saw very clearly that the one equals the other.... With Paul there was no difference. To be an artist was an element of the struggle. To be an artist was to strike a blow with a song, which in his voice and in his hands became a battle axe."[4] Thus, for Robeson, being an artist did not negate or detract from the role one could play in the fight against injustice. He saw no dichotomy which separated the art world from the political realm. Throughout his career he endeavored to conjoin these two binaries and in doing so left a legacy of artistic work that represented a unique fusion of art that reflected issues in contemporary politics.

To be sure, Robeson's politics were not always readily apparent in every play, or especially film, in which he starred. Looking at his early work in particular, one sees, for instance, a mixed heritage of imperialistic jingoism (as in *Sanders of the River*), a misguided and paranoid black leader (*The Emperor Jones*), and a stereotypical hallelujah-singing sharecropper (*Tales of Manhattan*). However, one must take into account the full scope of Robeson's work, including his politically induced decisions offstage, when assessing individual pieces such as these. For example, he denounced *Sanders of the River* and took a hiatus from acting in movies in the late 1930s because of his frustration with the demeaning portrayals of people of African descent in that medium. His interpretation of Toussaint L'Ouverture in 1936 in a politically inspired play written by a black author, C. L. R. James, offered a heroic black lead which countered the psychological descent into madness emphasized in Eugene O'Neill's Brutus Jones. *Tales of Manhattan* precipitated Robeson's final departure from the film industry because he saw little progress away from the traditional denigrating images of people of color. Thus, the growth of his political consciousness swayed the direction of Robeson's artistic career. Perhaps nowhere was this evolution toward becoming a politically motivated artist more evident than in the history of Robeson's three portrayals of Shakespeare's Othello.

Trinidadian intellectual C. L. R. James once penned in one of his letters to literary critics that "Shakespeare's characters are an embodiment of the assault upon the ordered conception of the medieval world...."[5] Writing during the European Renaissance, England's great playwright relentlessly questioned the political and social assumptions of the previous era by crafting nuanced and multifaceted roles that personified the new intellectualism of his time. *Othello*, for example, represented a rumination on the idea of blackness, which often symbolized evil in Elizabethan England. However, Shakespeare's Moorish character, though he was dark-skinned, was not the villain of the play but was a casualty in the tragedy. James's idea can also be applied to Robeson's rendering of the Moor of Venice. His Othello represented an assault on the previous conceptions of Othello as well as on the ordered notion of the racially segregated theater house. In 1930, Robeson was the first actor of African descent to portray Othello in London since Ira Aldridge in the mid-nineteenth century. The idea of a dark-skinned Othello was not universally accepted, so Robeson wrote articles and sat for interviews where he persuasively argued in favor of an African depiction of Shakespeare's character. In the middle 1940s, Robeson was the first African American to play Othello on Broadway, which was a historic accomplishment. However, Robeson took the issue of theater desegregation an unprecedented step further by insisting that the troupe would not perform to segregated audiences on the seven-month U.S. tour. Robeson, as a reporter for *The Worker* shrewdly pointed out, had pioneered the cause of dignity for the theater audience by refusing to subject them to racial segregation.[6] Finally, Robeson returned to the role of Othello for the 1959 Stratford festival. The nearly overwhelming reception for this performance, while probably not his best due to ill health, flew in the face of cold war repression by demonstrating the adulation which audiences abroad maintained for Robeson's triumph over his unconstitutional eight-year confinement in the United States. Thus, Robeson's Othello portrayals underscored the dignity of an African individual onstage and illustrated the amalgamation of his politics with his artistic career.

What Is the Role of the Artist in Times of Crisis?

The development of Robeson's maturity as a politically minded artist, as depicted through the three *Othello* productions, can also explicate the broader issue of the role of the artist in times of crisis. He intuitively recognized, as Susan Curtis has pointed out, that "cultural victories ring hollow when they are not accompanied by social and economic improvement."[7] Robeson not only fervently believed but tangibly exhibited through his life's work that political engagement was an inherent component of the role of the artist in society. He articulated this commitment in one of his most well-known speeches in 1937 during the critical moment of the Spanish civil war when he publicly avowed his antifascism and called on others to join the struggle. In this speech he explained that the artist had a distinctive role in fighting fascism because it "fights to destroy the culture which society has created. . . ." Fascism "makes no distinction between combatants and noncombatants." As a result, "the true artist cannot hold himself aloof." Robeson stressed the urgency of the situation, "The legacy of culture from our predecessors is in danger. . . . It belongs not only to us . . . it belongs to posterity—and must be defended to the death." Thus, it was vital to rally "every artist" and "every writer . . . who loves democracy" to join the battle.[8]

Robeson's defiant posture against fascism was prompted not only by the political threat of this authoritarian movement but also because the cultural legacy, the art of Western society was in jeopardy. Fascism sought to destroy political opposition as well as the organic, indigenous culture of the people. The art forms that blossomed out of the daily lives of the folk and sustained generations through their lively words, song, and life force could be destroyed. The only place for the artist, then, was to stand on the side of freedom, to be on the front lines to prevent such a disaster. Freedom, for Robeson, meant not solely political freedom and protection of civil rights but also artistic freedom and the freedom to pursue his livelihood.

Robeson's public pronouncement of his political principles came in the late 1930s as fascist clouds were gathering across Spain, Italy, and Germany. Because he spent much of that decade living in England, he had witnessed firsthand the coalitions built to counter this political force as they were taking shape. It was against this backdrop that Robeson's political awareness ripened and began to more overtly meld with his stage career. By the 1940s, when the United States was jolted out of its isolationism and began mobilizing, Robeson's antifascism was already firmly rooted and remained entrenched throughout the war. As the Second World War wound down and anticommunist reactionism began to prevail, Robeson's stance against fascism persisted. In the climate of the cold war, he spoke against the neofascist constituents in the United States that disregarded constitutional civil rights as well as sovereignty rights for colonized people arund the world. Thus, Robeson's antifascist perspective endured from the 1930s through the late 1950s whether the specter of fascism loomed over Europe or reared its head from the right wing of the U.S. government. As an artist, Robeson responded to political crises that were specific to the historical circumstances: the spread of fascism across Europe, the Second World War, full citizenship for African Americans, independence for European colonies, especially in Africa, and peace with the Soviet Union after the war.

Robeson's three productions of *Othello* occurred at pivotal moments in his career that reflected both the particular historical setting and his response to the political climate. Because of this unique positioning, the *Othello* productions act as guideposts which signal the transformation in Robeson's art as he became a consciously devoted, politically minded performer. Each of the *Othello* productions illuminated key ingredients in Robeson's artistic development. In addition, the time frame in which these revivals were produced shed light on fundamental aspects of his political life and the historical events which informed his politics. Analyzing these theater productions, or any of Robeson's work, in the absence of the political context would neglect the basis of Robeson's approach to art as a socially conscious endeavor. Using the *Othello* productions as a framework, this study will examine each of these revivals and the corresponding historical milieu as a means to elucidate the way in which an artist can perform in a politically charged environment should s/he choose to engage and respond to contemporary issues. Concurrently, this narrative inherently speaks to the pressure that society was capable of exerting on an artist who challenged mainstream political assumptions in an outspoken manner. Should an artist relent when government and social pressures endanger the artist's ability to practice his or her livelihood? For Robeson, the answer was a resounding and inspiring "no." The shifting political climate impacted and, at times, devastated Robeson's artistic career, but once he had committed to wedding his creative life, his means of making a living, with his political principles, that would be the enduring position from which he stood, as the resolute title of his memoir, *Here I Stand*, affirmed.

This exploration begins by introducing Shakespeare's play in the first chapter and offering an overview of important precedents, from Britain, the U.S. and the African American community, to Robeson's portrayal of the Moor of Venice. To provide context for Robeson's artistry, this chapter also looks at Shakespeare in the African American community and the importance of the black oratorical tradition to Robeson's acting methodology. Chapter two then closely examines Robeson's first portrayal of Othello in London in 1930, including the critical reception of the play and the obstacles that inhibited this from being a successful production overall. This experience was crucial to Robeson's growth as an artist and the development of his cultural theory. The next chapter, three, delves into Robeson's writing on culture as it blossomed in the 1930s. This decade was decisive in the maturation of his political thinking and was the key moment when his politics began to conjoin with his art. This progress is explored through fundamental events, including Robeson's portrayal of Toussaint L'Ouverture, his published writing on African culture, and his visit to the front of the Spanish civil war.

Chapter four analyzes the significance of Robeson's historic portrayal of Othello on the Broadway stage during World War II. The importance of this revival was embedded not only in the conscious decision to cast a black actor in the lead role but, moreover, that it responded to both the wartime context and the issue of segregation in the theater setting. The following chapter, five, discusses the blurring line between Robeson the artist and Robeson the activist in the 1940s. During this time, his political activities added depth to his Othello interpretation, while his political involvement can be conceptualized as performance outside of the formal theater. In all arenas, he advocated against fascism and for the dignity of the African American community. The ways in which Robeson utilized creative performative strategies to circumvent his confinement in the United States during the early cold war is dealt with in chapter six. Despite persistent government repression, Robeson maintained his internationalist antifascist analysis which emphasized civil rights for African Americans and self-determination for Africans. The final monologue of Othello remained prominent in his cold war repertoire, reflecting the importance of that role in his artistic legacy and the capricious passport ban which prevented him from again donning Othello's robes onstage.

Finally, chapter seven explores Robeson's third portrayal of Shakespeare's Moor in Stratford-upon-Avon in 1959. This triumphant moment recalled the pinnacle of Robeson's career, the Broadway *Othello*, while symbolizing his victory over the State Department's unconstitutional withholding of his right to travel overseas. This revival afforded audiences abroad the opportunity to affirm their support for him as both an artist and a citizen of great courage who had stood steadfastly against government suppression and emerged with his dignity intact. Significantly, this production occurred at a moment when cold war repression was ceding slightly, and independence for Africans, for which Robeson had so zealously advocated, seemed momentarily hopeful.

Robeson's path toward becoming a politically motivated artist encompassed some of the most weighty and controversial historical events of the mid-twentieth century. Yet, the true starting point on this journey must be much earlier, near the dawn of the seventeenth century, when England's most revered playwright sat down to pen a drama about a Moor in Venice.

CHAPTER ONE

An Introduction to Shakespeare's *Othello*

Most scholars agree that Shakespeare's *Othello* was written between 1603 and 1604, with its first recorded performance being staged in 1604. The King's Men, the company with which Shakespeare was affiliated, produced *Othello* on the first of November. King James had recently ascended to the English throne upon the death of Queen Elizabeth the prior year. It was, thus, a time of political transition in Britain. Times were also evolving for Shakespeare, whose company had previously been designated as The Lord Chamberlain's Men.[1] As with many of Shakespeare's plays, the plot of *Othello* was not original. In this case, it was loosely based on a tale in the *Hecatommithi*, a collection written by the Italian novelist and poet Cinthio (1504–1573) that dated from the mid-1560s. Lois Potter observed in her stage history that when *Othello* debuted, it was one of several plays on the contemporary stage that explored domestic themes. Also appearing in repertoire at this time were Shakespeare's *The Merry Wives of Windsor*, *Measure for Measure*, and *The Comedy of Errors*.[2] Perhaps Shakespeare did not feel that political commentary was appropriate during the shift from the stability of Queen Elizabeth's lengthy reign to a new monarch. Thus, *Othello* was one of Shakespeare's tragedies in which the question of governmental leadership was not thematically explicit. In this work, the Venetian Senate was firmly grounded and the authority of the Duke was unquestioned.

It can be argued that *Othello* was Shakespeare's chief exploration into the notion of racial difference. He wrote very few characters of African descent, the other primary character being Aaron the Moor in *Titus Andronicus*, although one of the suitors in *The Merchant of Venice* was also dark skinned. One might quickly characterize Aaron the Moor and Othello as embodying two basic stereotypes: the noble civilized Moor (Othello) and the savage African (Aaron). However, *Othello* was still a play that relied heavily on the racist assumptions of the day, particularly that Africans were prone to jealousy, gullibility, and inexplicable fits of passion or rage (as in Othello's epilepsy). At the time Shakespeare was writing, England was on the brink of colonial expansion and involvement with the trans-Atlantic slave trade. For example, the King James translation of the Bible would soon be distributed to many dark-skinned foreigners in an attempt to transform their perceived heathenism. Likewise, Othello had been converted to Christianity prior to commanding the Venetian armed forces. While Shakespeare did manipulate certain racial images, ultimately his work was a product of the protoimperialistic society in which he lived.

The idea of race in Shakespeare has been hotly contested over the centuries. Just as Shakespeare's writing reflected the perceptions of race in the early 1600s, the commentary on race in *Othello* necessarily has mirrored the perception of race at the historical moment in which the critic was writing. For example, British author and literary critic Samuel Taylor Coleridge postulated in 1822 that Othello "must not be conceived as a negro" because he displayed too much virtue for such a base characterization.[3] Coleridge's analysis remained influential for some time, for he was cited by a number of the critics who reviewed Robeson's 1930 performance of Othello in London. John Quincy Adams, writing during the U.S. civil war in 1863, was very critical of Desdemona as a woman who had sinned against nature in her love for the Moor. The idea of interracial marriage was anathema even to a northern opponent of slavery. He argued, "The great moral lesson of the tragedy of *Othello* is, that black and white blood cannot be intermingled in marriage without a gross outrage upon the Law of Nature. . . ."[4] William Winter, an influential American critic at the turn of the twentieth century when segregation laws were proliferating, praised actor Edmund Kean's decision to play Othello with lighter "tawny" makeup as opposed to black. He posited, "To take a cue from such expressions in the text as 'thick lips' and 'Barbary horse,' and make *Othello* a Negro, is, necessarily, to lower the tone of the interpretation."[5] The term "barbary" was an Elizabethan euphemism for barbarous and was used to reference people or places in Africa. In this passage, Winter argued against a dark-skinned Othello on the basis that most of the passages that refer to Othello as black were insults. Thus, they should not be taken literally. He did not, however, acknowledge the Duke's reference to Othello as black at the end of act I, scene 3 when the allusion to Othello's skin color was not an epithet but a compliment. Overall, Winter seemed to suggest that drama simply was not as tragic if it occurred to someone with dark skin.

On the other hand, more recent criticism offered new analyses. With the advent of postcolonial theory and cultural studies, Shakespeare's Moor has been reinvestigated. For example, Ania Loomba, in *Shakespeare, Race and Colonialism,* pointed out that as a dark-skinned character created by a British author and primarily interpreted by white actors "Othello remains trapped within a white view of Moors."[6] In her article "Casting Black Actors: Beyond Othellophilia," Celia R. Daileader worried that dark-skinned actors, even if given other roles early in their careers, were "being groomed for one role alone."[7] Similarly, Robeson longed to undertake Shakespeare's other great tragic heroes, but, unfortunately, no one will ever know what power Robeson as King Lear or Robeson as Macbeth might have achieved. These few examples illustrate that perceptions of race have evolved over the centuries according to the sociopolitical context. In the United States, the modern social construction of race has stemmed from the history of the trans-Atlantic slave trade and the implications of subjugating people of African origin as slave laborers for around two hundred and fifty years. The idea of racial inferiority grew out of the development of the early capitalist system and its need for vast quantities of workers in order to turn immense profits from the tobacco and rice plantations of British North America. Still, because colonial expansion was just taking shape during Shakespeare's time, delineating exactly what he meant by crafting a noble Moorish character can be relentlessly debated. Did he challenge the burgeoning racist stereotypes of the day? Or did Shakespeare simply modify the existing attributes of African foreigners? Was Othello a noble character at all? One question, however, can clearly be addressed: did Shakespeare write Othello as a black character? Without a doubt, he did. In addition to the textual references to Othello's skin tone, in Shakespeare's day Othello was portrayed onstage by an actor wearing dark makeup. Nevertheless, the idea of whether Othello was a black character has often been challenged as by critics such as William Winter. This issue was still prominent in the 1930 commentary on Robeson's first portrayal of the Moor.

How then might Shakespeare have been inspired to create a Moorish hero? There was interaction between Britain and the "dark continent" in the late 1500s and early 1600s. Trade networks were being established by

British ship captains at this time, and with John Hawkins's trade of three hundred slaves around 1562 the British officially entered the African slave trade.[8] In 1600, a diplomatic envoy from Morocco visited London and stayed for six months to consider a joint venture against Spain.[9] A portrait of this Moroccan ambassador was painted for Queen Elizabeth, and it represented what Shakespeare and his contemporaries might have perceived as a Moor of status.[10] Moreover, one of the most popular travelogues of Shakespeare's day was an account of tropical Africa from 1526 written by a man who was converted from Islam to Christianity (as was Othello), had traveled extensively through Africa, and finally settled in Italy.[11] This piece, *A Geographical Historie of Africa* by John Leo Africanus, was translated into English about four years before *Othello* was written and emphasized the African propensities toward jealousy and fits of passion that also appear in Shakespeare's text.[12]

Othello was portrayed with dark makeup from the earliest production when Richard Burbage (a friend of Shakespeare's for whom he wrote the part) played the Moor of Venice. This was the theatrical tradition until around 1812 when American actor Edmund Kean changed his makeup to a lighter tawny color. Marvin Rosenberg, in his seminal history *The Masks of Othello*, noted that this change corresponded with the entrenchment of plantation slavery in the United States. He contended that Burbage probably "played Othello black, rather than tawny, for this was the theatre tradition . . . until widespread Negro slavery. Othello changed to 'tawny' in the 1800's to free the role from the unfortunate connotations borne by that growing social evil. . . ."[13] Actors in the nineteenth century, then, wished to distance noble Othello from the debased characteristics that would be implied were he portrayed as a black man. By this time, ideas of racial inferiority were rooted in the social and political culture of the United States, whose economy was increasingly dependent on slave-grown cotton. Additionally, a study of the artistic renderings of *Othello* concluded that the Moor was depicted as black from 1760 to 1804.[14] This article corroborated the argument that representations of Othello changed from dark to tawny in the early nineteenth century.

A black activist and follower of Marcus Garvey, John Edward Bruce, published a slim volume in 1920, just ten years before Robeson's first Othello, which commented on the question of Othello's color. In it, he assailed the racism implicit in the trend toward a tawny Othello: "Modern tragedians in America and Europe who have essayed the role of Othello have bowed to the popular prejudice and portrayed the character as that of a white man or a man of tawny complexion."[15] It was Ira Aldridge, on the British stage, and later Robeson, in both Britain and the United States, who ushered a dark-skinned Moor back to the spotlight. Robeson, who was definitely versed in Shakespearean history, was well aware of the stage tradition. He remarked in an interview in 1930 that "in Shakespeare's own time and through the Restoration, notably by Garrick, the part was played [as] a black man. It is not changed until the time of Edmund Kean. . . . I feel that had to do with the fact that at that time Africa was the slave center of the world and people had . . . forgotten the ancient glory of the Ethiopian."[16] "It may finally be said," scholar Mythili Kaul pronounced, "that if Kean banished the black Othello from the stage, Robeson . . . succeeded in bringing him right back."[17]

It should also be mentioned that Shakespeare clearly alluded to Othello's skin color in the text. There were several references to Othello's skin tone, some of which were epithets uttered by Iago against the Moor. Interestingly, the term "black" was also used in Elizabethan English to connote something unholy or sinful (as in "black devil"). Shakespeare was manipulating this stereotype by creating a protagonist who was actually dark skinned but was *not* the primary villain. Shakespeare's Moor in *Titus Andronicus* (written about ten years before *Othello)*, Aaron, illustrated the more common archetype of a black character who was also villainous. Othello's temperament, on the other hand, was not so clear cut. He had virtuous qualities but fell prey to jealousy, gullibility, and Iago's machinations. Conversely, the amoral but non-African Iago was a much "blacker" character than Othello as a vision of evil. Yet, it was Othello's literal blackness that separated him from Desdemona's Venetian society. It was this sense of foreignness that accentuated Othello's misgivings which Iago, in turn, ruthlessly exploited. Thus, the color "black" often has a dual meaning in *Othello*, especially when invoked by Iago, which helped to illuminate Shakespeare's multilayered exploration of the theme of blackness.

The following quotations are examples of Shakespeare's references to Othello's color in the text. The first examples were racist insults. In act I, scene 1, Iago yelled up to Brabantio's window in the dead of the night, "Even now, now, very now, an old black ram / Is tupping your white ewe." During that same exchange, Iago referred to Othello as a "Barbary horse." In the following scene, Brabantio accosted Othello concerning his secret marriage to Desdemona and inquired why she would "Run from her guardage to the sooty bosom / Of such a thing as thou. . . ." On the other hand, near the close of act I, scene 3, the Duke pointed out to Brabantio that "If virtue no delighted beauty lack, / Your son-in-law is far more fair than black." In this instance, Shakespeare revealed that even though Othello was black skinned, he was still honorable. Later, in act III, scene 3, Iago has been poisoning Othello's mind with thoughts of Desdemona's infidelity. Othello deprecated his own lack of Venetian social mores: "Haply, for I am black / And have not those soft parts of conversation / That chamberers have...." Here, Shakespeare again played with the notion of blackness on several levels. For the phrase to be most effective, it would be uttered by a dark Othello who was disdainful of his skin color, which was the most obvious signifier of his cultural foreignness. Othello wondered whether he might have been more adept at maintaining Desdemona's love had he not been a black foreigner.

The nature of Shakespeare's fast-paced drama further necessitated a dark-skinned title character. The Bard set up Othello to betray and murder his wife in roughly six scenes. The only way this can be even remotely viable was if a radical effort was made to position Othello as an outsider to Desdemona's courtly Venetian society. The juxtaposition between the young, chaste, white Desdemona and the older, militaristic, dark-skinned Othello was paramount for the plot to work. Without these elements in place, the play had no hope of capturing the audience. This fact was not lost on several of the critics who wrote about Robeson's portrayal of Othello on Broadway. For instance, Rudolph Elie, Jr., wrote in *Variety*, "It was also the first time in modern times that the incredibly powerful tale . . . ever made sense."[18] The reviewer for *The Christian* stressed, "The use of a Negro actor . . . underlines the sense of division between him and the Venetians and lends credibility to the intensity of his passions."[19] Thus, a number of reviewers had an epiphany when they saw Robeson's dark-skinned Othello, because it was the first time they felt the plot had ever succeeded.

Major Portrayals of Othello Prior to Robeson

After its debut in 1604, *Othello* became "perhaps *the* leading tragedy of the early 1600's."[20] The play was produced in New York as early as the 1750s when Lewis Hallum's company performed it as part of their repertoire while visiting from London. Moreover, *Othello* was one of the established Shakespearean pieces produced in America continuously between the Revolutionary War and the War of 1812.[21] Spranger Barry was "the eighteenth century's most popular Othello" in London and played the Moor in "an upward, triumphal progression through extremes of beautifully expressed emotion, rather than a descent into brutality, diseased imagination, and self-loathing."[22]

Several of the memorable Othellos from the early nineteenth century included Edmund Kean, William Charles Macready, and Junius Brutus Booth. Edwin Forrest was also a favorite who emphasized Othello's physical prowess and was said to be a "distinctly American" Othello.[23] Charles Macready, though he displayed impeccable Victorian mores in his private life, was Forrest's "violent and animal-like" British rival. In fact, fans of Forrest actually rioted outside of the Astor Place Opera House in New York when Macready played Othello there in 1849.[24] As one could imagine, the Astor Place riot became a landmark event in American theater history. Junius Brutus Booth had several sons who also became actors, including Edwin and John Wilkes. John Wilkes Booth was known for his erratic behavior, and it was said that his Othello would once have actually smothered the actress playing Desdemona had he not been thwarted by concerned actors rushing in from the wings.[25] Nevertheless, John Wilkes Booth was probably better remembered in the history books as the assassin of Abraham Lincoln, his unsuccessful near-suffocation of a vulnerable Desdemona notwithstanding. Yet, it was Edmund Kean who defied the stage tradition on two important fronts. He was short and known for his incessant movement, whereas Othello had traditionally been portrayed with an imposing physical presence.[26] Additionally, Kean altered Othello's complexion to a lighter tawny rather than a darker black. To assume that all actors followed Kean's lead would probably be an oversimplification of the complex interplay between race and stagecraft.[27] However, according to Lois Potter's stage history, "his choice influenced many nineteenth century actors."[28] Robeson's Othello followed the earlier tradition, before Kean, of a dark-skinned Moor who was not inclined to move about the stage a great deal but relied more on the impact of his towering physical frame.

Probably the most notable Othello from the late nineteenth century was Italian Tommaso Salvini. He toured Britain and the United States in the mid-1870s and introduced a new, more brutal Othello to audiences. Salvini was viewed as exotic to the Anglo-Saxon audience for his passionate acting technique and his insistence on playing Shakespeare in Italian.[29] Constantin Stanislavsky described Salvini's performance as vividly depicting Othello's descent from "the heights of bliss to the depths of destructive passion."[30] Interestingly, Salvini maintained that Desdemona's murder should be obscured from the audience behind the bed curtain while he juxtaposed Othello's suicide with "extreme exhibitionism."[31] Salvini's onstage passion was often attributed to his Mediterranean heritage. Thus, he offered a marked contrast to the Anglo-Saxon Victorian tradition of Othello as portrayed by his contemporaries.

In addition, the U.S. minstrel tradition of *Othello* needs to be acknowledged. Shakespeare was more available to the masses in the early to middle nineteenth century partly because his works were portrayed not only in formal theaters but also in a variety of venues from inns to makeshift stages in the countryside. Furthermore, his plays were frequently satirized in vaudeville and burlesque shows. Lawrence Levine commented on the ubiquity of Shakespeare during this century: "The significance of the national penchant for parodying Shakespeare is clear: Shakespeare and his drama had become by the nineteenth century an integral part of American culture."[32] This is particularly relevant to an examination of the stage history of *Othello* because of the link between the popularity of this play in the United States and the blackface stage tradition of the nineteenth century. A recent study of Shakespeare in the United States from 1835 to 1875 argued, "A connection between Othello and minstrelsy . . . suggests strongly that audiences were looking at the two in the same way [for] . . . a comical, at times even buffoon-like, or crazed Othello seems to mark both types of performances in the period."[33] Because Shakespeare was not relegated solely to refined theaters for the upper classes, Othello was widely interpreted in a variety of forums.

Various incarnations of Othello, such as *Desdemonum* and *O-Thello and Dar's-de-Money*, appeared on the minstrel stage. They featured themes from *Othello* (jealousy, miscegenation, misogyny) presented in a shortened framework (sometimes just a scene or two) and, occasionally, painted Desdemona in blackface as well as Othello. Presenting Othello's spouse in blackface might have been a reference to the contemporary fear that a white woman who married a black man would soon appear to be black.[34] There was but a fine line between *Othello* as presented in the formal theater and on the minstrel stage, for many of the great Othellos of the theater (like Macready, Kean, and especially Salvini) emphasized the Moor's savage characteristics.[35] Thus, Robeson's assumption of the role in the twentieth century, accentuating Othello's dignity as a dark-skinned actor, defied a multifaceted tradition of racism that spanned not only the formal theater but the minstrel stage as well.

The changing attitude in the United States toward Shakespeare and the theater by the late nineteenth century should also be noted to contextualize Robeson's impact on the stage history of *Othello*. As early as the 1880s,

Shakespeare was becoming entertainment for the elite rather than popular amusement enjoyed by all classes as it had been earlier in the century. Lawrence Levine documented the trajectory of this shift in his book *The Unpredictable Past*. Levine postulated that during the late nineteenth century "cultural space became more sharply defined, more circumscribed, and less fluid than it had been."[36] He maintained that knowledge of Shakespeare's texts was widespread in the early 1800s as depicted comically by Mark Twain's roguish characters, the duke and the king, in *Huckleberry Finn*. In this novel, two lower-class hucksters misquote a soliloquy of Hamlet's, and Twain relied on the audience's intimacy with Shakespeare for the punch line.[37] Levine contended this would probably not be possible by the turn of the twentieth century once Shakespeare was increasingly reserved for the upper echelons of society in the "proper" theater. He explained, "If Shakespeare had been an integral part of mainstream culture in the nineteenth century, in the twentieth he had become part of 'polite' culture—an essential ingredient in a complex we call, significantly, 'legitimate' theater."[38] However, there were efforts to reverse this cultural shift in the twentieth century.

By the Popular Front era of the 1930s and early 1940s, New Deal liberalism sparked a movement which aimed, in part, to make theater more accessible to the masses. For example, numerous productions of Shakespeare were funded through the Works Progress Administration's Federal Theatre Project (FTP), including Orson Welles's experimental all-black production of *Macbeth* in 1936. Additionally, one of the aims of the FTP was to "bring the theatre to the people by making the shows free to the public and by introducing theatre to localities outside urban centers."[39] In the spirit of the Popular Front, the Broadway *Othello* starring Robeson in the early 1940s appealed to and was supported by diverse audiences during its extended run from the summer premiere in 1942 to through the U.S. tour in 1944–45. These shows were often sold out or standing room only. Critics noticed the unique assemblage of people who attended these shows. Because of Robeson's unique charisma and activism, he was beloved across class lines, and people of all strata and colors flocked to see his *Othello*. For example, on the West Coast, in Los Angeles and San Francisco, special showings of *Othello* were sponsored by trade unions and a black advocacy group, the Council on African Affairs. Margaret Webster's theory of directing was focused on the idea that Shakespeare should not be relegated to the dusty shelves of a library. Her production was intentionally slimmed down and sped up to be more accessible to wide-ranging audiences. But it was the combination of Robeson's persona and his activist ties that enabled the

Broadway *Othello* to reach an audience far more vast and diverse than the average "legitimate" Shakespearean production.

African Americans, Shakespeare, and Oratory

A mythology of sorts has grown around Paul Robeson's legacy as the first African American to play Othello on the professional stage. To be sure, he was the first African American to portray Othello on Broadway. Yet, there was a history of African Americans who had played Shakespeare's Moor prior to Robeson, the most notable of these being Ira Aldridge. Aldridge, the "African Roscius" as he was known, never played the role in the United States but achieved great fame in Britain and Russia. He was dubbed the "African Roscius" after Roscius, who was a Roman actor born into slavery and praised for his stagecraft. There were other predecessors to Robeson's Othello who are worth mentioning, for they illustrate the prominence of the Bard in the African American community and the tenacity of actors who produced Shakespeare under circumstances when black actors were rarely perceived as serious artists of merit. Thus, while Robeson's preeminence in the stage history of *Othello* cannot be disputed, his performance was not completely without precedent.

Errol Hill's monograph *Shakespeare in Sable* is an essential text for anyone examining African Americans in Shakespeare. He observed that there was little space for a committed black actor on the American stage, particularly in the nineteenth and early twentieth centuries. Some actors, such as Samuel Morgan Smith, who was born in the United States in the nineteenth century, followed in the footsteps of Aldridge and eventually migrated to England to pursue an acting career. This was due to the fact that in the United States no black actors were accepted by legitimate white companies in the 1800s.[40] Although rare, black companies did exist, such as the short-lived group headed by actor James Hewlett, which performed at William Alexander Brown's African Theatre in New York. Their opening performance in September 1821 was a revival of Shakespeare's *Richard III*. Due to harassment, finding a permanent home for the acting troupe was problematic.

The African Theatre endured for only three season, but they produced at least ten productions. Of those, two were plays by Shakespeare (*Richard III* and *Othello*), and two other productions included scenes from *Macbeth*, *Julius Caesar*, and possibly *Romeo and Juliet*. The emphasis on

Shakespeare in the African Theatre's repertoire underscored his popularity in the United States during the nineteenth century. Hill further characterized Shakespeare's status among African Americans: "Indeed, stagestruck youths and adults from the city's black community would frequent the segregated upper gallery of the Park Theatre [New York's leading playhouse] to keenly observe the manner in which these admired English stage veterans presented Shakespeare's heroes."[41] It was no surprise, then, that the African Theatre offered their own interpretations of Shakespeare for the few seasons they were operational.

By the late nineteenth century, following Emancipation and Reconstruction, according to Hill there was a "marked increase in dramatic activity among African Americans." Shakespeare remained esteemed during this period also. In the 1880s, the decade prior to Robeson's birth, Hill counted eighty-six recorded productions by African American troupes, and about one-third of those were Shakespearean plays.[42] In the early twentieth century, Shakespeare's plays were being mounted by students at Historically Black Colleges and Universities (HBCUs). For example, from 1905 to 1910, with the exception of 1909, students at Atlanta University put on a play by Shakespeare every year under the direction of Adrienne McNeil Herndon.[43] The reputation of the students must have been growing, for *The Crisis*, the journal of the National Association for the Advancement of Colored People (NAACP), ran a two-page photo spread of their 1912 revival of *Twelfth Night*.[44]

From 1915 to 1932, the Lafayette Players worked out of the Lafayette Theatre in New York City's predominantly African American Harlem neighborhood. This group has been described as "the first major professional Black dramatic company in America."[45] Even though the Lafayette Players did not produce Shakespeare themselves, the theater hosted *The Comedy of Errors* and *The Taming of the Shrew* in 1923. It was probably the success of the Lafayette Players, moreover, that led Edward Sterling Wright to stage his notable revival of *Othello* at the Lafayette Theatre.[46] This all-black production was mounted in 1916, about three years before Robeson moved to Harlem. Wright's *Othello* was performed in both New York and Boston for the tercentenary anniversary of Shakespeare's death. Many theater goers were excited or at least curious to see the cast of black actors, for the *New York Times* commented that an audience of fifteen hundred packed the house for the first night of this novel *Othello*.[47] When the production went north to Boston, the *Herald* also lauded Wright, who "shines by comparison with some of [his] predecessors who had to stain their faces to meet

[the] requirements of [the] part."[48] In addition, this successful production was praised by none other than Sir Herbert Beerbohm Tree, an eminent British tragedian, who was the guest of honor at an opening performance. He personally praised Wright, who played Othello, and the entire cast: "All the people of every clime, complexion, and degree are taking part in these celebrations and it would be, I am sure, a pride to Shakespeare himself to know that his works were being played by your people."[49] That was no small praise coming from Sir Tree, who helped found the Royal Academy of Dramatic Art and had played many of Shakespeare's memorable characters.

It was indisputably Ira Aldridge, however, who achieved the greatest stature of any African American stage actor prior to Robeson. Aldridge was born in the United States in the early nineteenth century. The obstacles for an actor with aspirations of tackling serious stage work were immense at that time. Aldridge decided to pursue his career abroad and departed for Britain in 1824. It was in England and on tour across Europe and Russia that Aldridge established his Shakespearean repertoire. He performed over forty roles, including Othello, the noble Moor, as well as Shakespeare's villainous Moor, Aaron from *Titus Andronicus. The Standard* newspaper critic asserted, prior to seeing Aldridge, that, as a contemporary of such renowned actors as Edmund Kean, it was "most hazardous" for him to take on the role of Othello beneath the shadow of these forerunners. Yet, following the 1833 performance, the reporter applauded Aldridge, saying that "the result showed that the African Roscius was fully justified in making the bold attempt."[50] A skeptical *Times* reviewer in London found his accent "unimpressive" but had to admit that "Mr. Aldridge was extremely well received" by the audience.[51]

Aldridge, remarkably, accomplished a feat that few black actors, including Robeson, have ever achieved. Despite some notable exceptions, such as Ray Fearon's Romeo with the Royal Shakespeare Company in 1997, black actors today still struggle with typecasting based on skin color. However, Aldridge successfully portrayed Shakespearean characters that were not written specifically as black roles. Aldridge embodied, for example, King Lear, Macbeth, Hamlet, Richard III, and Shylock. He also received numerous awards and medals for his artistry. Therefore, Aldridge was noteworthy in the stage history of Shakespeare as the first major African American talent. Errol Hill took the praise for Aldridge further, asserting that he was "the most accomplished American actor in nineteenth-century England and Europe and one of the finest Shakespearean interpreters of all time."[52]

Many reviewers placed Paul Robeson's Othello firmly within the lineage of Aldridge's portrayal. Indeed, in 1930, Robeson was the first actor of color to play Othello in London since Aldridge. Robeson was fully cognizant of the torch being passed to his generation. Aldridge's youngest daughter, Amanda, an accomplished vocalist, was living in London in the 1930s and had given Robeson voice lessons. Just prior to Robeson's debut, Amanda bestowed on him the gold earrings worn by her father onstage as Othello. Thus, Robeson was a direct descendant of the tradition of Ira Aldridge, who also spent much of his life abroad and was beloved in Russia and throughout Europe. More important, Robeson was fully conscious of this vital lineage.

Robeson was an inheritor of another important cultural legacy in the African American community: the elocutionary tradition. The art of speech making was tied closely to the African American church but was also connected to reciting Shakespeare. Errol Hill and James Hatch have argued that drama was often frowned upon by the black church in the late nineteenth century. Yet, they point out that "future ministers and teachers studied rhetoric and elocution, which included Greek and Roman orators. The art of declamation, with its rhetorical flourishes, led to the recitation of the Bible and Shakespeare aloud."[53] This tradition of oral transmission had deep roots in the African American community. When Africans were forcibly transported to North America for their labor, they brought with them the patterns of expression from their continent. Self-expression was paramount during the slave era, as Roger D. Abrahams explicated in his article "Traditions of Eloquence in Afro-American Communities." He wrote, "We see here the tremendous importance attached to speech in all its forms: the use of talk to proclaim presence of self, to assert oneself vocally in the most anxious and the most unguarded situations." He also noted "the importance of a highly formal and decorous approach to language in both the intercultural exchanges and in intra-group activities."[54] Asserting oneself vocally in various forms like preaching, storytelling, or toast making was a vital legacy passed down from African forebears. It was also essential to an enslaved people who were forbidden to learn to read and for whom gaining access to reading material was dangerous, even life threatening. Because of factors such as African traditions and the prohibition on literacy during slavery, there has been historically a "greater emphasis on the oral tradition in black culture."[55]

How was Robeson an inheritor of this legacy? First, Robeson's family was directly linked to oral tradition through the church. His father, William D. Robeson, was a minister, and his older brother, Ben, also became a preacher in the A.M.E. Zion church. The church, then, played a central role in Robeson's childhood as it did in the larger black community in the late nineteenth and early twentieth centuries. Robeson, who was born in New Jersey in 1898, was only one generation removed from slavery. His father had escaped from North Carolina and settled in the North where he ultimately married, raised a family, and ministered to the black community. Black churches like Reverend Robeson's provided much-needed support for African Americans who faced poverty and discrimination on a daily basis. The church offered both an emotional outlet and a center for socialization. Music and elocution were essential aspects of the worship services. These influences from Robeson's early life were manifested in his career. As a concert vocalist, Robeson focused on African American spirituals in addition to other forms of folk music. Oratory was a primary facet of Robeson's career as a performer.

Robeson proved himself to be a successful orator even at a young age. In his memoir from 1958, Robeson recalled being a "prize debater" in high school as well as a "diligent student of my father's artistry of speech." In 1915, he entered a statewide oratorical contest in which he placed third. He was somewhat amazed, in retrospect, at his recitation of a fiery abolitionist's speech before the mostly white audience. "But there I was," Robeson recollected, "voicing, with all the fervor and forensic skill I could muster, Wendell Phillips' searing attack on the concept of white supremacy!"[56] One can visualize the teenage Robeson standing erectly on the stage, striving to perfect his diction and all the while probably shocking his audience with the substance of Phillips's eulogy for the black revolutionary hero Toussaint L'Ouverture! Robeson admitted that, at seventeen, he did not fully comprehend the content of this speech, but it seems altogether appropriate that his entrée into public oratory drew upon the tradition of abolitionism and invoked the struggle for justice for his people.

This trend continued throughout his college years at Rutgers where he seldom lost a major oratorical contest. The years 1915–1919 were turbulent ones in the United States. Booker T. Washington's death in 1915 signaled the beginning of a new generation of African American leadership. During this time, President Woodrow Wilson segregated the federal buildings in Washington, D. C., which offered a glaring symbol of government sanction to racial discrimination. Perhaps even worse, Wilson hosted the premiere of the film *Birth of Nation*, which glorified the Ku Klux Klan, at the White House. Lynching and race riots continued across the country even as the United States sent troops over to the European theater of World War I.

Meanwhile, young Robeson was using the platform of elocution at Rutgers to speak out about positive social change. Publicly addressing such issues, especially in wartime, was particularly courageous. This was around the time when suffragettes were jailed for silently picketing the White House during the war. Soon Congress passed the infamous Espionage Act which was ultimately used to silence political radicals. Nevertheless, Robeson, when asked to speak at commencement in 1919, composed an address titled "The New Idealism." In it, he "declared that his generation must struggle for peace, fight against poverty, prejudice, and the demoralization of the human spirit."[57] The notion of "struggling for peace" foreshadowed his activism against going to war with the Soviet Union in the early cold war. Robeson indeed stayed true to the values he articulated as a prescient youth.

By the time of his acting debut in New York the following year, Robeson was not unfamiliar with the idea of standing before an audience. He had already done it many times as an elocutionist. One can conceive of Robeson first as an orator who subsequently sang and performed in dramas. In fact, in his book *The Oratory of Negro Leaders*, Marcus Boulware characterized Robeson as "probably the only Negro orator who combined singing, acting, and speaking."[58] Just as his early life in the church stimulated his concert repertoire, Robeson's exposure to his father's oration coupled with his own forensic activities in high school and college informed his stage persona. Robeson's vocal presence was a noteworthy theme that recurred in the reviews of his three portrayals of Othello. Based on its prominence in the contemporary notices, Robeson's baritone and vocal intonation were prominent aspects of his interpretation of Othello. His vocal bearing was fostered by the oral tradition passed down through his father, who personified the elocution mastered by an enslaved people. The seed of oratorical heritage was planted early in his life and remained a prominent aspect of his onstage appearances. His voice was, of course, unmistakable and part of what helped secure his success and widespread appeal. In 1930, however, Robeson faced a new challenge: his first attempt at Shakespeare on the professional stage. His diction would be tested by Elizabethan English. His acting had to hold its own as lead in a classic tragedy. Would Robeson, at thirty-two, be up to this momentous task so early in his career?

❖ ❖ ❖

CHAPTER TWO

Robeson's Professional Debut as Othello

"The Root of the Racial Question": Robeson on Shakespeare in 1930

In the spring of 1930, the United States was still reeling from the shock of the stock market crash the previous autumn. However, the full onslaught of the depression was not yet apparent. The unemployment rate had not hit the epidemic proportions that it would by 1932. The young Communist Party in the United States began to take a more radical stance by opposing the American Federation of Labor (AFL) and organizing in the South among the textile workers in Gastonia, North Carolina. The party would also soon try to unionize sharecroppers in Birmingham, Alabama. For Paul Robeson, 1929 had been a successful year. He toured concert halls in Europe and Britain and wound up the year singing to a full house at Carnegie Hall in New York. In May of 1930, Robeson's new onstage venture was in Shakespeare's *Othello* in what turned out to be a rather dreadful production.

Robeson recalled fondly in his memoir how an English teacher had coached him through his first attempt to portray Othello in high school.[1] In 1917, Robeson was likened to an Othello of the football field. A reporter commenting on a game between Rutgers and the Naval Reserve team that year remarked, "It was Robeson, a veritable Othello of battle, who led the dashing little Rutgers eleven to victory. . . ."[2] One can picture the young Robeson darting across the grass, the sole African American on the Rutgers team, dominating the field and guiding them to conquer just as Othello commanded the Venetian troops. How prophetic it was that this sports journalist utilized a Shakespearean metaphor. Of course, it was not until 1930 that Robeson, the actor, had his first opportunity to portray the Moorish general on the professional stage. Robeson's research for this Shakespearean role and his apparent misgivings as opening night approached have been well documented in contemporary interviews. These conversations with Robeson also illuminated his interpretation of Othello's character and the play as a whole. It was clear that Robeson carefully prepared himself for the role. He explained, "As a rule I like to think things out for a very long while. . . . I always first come to a good solid understanding of a character. . . ."[3] Robeson further observed, "I have studied him [Shakespeare] closely since I was a boy of fifteen, and still I am striving to learn more."[4] His early exposure to Shakespeare underscored the prominence of the playwright in the black community. Still, Robeson admitted that he considered portraying Shakespeare's Moor in London with some trepidation.

A chief concern of his was mastering the king's English pronunciation, as British critics were sticklers for proper enunciation. Robeson understood that, as George Bernard Shaw once pointed out, the United States and England were two countries divided by a common language. Robeson jested to one audience, "Playing in London one must try not to offend the English ears too much as we Americans distress them with our speech almost as much as they amuse us with theirs."[5] But the issue was, in fact, a serious one for he "felt that [it] was more of an ordeal to play Othello in London" because of the language barrier. He continued, "I found your vowels hard to remember . . . so I did some research. I bought Shakespeare's plays with their original spelling. . . . And I understood why you put in all those vowels [that] Americans leave out."[6] Robeson was self taught in numerous languages from Russian to Welsh. His affinity for languages prompted him to approach his study of the king's English as he would any other foreign tongue.[7] After a successful opening night he could comfortably confide, "I took the part of Othello with much fear. Now I am happy."[8] Indeed, Robeson was "thrilled to know London is pleased with me. I can say frankly that I never had any first night feeling of glamour. I just expected that you would not like me."[9]

Robeson's knowledge of and admiration for the Bard was also apparent in his commentary on the role. He asserted, "Shakespeare was a great human being who saw no character from one angle. His creations are therefore consistent, but many-sided: and each of their phases is emphasized."[10]

Additionally, Robeson highly regarded the playwright's "superb sympathy for the under-dog."[11] Yet, the challenge of Shakespeare was the latitude he provided the actor. "I gradually realised [sic] that a great deal of what Shakespeare intends to convey is left to the actor," Robeson noted. "It is of no use [to] merely declaim his lines—they must be given with all the loving feeling of which a man or woman is capable."[12] Probably due to this nuance in *Othello*, Robeson had difficulty interpreting the version of the play produced in London in 1930 by Maurice Browne and Ellen Van Volkenburg, who had slashed the poetry of Shakespeare indiscriminately. Many critics felt they were irresponsible in this and had ruined the play. It also troubled Robeson's artistry. He disclosed, "I think the contrast between Shakespeare's original and the 'cut' version which I had to learn prevented me from seeing Othello as a complete personality."[13] Unfortunately, this was just one example of many instances where poor producing inhibited Robeson's debut performance.

Robeson's faith in Shakespeare as a writer was also reinforced by his interpretation of the role of race in the tragedy. He emphasized passionately, "To me it is extraordinary how Shakespeare, at that time was able to get to the root of the racial question. I feel it here [he strikes his breast]." Robeson subsequently drew an illuminating modern-day parallel to the Senate scene (act I, scene 3) in *Othello*. This commentary shed light on Robeson's strong connection to the play: "[A]s Othello I walk into the Senate, among all those people who in their hearts hate me, but fear me and know they must use me. I have known instances of the same sort of thing to-day; when, for example, the only skillful physician in town has been a Negro and the people during an epidemic have had to go to him to be saved from death. Shakespeare grasped this principle perfectly and Othello is, if anything, more apt to-day than when it was first written."[14]

Frequently, the play has been considered solely as a study of sexual jealousy. However, some critics maintained a more subtle interpretation linked to Othello's sense of honor. James Agate, a reviewer for the prominent London *Sunday Times*, posited, "Othello conceives Desdemona's death not as a murder but as a sacrifice, and kills her not out of passion but because her conduct has shaken the world from its propriety."[15] Richard Watts in the *New York Herald Tribune* and the reviewer for the *Boston Herald* both observed that Robeson's interpretation especially highlighted the fact that Othello had been dishonored. Thus, for Robeson, the crux of Othello's motivation was protecting his honor rather than merely acting out of jealous passion.

Robeson consciously emphasized this issue of Othello's honor. It was Othello's nobility and dignity that he underscored in the Senate scene. Venice needed Othello's military guidance and held him in high esteem. Simultaneously, Othello believed in the virtue of Venetian society, as exemplified in the purity of Desdemona's love for him. When he felt that his wife had been disloyal, Othello's honor was betrayed. Robeson explicated his position: "I feel the play is so modern, for the problem is the problem of my own people.... It is a tragedy of racial conflict, a tragedy of honour [sic] rather than jealousy. Shakespeare presents a noble figure.... He is important to the State.... Desdemona loves him and he marries her, and then the seed of suspicion is sown. It is because he is an alien among the white people that his mind works so quickly, for he feels the dishonour [sic] more deeply. His colour [sic] heightens the tragedy."[16] The point of honor over jealousy may seem moot on the surface; however, if the play was primarily about sexual jealousy then Shakespeare would merely be reinforcing the stereotype of the passionate jealous savage from Africa as characterized by Leo Africanus in his travelogue, which was widely known in Elizabethan London. If Robeson believed the heart of *Othello* to be solely jealousy, then it could not be illustrative of "the problem of my own people." Furthermore, Robeson asserted in another interview that Othello's "jealousy was in no way an inferiority complex."[17] This statement represented an important refutation of the critics who described Robeson's portrayal of Othello as fraught with a melancholy sense of inferiority.

Another point upon which Robeson disagreed with the critics was the issue of Othello being portrayed as an Arab rather than an African. This had been a longstanding debate since at least the early nineteenth century. One reviewer summarized that Othello "must not be conceived as a Negro, but a high and chivalrous Moorish chief."[18] As would be expected, controversy arose in London concerning Robeson, a dark-skinned African American, playing Othello, a character whom many critics, scholars, and theatergoers traditionally held to be a light-skinned Arab of North African descent. Naturally, these arguments stemmed from the racism of the culture in Britain but, nevertheless, the debate raged and probably increased the popularity of the production. Ironically, and amusingly, critics who fussed about a "Bantu" or an "Ethiopian" (dark-skinned actor) playing Othello had no qualms with a white European portraying the Moor.

The question of Othello's skin tone or racial heritage spilled over from the drama reviews into the editorial pages of London's *Daily Mail*. A couple of readers were moved to comment on the ongoing debate in letters to the editor. One reader of the *Daily Mail* who was "shocked to find the part of Othello taken by a negro" weighed in with a detailed summary of Moorish lineage, arguing that "all authorities emphasise [sic] the point that Othello was not a negro" and, moreover, he was "the victim of private malignity (not race hatred)."[19] Several days later, a provoked reader retorted, "Of course, everyone knows that a Negro is not a Moor, but neither is an Englishman . . . surely it is more fitting that the part should be played by one of natural colour [sic] than by a man whose skin has to be stained brown?"[20] It is interesting to notice that while the word "Negro" was not widely capitalized in the American press until the 1950s, this respondent took the care to do so.

In light of the debate stirring, Robeson cogently articulated his position on Othello's racial persuasion for British and American papers. On the question of the North African Moor versus the dark-skinned African, Robeson held that "[t]here are very few Moors in Northern Africa without Ethiopian blood in their veins."[21] (The term "Ethiopian" commonly referred to any dark-skinned person from non-Islamic Africa.) Robeson also astutely pointed to the stage history of the play. In a London interview that was broadcast across the Atlantic by radio, he observed that in Shakespeare's time the part was portrayed with darkened skin. Subsequently, "it changed around the time of Edmund Kean," as noted in chapter one.[22] This illustrated the depth of Robeson's study on the role. Indeed, the stage tradition of a "tawny" rather than a darker Moor of Venice began with Kean in the early nineteenth century and continued, with a few exceptions, until Robeson's 1930 performance. Robeson also adeptly reasoned that this transition was related to slavery. By the early 1800s, the African slave trade had been operating and yielding profits for over two centuries. Although the British outlawed the trade in 1807 and the United States followed in 1808, slave traffic was not completely halted and Emancipation was still decades away. In the first half of the 1800s, theories on the inferiority of dark-skinned people proliferated as the abolitionist movement grew and the need to more staunchly defend slavery became imperative to protect the thriving cotton industry. Thus, if Othello was to be interpreted as a noble character and a leader of men then it was logical, even crucial, to the racial theories of the time that he not be viewed as black.

Additionally, Robeson cleverly played on the idea of the "one drop rule" in America to defend his dark-skinned portrayal. In the United States, particularly the South, one was infamously considered to be black if there was but one drop of African blood in his lineage. Robeson poked fun at this ridiculous assumption and suggested that "since he [Othello] came from

Africa he must have had some Ethiopian blood in him. And as one drop of white blood in a Negro is supposed . . . to account for all his abilities . . . so surely I am justified in taking the drop of Negro blood in Othello as the basis of my interpretation of him."[23] Finally, Robeson concluded that the petty distinction between shades and hues was of little consequence in the end: "In any case, I feel that Shakespeare merely wanted to draw a character as far removed as possible from a white woman. He was probably the first man ever to refer to what is known today as the 'colour [sic] bar.'" Still, the question arose again in a 1933 interview. At this time, Robeson stated confidently that "there was some critical discussion when I played 'Othello' in London as a black man, but [A. C.] Bradley, the great Shakespearean critic, using Shakespeare's text and the tradition of the theatre, said that any interpretation other than mine was nonsense."[24] As a humorous aside, one reviewer of the 1930 London production noticed after the opening, "Paul Robeson's make-up, despite his natural advantages, seems to take as long as that of any European actors who play Othello."[25] Even though Robeson did not need dark makeup, it appeared that he still required considerable time to get into his costume, which included a short artificial beard.

In 1930, Robeson expressed a desire to play Othello in the United States, particularly in New York. He feared, however, that "they certainly wouldn't stand in America for the kissing and for the scene in which I use Miss Ashcroft roughly." So he "wouldn't care to play those scenes in some parts of the United States."[26] On another occasion he was more sanguine: "I am positive that in the enlightened sections of the United States there can be only one question: Is this a worthy interpretation of one of the great plays of all times?"[27] And what about those onstage kisses with Peggy Ashcroft, his first Desdemona? Reporters in London were certainly intrigued, for these kisses generated several headlines. For her part, Ashcroft remained nonchalant with the press, merely remarking that the kisses were "just necessary for the play."[28] However, there had been more going on backstage. Much to her chagrin, Robeson's wife discovered afterward that Robeson and Ashcroft had an affair during the run of *Othello*. Years later Ashcroft recalled in a biography, "How could one not fall in love in such a situation with such a man!"[29]

Robeson was optimistic to the press concerning the reception a dark-skinned actor would receive in London. He pointed out, "I was a little disturbed myself when I started rehearsals and rumors that there might [be] objection to a coloured [sic] actor playing with a white girl came to my notice. In my heart I felt that in London trouble could not possibly arise on racial grounds."[30] Yet, Robeson knew that London's color bar was alive and well in the 1930s. It had been documented by various writers and was demonstrated by Robeson's own experiences. The racial language employed by the critics who reviewed Robeson's Othello in 1930 reflected the culture in which they lived. Some of them actively denied that color prejudice existed in London. On the other hand, people of color who spent time in London during that period told another story.

C. L. R. James, who was a recent immigrant from Trinidad, compiled his first impressions of London in the early 1930s in a series of essays. He summarized, "The average Englishman in London is, on the surface, quite polite. . . . But nevertheless the average man in London is eaten up with colour [sic] prejudice."[31] An illustrative article from 1934 by D. F. Kanaka, who identified himself as the "first coloured [sic] president of the Oxford Union," bravely asserted, "Hotels in England have refused admittance to prominent Indians and to celebrated coloured [sic] stars from the States." Yet, "It is not often that the British public hears of these individual instances." He concluded hopefully, "If English people realised [sic] the gravity of the injury they inflict on coloured [sic] people, they would perhaps not insist in enforcing the Colour [sic] Bar to the same extent as they do now."[32]

Kanaka might have had Robeson in mind when he noted that celebrated stars had been stymied by the color bar in England. In 1929, Robeson and his wife were prevented from entering the restaurant at the Savoy, a prominent London hotel. The ensuing protest uncovered other stories of discrimination, and a minister of parliament raised the issue before the government. The controversy even sparked the interest of the press back in the United States as the *New York Times* ran several related articles on the incident in October and November of 1929. The next year, when *Othello* opened, producer Maurice Browne assured the *Daily Sketch* newspaper that "no single letter of protest" had been received at the theater.[33] Still, Peggy Ashcroft recalled to a biographer that she and Sybil Thorndike, who played Emilia, got "rather unpleasant letters saying 'East is East and West is West and no more theatres where you play for me after this.'"[34] The attitude of the sender of that letter was not unique. One theatergoer frankly admitted to a reporter, "We all know that if a white woman marries a coloured [sic] man she renounces her God and country, and is held in contempt by all her . . . relations."[35] While perhaps it was not as outwardly apparent as the strict segregation in the United States, London certainly was not immune to racial discrimination.

Because Robeson's political consciousness was just beginning to take shape, his views on *Othello* and Africa were not yet completely honed in 1930. For example, he suggested that "anyone who approaches Othello [as a role] must remember that part of him which is crude savage, and makes him murder his wife. . . ."[36] In this instance, Robeson sounded as if he was acknowledging the denigrating stereotype of the African savage. Then again, murdering one's wife was not exactly refined behavior. On another occasion, he mentioned that when playing Othello, he endeavored to "allow the essential simplicity of his character to come into its own."[37] Again, this seemed to confirm the archetype of the simple-minded African that continuously appeared in European characterizations of people of color.

He put forth a similarly puzzling contention in another interview when discussing Othello's lineage: "If Othello had been a crafty Moor, he would never have listened to Iago. Moors were more subtle than the Venetians themselves. But the play demands a simple, direct black."[38] By this logic, Othello should be portrayed as black because Africans were less scheming than Moors and, therefore, would be more vulnerable to Iago's insinuations. This reflected the commonly held assumption among African Americans that Africans were somewhat primitive and needed to be redeemed or civilized. At this point, Robeson's pondering on *Othello* and Africa was not yet fully conceived. In the 1930s, after *Othello*, he interacted with educated Africans in groups like the West African Students Union and the League of Coloured Peoples in London. He also learned important lessons from artistic work like *Sanders of the River* (1934) for which he was reprimanded in the black press for reinforcing African stereotypes linked to imperialism. As will be explored in the next chapter, Robeson sharpened his theoretical stance on African culture throughout the 1930s. Thus, by the time of the Broadway *Othello*, Robeson's interpretation had matured, and he connected the play directly to current political issues including World War II and racial segregation.

Background on the 1930 Production at the Savoy Theatre

Shakespeare's play was adapted for the London revival and directed by American actress Ellen Van Volkenburg, who jointly produced the show with British actor/producer Maurice Browne. The pair had been married and had founded together the Chicago Little Theatre in 1912, which had a reputation for experimental drama. By the late 1920s the team was in Britain, and Browne was known for taking investment risks on the West End for better or for worse. His production of *Journey's End* was a critical and financial success, but he lost money on many of his ventures. Browne was an ambitious producer and, in May of 1930, amazingly had three productions running on the West End simultaneously: Robeson's *Othello* at the Savoy, John Gielgud's *Hamlet* (with the Old Vic Company) at the Queen's Theatre, and Alexander Moissi's *Hamlet* at the Globe Theatre. Perhaps it was not surprising, then, that the critical reception of Browne's performance as Iago was not complimentary. He finally admitted in June, when he resigned the part to his understudy, that "the strain of management, and the time involved told on my acting—as the critics did not hesitate to point out."[39]

The initial response to *Othello* was promising, as box office returns amounted to twenty-two hundred pounds for its first seven performances. Yet, Browne later revealed to the *Sunday Dispatch* that *Othello* might have paid higher dividends "had not the salary list been so heavy." Indeed, Robeson was paid three hundred pounds a week, according to Browne.[40] The *New York Times* had also reported back in 1929 that Robeson would make a record salary for his performance.[41] Yet, Browne's penchant for risk taking and acumen as a producer must have told him that he needed Robeson for the show. If Browne had not taken a chance by offering Robeson the lead in *Othello*, this production almost certainly would have quickly been forgotten. The mutilated script, inadequate lighting, bulky sets, and mediocre company were perhaps only redeemed by Peggy Ashcroft's and Sybil Thorndike's memorable interpretations of the female roles Desdemona and Emilia. And, of course, Robeson's Othello, whether one praised or criticized his performance, was historic.

How did Robeson prepare for his debut as Othello? It was clear from his interviews and commentary that he was versed in the history of the play and had ruminated upon his position regarding Othello's race. Through his study of the text, Robeson's wife, Eslanda, noted in her 1930 biography that he had "learned his lines more than seven months before he was contracted to report for rehearsal." She further recounted that at this time he was "happy in his work."[42] *The Observer* reported that none other than Amanda Aldridge had been reading the play with Robeson. Aldridge conveyed to a reporter that she was planning to attend opening night and was especially looking forward to seeing Robeson as Othello because she had never been able to watch her father perform since he had died when she was only a year old.[43] Andrew Bunie and Sheila Tully Boyle's biography depicted Robeson as maintaining a heavy schedule of concerts and film work which left him only six weeks in which to prepare for the play. They suggested that his possible procrastination was motivated by apprehension about tackling his first Shakespearean role.[44] Unfortunately, formal rehearsals with Van Volkenburg and Browne did little to assuage Robeson's worries.

Eslanda recorded in her diary the tense weeks leading up to the May premiere. In mid-April, Robeson was describing rehearsals as "hopeless" and "dreadful." As opening night approached, Eslanda described Robeson as being "wild with nerves" and the Browne/Van Volkenburg duo as "hopeless amateurs." Despite the dearth of support Robeson received from the production team, he had a houseful of benefactors to assist him through this rite of passage. James Light, a director with whom Robeson had worked on *The Emperor Jones* with the Provincetown Players in New York, was in town and "working madly over the play with Paul." Max Montesole, who played Cassio in the revival, was a veteran Shakespearean actor and was, according to Eslanda, "working like blazes" with Robeson on his part after hours. Peggy Ashcroft also came by for the informal sessions held at the Robeson residence, which Eslanda portrayed as being a "boarding house" the week prior to the opening.[45] Robeson corroborated the tense circumstances in an interview: "You do not know how worried I was. I expected ... to have more real guidance. I was so worried that I nearly gave up the idea." Luckily, Montesole was on hand to spend "hours and hours helping to perfect me in my part" and James Light "came over to help me psychologically."[46] Thus, despite Robeson's analysis of the play's text, his technical preparation was largely patched together hastily outside of the official cast rehearsals. Because of these factors, coupled with his overall lack of maturity as an actor, Robeson was later somewhat dismissive of his first performance in *Othello*. Though the 1930 production was a vital growing experience for Robeson, it would have been difficult to be proud of the final product in this case.

What elements detracted from the potential success of this production? According to the promptbook, it was arranged into four acts with three intervals, making for a lengthy and disjointed program.[47] In the Broadway production, Margaret Webster took exactly the opposite approach, arguing that *Othello* can only be played very swiftly so as not to give the audience any time to consider the logic of the plot but to depend solely on the momentum of the emotions displayed. This proved to be a more effective strategy. Certainly, the audience at the Savoy Theatre must have been dragging by the third intermission. In addition, the stage was overcrowded with extras, irrelevant dance numbers were inserted, the lighting was too dark, and the set distanced the action from the viewers. Thus, the overall production had serious liabilities, the worst of which may have been the bungled portrayal of Iago. The reviewers who were critical of Van Volkenburg and Browne's production did not mince words when outlining the handicaps of this revival.

Perhaps as a marketing strategy, Eslanda Robeson's biography of her young husband was released the same month that the London revival opened. *Paul Robeson, Negro* was reviewed in major London newspapers, and a few critics reviewing the play had first familiarized themselves with Robeson's life through Eslanda's book. The timing of the book was alluded to by W. Keith, writing for *The Star*, who noticed, "Mrs. Robeson declares that his acting of Othello is an old intention long deferred."[48] Reviewers noted that the biography honored Robeson and the race he represented. The *London Times* critic observed, "The implications of the title of the book are obvious enough in a sense. . . . The racial pride and the enthusiasm for negro culture of both the writer . . . and the subject of it are very deeply expressed."[49] A reporter for the *Observer* opened, "Racial pride is finely displayed in the title of Mrs. Robeson's simple, almost naïve, story of her husband's life."[50] He concluded about Robeson, "He stands for his race. And how well he stands for it." Yet, Eslanda's account was not uniformly appreciated, for the *Daily Herald* complained, "It is a paean of praise rather than a biography."[51]

According to volume one of Paul Robeson, Jr.'s monograph on his father's life, parts of Eslanda's chronicle angered Robeson when it was published. The younger Robeson confirmed, "There was a wide gap between the 'Paul' depicted by Essie and his public personification of dignity, discipline, and dedication."[52] Unfortunately, Eslanda's manuscript was more a subtle revelation about the frustrations in her marriage to Robeson than an objective assessment of his life and career. On one hand, Eslanda portrayed Robeson as genial and affable even as his celebrity grew. She described a street scene in Harlem: "When Paul Robeson walks down Seventh Avenue . . . at every step of the way he is stopped by some acquaintance or friend who wants a few words with him. And always Paul has time for those few words."[53] On the other hand, she presented Robeson as idle and unfocused. Throughout the book, she seemed to highlight her aggravations with Robeson by pointing out her perceptions of his flaws. She grumbled about his predilection for "sprawling" in an easy chair at home rather than sitting "properly."[54] She complained about Robeson's lack of ambition in obtaining a job once he completed his law degree: "Paul was very lazy. He was not the person to think out what he would do or wanted to do and then go out and try to do it."[55]

Against his indolent habits, Eslanda rendered herself as conscientious and diligent. For example, she depicted a bustling scene in which the Robesons and pianist Lawrence Brown barely missed a train from London's Victoria Station. A fuming Eslanda was juxtaposed with an unruffled Robeson, much to her dismay. Robeson, in her dialogue, giggled, "What tickles me so is the fact that she's mad because it's a reflection on her efficiency and her dignity as a manager—not because we missed our connections . . . ."[56] The dialogue she wrote between herself and Robeson in the biography sounded almost wistful as if she was imagining the conversations that she wanted to have with him but, in reality, they were not communicating. She observed to Paul during a discussion about the possibility of his infidelity: "[B]ut you don't know what I mean. So we're talking about quite different things—as we often do."[57] In the matter of his career, Eslanda portrayed herself as being more ambitious than her husband and having to motivate him. Concerning *Othello*, according to her narrative, she nudged Robeson into agreeing to Browne's production. Robeson queried, "Do you think I could play Othello now, if I worked at it?" Eslanda replied, "I know you can, silly." At her prompting, Robeson concluded, "All right, I'll do it. I'll tell Maurice Browne so the next time he asks me. . . ." Eslanda then praised his decision by saying, "Attaboy" and placed a "resounding kiss on his cheek."[58] Paul Robeson, Jr., astutely pointed out in his biography that this representation of Robeson's decision to play Othello was "especially misleading" and that Robeson's "hesitations about that production had more to do with his well-placed misgivings about Maurice Browne and less to do with his doubts of his own abilities."[59]

Eslanda's concluding remarks in her biography envisioned Robeson as an almost stock happy-go-lucky black character: "He leaves a trail of friendliness wherever he goes, this Paul Robeson, Negro, who, with his typically Negro qualities—his appearance, his voice, his genial smile, his laziness, his child-like simplicity—is carving a place as a citizen of the world. . . ."[60] Yet, as can be seen in Robeson's 1930 commentary on Shakespeare, he was clearly more studied and complex than this description insinuated. Eslanda's lack of confidence in the security of their marriage had prompted her to caution Robeson, through the writing of the biography, that she was not afraid to speak about him publicly. Paul Robeson, Jr., offered the following analysis of Eslanda's biography: "Paul now read it as an unmistakable warning to him: If you even think of replacing me as Mrs. Paul Robeson, beware of my wrath."[61]

Perhaps there was also another interpretation of Eslanda's conclusion. Eslanda might have been intentionally portraying her husband in a fashion that would be palatable to the critics and audiences who would soon see him play Othello onstage. Her emphasis on geniality, simplicity, and laziness would not be an affront to potential patrons who would be purchasing tickets to see the revival. Her characterization of Robeson presented typical perceptions of black people in that time period. Thus, the critics who reviewed Eslanda's book easily accepted this representation of Robeson and mainly praised her assessment. Many of the *Othello* reviews underscored similar racialized attributes of Robeson onstage such as simplicity and naturalness in his voice and appearance. The theme of Robeson's dignity, while not accentuated in Eslanda's biography, was fundamental to his public persona and his interpretation of Othello. Although dignity was more apparent in the reviews for the Broadway and Stratford productions, it did not go unmentioned in the notices for the London revival.

Critical Reception of the Savoy Production

Before one delves into the British reviews, it is important to mention that the major African American newspapers eagerly reviewed Robeson's portrayal of Shakespeare's Moor in London. The *Chicago Defender* placed Robeson squarely in the tradition of Ira Aldridge and noted that on opening night "one of the most interested persons in the vast audience was Dame Madge Kendal who played Desdemona to the Othello of Mr. Aldridge 65 years ago." (Kendal was only seventeen at the time of that production.) The reviewer for the *Defender* also commented on the debate as to whether Robeson should play the Moor and noticed that "the controversy led to the box offices of the theater being flooded with requests for tickets."[62] The reporter for the *Afro-American* in Baltimore was also scanning the crowd and observed that "colored people sat dotted about the audience." This article, also acknowledging the controversy, saw one disgruntled audience member exit the theater but concluded, "There was no other murmur that I heard." The reviewer emphasized, "There was no protest . . . in the theater," even when Robeson kissed Ashcroft "full on the lips" several times.[63]

All of the reviewers in the black press underscored the praise Robeson received from London critics. However, the *Pittsburgh Courier* admitted that the production as a whole was "far from a masterpiece" and that the cuts to the script were "clumsily managed." When this reporter remarked that the producers were considering taking the show to New York, he suggested that if they do so, "It might be just as well to pick another Iago."[64] However, another article in the *Courier*, by Ivan Browning, recognized Maurice Browne's shrewdness as a producer. Browning asserted, "Mr. Browne has done something which all right thinking Negroes will highly appreciate. He turned a deaf ear to the harshest criticism possible and gave Robeson his big chance."[65] While they recognized the downfalls of the overall production, reviewers for the black press were, nevertheless, proud of Robeson's London debut as Othello.

Assessing contemporary reviews of a revival is always intriguing, as this attempt can reveal more about the critics and their societies than the production at hand, especially when discussing the issue of race. As with reviews of any piece of art, they offer glimpses of the play but from very subjective viewpoints. Nonetheless, reviews are instructive, sometimes in surprising ways. A basic pattern emerged from the contemporary reviews of the 1930 *Othello* production at the Savoy Theatre in London. One critic summed up the general reaction to Robeson well: "I am sure that many playgoers will go into rhapsodies over Paul Robeson's performance . . . while others will take a less enthusiastic view of his acting. I think that the latter will allow that Paul Robeson possesses dignity and a magnificent voice, and that he has his big moments, but . . . when speaking possesses very little range and, in consequence, his delivery is inclined to become monotonous."[66] This represented a pretty fair assessment of the reviews. The reviewer understood that there would be critiques of Robeson's acting which even he realized was not fully cultivated at this early point in his career. Yet, this reviewer acutely perceived that even those who were "less enthusiastic" about Robeson's technique would still allow that Robeson possessed dignity and a splendid voice. Dignity, here, was recognized as crucial even if Robeson's acting ability was not fully conceived. As for the overall production, almost all of the reviewers agreed that Peggy Ashcroft's baptism into Shakespearean drama signaled an important new personality on the London stage. Similarly, nearly everyone felt that Dame Sybil Thorndike probably stole the show as Emilia. Unfortunately, there was a comparable uniformity of opinion that Maurice Browne's Iago was unconvincing.

By and large, the reviews can be divided into three categories: those which praised both Robeson and the production, those which praised Robeson but were critical of the production, and those which were critical of both the production and Robeson. Racial stereotyping was replete within all of these groups. Robeson had to face the tough London critics without ever having played Shakespeare on the professional stage and with only a weak production team on his side. Needless to say, he was nervous opening night! Yet, the critics were aware of these liabilities and many took them into consideration.

On the whole, about twice as many critics endorsed Robeson as were critical, even if most had at least a few reservations. The breakdown was similar for the production: roughly twice as many reviewers criticized the production as favored it generally. This mixed reception foreshadowed some of the criticisms of Robeson's acting that were revisited when the play was revived on Broadway. However, the language employed by reviewers in 1930 was probably more overtly racist than for the two subsequent productions. Most important, the London production was a learning experience for Robeson, and it whetted the appetite of the theater world for another course of Robeson as Othello.

In the reviews which endorsed Robeson's performance and the production overall, several themes appeared. First, there was general praise for Robeson. For example: "His portrayal of Othello consolidated his position as one of the finest actors of the day."[67] A critic observed that Robeson "has identified his own people with the tragedy," and he continued, "For nobility of mind and beauty of speech, it is difficult to imagine a better rendering."[68] The reporter for the *Irish Times* felt that Robeson's portrayal was "remarkable for its fine accomplishment."[69] "The shade of William Shakespeare," began the *Hampstead Express*, "would have counted himself well served" had he been in attendance opening night.[70] Interestingly, the reviews that were less critical of Robeson tended to be from outside of London in towns such as Sheffield, Croydon, Dublin, Bristol, Manchester, and Leeds, to name a few. Thus, the critics in the metro area, as would be expected, seemed to be the hardest to please.

Several of the critics in favor of Robeson were not bothered by his accent. "No doubt," one reviewer exclaimed, "but it will be agreed that his success in managing the troublesome word is noteworthy."[71] This was a thorny issue, however, for even reporters who praised Robeson occasionally picked up a note of the American accent. Moreover, a number of reviewers believed that the poignancy of Robeson's Othello was based on more than his color. The *Newcastle Chronicle* reviewer posited that Robeson "did more than merely by virtue of the colour of his skin add piquancy to this production."[72] Critic Thomas Moult agreed, "Mr. Robeson lends a certain verisimilitude to his part through the fact that he is a coloured actor.... But Mr. Robeson is not simply a black man. He is a very fine tragedian, and his acting would of itself make this drama... the second best selection... of the West End theatres."[73] There were no less than four Shakespearean revivals on the West End at this time, including *The Merchant of Venice* and two productions of *Hamlet*.

Conversely, several reviewers found plenty of reason to extol Robeson but, nevertheless, felt his acting revealed a lack of experience. For instance, one critic carped, "At present he [Robeson] is too soft." Yet, he concluded in a positive vein, "But all the power that the part calls for is there. It only seems to await control and discipline."[74] Another critic, who wrote under the pen name "The Candid Friend," had a similarly bifurcated response: "I do not doubt that there was an immaturity in the actor." Still, "It was a dignified and impressive rendering though it nowhere encompassed the part's full greatness."[75] This reviewer's anonymous response was a good example of a critic who felt Robeson's interpretation left room to grow but still perceived his dignity onstage. Elizabeth Montizambert, a rare female critic who was writing for a Canadian newspaper, exclaimed, "This is the last Othello I shall see; any other would suffer by comparison." While she noted his inexperience, she felt it was an asset for Robeson. She explained that Robeson's "inexperience and lack of the usual theatrical cocksureness and time-worn technique only enhanced the sincerity of this remarkable interpretation." She concluded, "He did not seem to act the Moor, he was the very incarnation of Othello...."[76]

Some reviews that supported Robeson did so by invoking racial assumptions. One reporter opened with the dubious phrase "I have no colour [*sic*] prejudice but," he continued, "looking at Paul Robeson's Othello... it is impossible to see in him the noble Moor that Shakespeare intended. Othello belonged to one of the oldest and haughtiest aristocracies in the world, at the Savoy he was just a flat-footed negro with a prognathous jaw."[77] Yet, surprisingly, the same reviewer paid tribute to Robeson's "magnificent voice" and actually encouraged the reader to attend the Savoy production! The *Sheffield Telegraph* called upon several stereotypes of dark-skinned people. This reviewer was awed by Robeson's "most virile performance" which was "an especially African interpretation, savage, fervently amorous and rhapsodically sentimental."[78] Robeson's speech before the Duke and Senate (act I, scene 3) was considered by the *Scotsman* to be "a simple man's recital of the simple facts." This may sound insulting in retrospect, but Robeson himself believed at this time that Othello should be played as a "simple, direct black." Still, this reviewer felt that Robeson's interpretation "places him at once in the front rank of Shakespearean actors."[79]

The scenes in which Othello exploded with jealousy were especially engrossing to those reviewers who perceived that Robeson's African sensibility would be particularly useful in these moments. The *Church Times* characterized Robeson's "flood of turbulent passion" as "primitive, child-like, [and] uncontrolled."[80] A review for *The Stage* maintained that "until Mr. Robeson began the quick savage pants, expressing Eastern passion, in the ... Jealousy scenes ... one had no thought of discussing the moot point as to whether Othello should be merely a swarthy ... Moor or Arab."[81] Similarly, a writer for the *Western Morning News* reported, "The play's chief fault, the suddenness of Othello's abandonment to jealousy, is counteracted by the lack of restraint which seems natural in a colored actor...."[82] These critics argued that Othello should be played by black actors because they were more credible savages.

This theme of atavism was especially prominent in the 1930 reviews. As Richard Dyer has pointed out, "Faced with a black man, Paul Robeson, playing Othello, white critics easily expected this primitivist interpretation and when they did not get it were disappointed...."[83] The critic from the *Christian Science Monitor* illustrated this idea well. He lamented that "while this Oriental [Robeson] towers with rage, he never seems quite to lose control ... and become the savage." This was because "those familiar with Orientals," as this reviewer presumably was, "will realize how completely the veneer of civilization is apt to give place on provocation to savagery."[84] He sounded rather disenchanted that Robeson, though black, did not rise to the level of savage passion he would have expected. However, this critic did concede that because the play was so "frightful," any actor would have trouble playing a convincing Othello. Still, these critics, even though their language was laden with racial platitudes, did endorse the production overall.

In the reviews that lauded Robeson while critiquing the production, a few patterns emerged. These critics favored Robeson's performance and usually Ashcroft's and Thorndike's as well, but outlined the major problems of the production. C. B. Purdom extolled Robeson: "Without question, Robeson gives us the most impressive Othello that this generation has known ... I have praised Robeson as he deserves; but he suffers from the general character of the production."[85] A reporter for the *Sunday News* described the revival as "a curiously uneven production." Yet, he was sure of Robeson's achievement: "There are no half measures about his success. It is an out and out triumph."[86] Another reviewer ventured, "If it is a success, it will be due solely to Mr. Paul Robeson...."[87] The critic for the *Eastern Daily Press* agreed: "He clearly felt the part as nobody else on the stage did. It was as [if] it were an incarnation of his desire to show what his race could do."[88] If Robeson was a success, then what, according to these reviewers, were the chief liabilities of the production?

First, there was the problem of the length of the show with its three intermissions. Apparently, Browne and Van Volkenburg did not understand that "a good production of the play should carry us swiftly on."[89] Next, there was difficulty with the lighting. The play's program even admitted that "no attempt has been made to light the scenes, particularly the exterior scenes, realistically...." This was, in theory, going to preserve the aesthetic value of the sets as designed by painter James Pryde. (This was his first attempt at set design.) However, the lack of lighting, while perhaps visually appealing, was not practical or suitable for theater viewing, as the critics hastened to point out. Critic Hannen Swaffer bemoaned the lack of lighting, saying "how dark the stage was and how dull the play seemed, except when Robeson was dominating the stage."[90] Another reviewer groaned that "the dark stage is killing Shakespeare."[91] To complicate matters further, the ill-lit sets must have been rather bulky to move because several reviewers groused about the noisy scene shifters. All in all, the critic for the *Daily Telegraph* chided director Ellen Van Volkenburg for the "distressing preciosity" of the production and suggested, in the future, she should "distrust her tendency to overload her structure with decorative detail."[92]

Regrettably, Van Volkenburg's overbearing artistic vision did not end with the inadequate lighting and poor set design. One reporter complained that the production tended to be "fussy," for it had "too much play with torches and trumpets, and one little dance . . . which was too irrelevant to be effective."[93] The extraneous dance was particularly odious to one reviewer who explained that "two young ladies burst forth into an unnecessary and exasperatingly slow dance." The audience did not approve either, for "[t]hey went off to practically no applause at all."[94] Furthermore, the role of the clown did little to further the plot and was often cut from the *Othello* script. Van Volkenburg, curiously, decided that the clown should remain. This prompted the reviewer for the *Sunday Express* to sigh, "One of Shakespeare's stupidest clowns was allowed to bore."[95] According to the promptbook, the superfluous business on the stage amounted to a surging twenty-one extras that were listed on the program as "Senators, Officers, Gentlemen, Musicians and Attendants," not to mention an additional two

2.1 Paul Robeson as Othello in 1930. Photographs and Prints Division, Schomburg Center for Research in Black Culture, The New York Public Library, Astor, Lenox and Tilden Foundations.

Trumpeters, two Attendants for Desdemona, three Ladies of Cyprus, and apparently one tank with fish and water lilies!

The costuming was also problematic. One critic stated simply that Robeson "did not look well in his Venetian clothes."[96] The costuming trouble inhibited Robeson's performance, according to some critics. One reporter suggested, "Bad costuming was probably accountable for Paul Robeson's lack of impressiveness in the first two acts."[97] Photos substantiate the opinions of these reviewers (figure 2.1). Robeson was decked out in almost comical Renaissance-era regalia with puffy sleeves, tights, and rather unsoldierly decorative shoes. The promptbook described his costume for act I as "Green cloak trimmed with fur. Green and gold headdress.

Green tights and green shoes." He later donned a similarly fashioned plum cloak with plum tights and "Black shoes trimmed [with] plum velvet" in act II. This seemed hardly to be the attire of a respected military leader. Robeson's wardrobe would have been more appropriate, perhaps, for a ballet version of *Othello*. Sybil Thorndike corroborated the costuming issue in a biography: "I don't think Paul Robeson's [Elizabethan] costume was right for him." However, she remembered, "In his white robe at the end he looked superb. . . ."[98] The simple white robe, which he wore during the bedroom murder scene, was more understated and appropriate for the circumstances of the final act.

Not only were the sets scantily lit, but the staging of the production prevented the audience from engaging with the characters. Shakespeare's plays were originally produced, as at the Globe Theatre, with few props on a small apron stage. The "groundlings," who paid a small sum to stand for the performance, were close enough to touch and lean upon the stage on three sides. Thus, it was a very intimate and interactive environment. The revival at the Savoy, disappointingly, produced the exact opposite effect. The sets were distanced from the audience by two obstructing sets of stairs. Noting the steps, one critic opined humorously that this production would be more aptly titled "Murder on the Second Floor."[99] Edward MacDonald reprimanded the producer because "[t]his Othello is played without reference to the audience." And he reminded Van Volkenburg that Shakespeare "relied on the sweep and colour [sic] of his words . . . to express the setting of his drama."[100] With the script, again, the producer/director team opposed the traditional approach. It appeared that Van Volkenburg wished to emphasize artistic embellishments rather than the scope and vision of Shakespeare's language. One critic who was appalled with her lack of regard for the script described it as having been "somewhat mutilated" with even "modern words" substituted in the text.[101]

A number of critics were concerned that the action of the play was too remote. Ivor Brown believed this curtailed the potential power of Robeson's portrayal for "[h]ad he been playing Elizabethanly [sic] . . . so that we had his frenzy and agony in our very midst instead of at a mitigating remove, I think we might have shuddered back in our seats and wanted to slink away."[102] This was a vital point since *Othello* was a very personal play as a portrait of a man dishonored in his marriage. The most crucial scenes depended solely on the dynamic between Othello and Iago. In order for the plot to be at all feasible, the audience must believe in Othello's private agony and internal conflict. Additionally, the bloody climax occurred in

Othello and Desdemona's bed chamber. What could be more intimate? Yet, the bed in this production (which had enormous posts that towered over Robeson's six-foot-three frame) was placed at the top of the staircase at an angle, which definitely made the action more removed from the viewers and, therefore, less penetrating. If the audience could not participate closely in the emotional climax, then the play was rendered powerless.

Lastly, the portrayal of Iago must be considered a liability. This was most lamentable because his contaminating of Othello's mind was central to the plotline. The entire pulse of the play hinged upon the dynamic between Othello and his corrupter. However, Maurice Browne, the producer, mistakenly cast himself as the chief villain. The interaction between Browne and Robeson was not at all convincing, which inhibited the viability of the plot. A reporter characterized Browne's Iago as being "a restless, skipping, tripping nonentity."[103] The critic for the *Curtain* felt that "When Othello and Iago are on the stage together [it] is a solo performance by Othello."[104] Ivor Brown, writing for *The Observer*, proclaimed Robeson's Othello to be "as sturdy as an oak." Yet, Browne's Iago could not match this interpretation, for "the bigger your Othello, the bigger your Iago must be." He concluded, "Mr. Robeson's Moor is an oak brought down by a gimlet."[105] Thus, everything that encompassed Van Volkenburg's ostentatious artistic vision, from the lighting and sets to the script and costumes, as well as Browne's deficient portrayal of one of the leads, all represented impediments to the success of the Savoy production.

Finally, the reviews that were critical of both Robeson and the overall production must be examined. This discussion will focus on the critiques of Robeson, as the principle faults of the production have been noted. E. A. Baughan in the *Daily News* summed up his perception of the revival: "Never, then, have I been present at a performance of 'Othello' which has moved me less."[106] The negative view of Robeson's race was summarized in the *Daily Sketch*: "What special quality did Paul Robeson bring to Othello because of his race? Chiefly the knowledge that the Moor was . . . a slow-witted creature; [and] . . . easy prey to . . . Iago."[107] The primary complaints against Robeson, then, included a failure to master English blank verse, an overall lack of technique, and his possessing dark skin.

His trouble with the language was prominent and appeared even in some reviews that endorsed Robeson. There was an interesting divide on this problem: some critics were able to overlook it in favor of the overall performance, given Robeson's inexperience with Shakespearean acting. Others, however, had little patience when an actor muddled the Bard's poetry. This question also spoke to the larger difficulty of Robeson's acting technique. The favorable reviews sometimes noticed his lack of experience but felt that it enhanced the naturalness or simplicity of his performance. The critical reviews, on the other hand, seemed frustrated with this trait of Robeson's. For example, A. E. Wilson in *The Star* complained of Robeson's "monotony" and "rather wooden attitude."[108] James Agate, writing in the London *Sunday Times*, expressed that "Mr. Robeson, alas, failed not only to show mastery of the grand style, but also to indicate any idea of its existence! He said the lines with a casualness which amounted almost to the meaningless."[109] No less harsh was the critic in the *Empire News*: "I trust he [Robeson] realises [sic] by now that the great and deserved esteem in which he is held as a man [and] as a singer . . . is insufficient excuse for what might not inaptly be described as 'messing about with Shakespeare.'"[110] Another reviewer invoked his lack of technique on racial grounds, saying that "his acting has been naïve and entirely without sophistication. . . . It is as if the negro took to 'play acting' with something of the delight that a child has in it as a game."[111] One must bear in mind, however, that Robeson's approach to the character was "simple" and "direct" even though that might not have fulfilled the expectations of certain critics.

One of his fellow actors also commented on Robeson's technical ability. Sybil Thorndike was at this time a seasoned and respected Shakespearean actress. Many, indeed most, of the reviewers agreed with the assessment that "Sybil Thorndike's playing of Emilia [was a] performance given in the true spirit of Shakespeare and acted as it should be acted."[112] She reflected on working with Robeson in a biography: "He was such a dear person—and how he worked! He was potentially a fine actor, but he hadn't the technique of acting . . . . In our big scene together I used to have to go on saying, 'This is *your* scene. Take the stage.'"[113] This criticism had some merit, for he had not been rigorously trained as a tragedian. Clearly, Robeson had a genuine, organic talent for acting, but he was not an experienced Shakespearean actor nor did he receive the guidance of a competent director in this production. Nevertheless, Robeson's vocal ability was probably his greatest asset, and, in the British tradition, elevated speech was essential to playing Shakespeare. While he may not have mastered dramatic technique, he could rely on his background in elocution and his vocal aptitude.

Another recurring critique of Robeson recalled the Arab Moor versus Ethiopian debate. Quite a few critics were not convinced by Robeson's portrayal because they could not reconcile a dark-skinned actor playing Othello. One reporter appreciated Robeson's fine voice and asserted that it was more of an asset to him than his race, for "Othello is not an Ethiopian, but a Moor."[114] Alan Parsons, in the *Daily Mail*, could not fully accept Robeson: "Yet, the man [Othello] was a Moor and not an Ethiopian and though I was continually moved by his splendid, vibrant voice . . . I had throughout a disquieting feeling that it was not quite right, that this was not the *real* Othello."[115]

Complaints of Robeson's physical carriage were also related to his race. Numerous reviewers detected an inferiority complex in Robeson's gait and stage presence, which they attributed to his being from an oppressed race. This, they alleged, unduly inhibited Robeson's ability to play a commanding general from royal lineage. One reporter ascribed Robeson's art to that of "the born underdog."[116] James Agate elaborated: "He walked with a stoop, his body sagged, his hands appeared to hang below his knees and his whole bearing . . . and diction were full of humility and apology, the inferiority-complex in a word."[117] Another critic felt Robeson appeared to be "a member of a subject race, still dragging the chains of his ancestors. He was not noble enough. . . . He did not tower. He seemed to me a very depressed Othello."[118] The reporter for *Country Life*, George Warrington, observed how Robeson "slunk off the stage" rather than exiting as a victorious general and ruminated, "It is possible that he is afraid that his assumption of arrogance might be mistaken for the insolent assumptions of the less educated of his race."[119]

On the other hand, one critic opined that Robeson's "falling short of our highest hopes was not his fault, but due to the poverty of his support."[120] Indeed, playing Othello to a completely ineffectual Iago must not have been painless and could be reason enough to appear melancholy on stage. Doubtlessly, Robeson recognized that the production was weak, the costumes inappropriate, and the lighting poor. Additionally, he was inexperienced and he was not being directed capably. A number of reviewers understood that Robeson's performance suffered from poor direction. For example, critic M. Willson Disher was severely disparaging of Van Volkenburg's blocking decisions. He utilized the example of Othello's "It is the cause" speech in act V and rebuked her for breaking up the soliloquy by having Robeson unnecessarily walk across the stage. Disher seethed, "The only fit punishment for this is that Miss Van Volkenburg should wear a dunce's cap and be stood in a corner of the foyer. Has she never heard that poetry must flow or cease to be poetry?"[121]

In her diary, Robeson's wife, Eslanda, frankly expressed her frustrations with the ineptitude of both Browne and Van Volkenburg. On April 16, a few short weeks before the opening, she sighed, "Rehearsals continue [to be] dreadful. Nellie [Van Volkenburg] doesn't know what it is all about.... I don't believe she knows anything about the theatre at all. In any case, she can't help Paul. She can't even get actors from one side of the stage to the other. Poor Paul is lost." After the initial reviews came out, Eslanda confided in her diary, "Nellie and Maurice [Browne] caught the hell they so well deserved. Paul is worn out and nervous from the strain."[122] Other cast members shared the prevailing disaffection with the whole experience. Peggy Ashcroft recalled in a biography that although she had been excited about her Shakespearean debut, it was also "desperately disillusioning because it was a perfectly terrible production."[123] A biographer of Dame Sybil Thorndike summarized the climate backstage: "a generally uneasy time was had by all."[124] Thus, while there might have been valid grounds upon which to critique Robeson's debut performance, these criticisms must be put into the context of what was a deficient production overall.

The significance of the 1930 Browne/Van Volkenburg revival was that it opened the door to Robeson's interpretation of Shakespeare's Moor. It was a generally poor production and the reviews for Robeson's performance were mixed. Yet, it gave Robeson a starting point from which he would grow. The production was historic and generated press attention because of its dark-skinned leading actor. This helped cultivate the idea of Robeson one day portraying Othello in New York. Those in the theater world who embraced the notion of Robeson playing this role on Broadway wanted to see what he could do in a top-notch production. One of these people was Margaret Webster, who saw Robeson in 1930 and felt he might have some potential. She recalled the Savoy production when Robeson approached her years later about staging an *Othello* revival in the United States. In this way, the 1930 *Othello* was a bridge in Robeson's career between his early film and stage work and what would become his most beloved and historic characterization. He broke new ground in his debut as Othello and, thus, developed a more clearly defined idea of where he wanted to take the role when he returned to it twelve years later. In the interim, his position on African culture and involvement with politics ripened throughout the 1930s. These years of maturation were fundamental to the more discerning and politically acute interpretation he brought to the stage when he once again donned the robes of the Moorish general.

❖ ❖ ❖

CHAPTER THREE

A Burgeoning Political Consciousness

Robeson in the 1930s

In 1938, Paul Robeson visited Spain and was very moved by the courage and energy displayed by the residents of Madrid who had mobilized against fascism. While there, he sat for a brief interview in which he discussed the current civil war as well as his artistic endeavors. He explained how, early in his career, he had been eager about the prospect of playing Brutus Jones in Eugene O'Neill's play *The Emperor Jones* because in it he "saw the possibilities that a Black [actor] had in dramatic art."[1] However, he continued, "I must tell you that for me this was only a point of departure, a means to do more basic and important things, since it was necessary in a country like mine to demonstrate first that a man of color had artistic sensibility, and could walk the stage or pose before a movie camera with the same presence as the whites, and sometimes with greater presence. That is why I later portrayed *Othello*, and I am now preparing to do *King Lear*." Robeson viewed Brutus Jones as a jumping-off point that would propel him into weightier, serious roles like Othello. Although Robeson never performed in Shakespeare's *King Lear*, his interest in the role illustrated the high regard with which he held such classic characters in the Western canon.

Moreover, as the quote above implied, Robeson considered his first foray into Shakespearean theater, with *Othello* in 1930, to be a building block that would demonstrate his acting ability and stage presence, and would enable his career to progress. Through the 1930s, Robeson achieved greater stature as an artist while his resume grew to include numerous film and stage credits as well as scores of concert tours, which were always especially well received. More important, the trajectory of this decade can also be charted by the public emergence of his political advocacy. His burgeoning consciousness was of enormous significance to his interpretation of *Othello* on Broadway. One cannot fully understand the New York *Othello* without considering his political involvement, and any investigation of his politics must examine the transformative decade of the 1930s.

What were the principle influences on Robeson's life during this period? First, he resided in London for most of this decade, although he did travel to the U.S. for a few projects, like the film version of *Show Boat* in 1935. Robeson also journeyed throughout the U.K. and across Europe on concert tours, which broadened his perspective on folk music and introduced him to the working classes, left-wing artists, and intellectuals in a number of regions. Of great import was his first visit to the Soviet Union in 1934. Robeson referred to this trip often in speeches and interviews throughout his life, for he truly felt emancipated by the lack of racism he experienced there. Robeson was not alone in this regard. The welcome extended to African Americans by the Soviet Union offered a stark juxtaposition to the skyrocketing unemployment and discrimination New Deal programs dealt to African Americans back in the U.S. Other African Americans, like Langston Hughes, W. E. B. Du Bois, and Claude McKay, who traveled there in the 1930s felt unshackled by the antiracism of the Soviets and some, like William Patterson, James Ford, and Harry Haywood, believed that Communism could be a progressive force in the United States.

Robeson was impressed that the Soviet Constitution outlawed discrimination. This would have been particularly poignant to Robeson because his senior thesis at Rutgers, "The Fourteenth Amendment, The Sleeping Giant of the American Constitution," focused on citizenship rights in the U.S. Constitution. Robeson also decided to send his son to a Russian school in 1936 to protect him from the shroud of bigotry during his formative years. It was in Moscow that Robeson interacted with African American attorney William Patterson, who became a leader in the U.S. Communist Party and a friend of Robeson's. They worked together with the Civil Rights Congress in the late 1940s and early 1950s. One of their most significant collaborations was on the petition *We Charge Genocide* that both men, Robeson in New York and Patterson in Paris, presented to the United Nations in 1951. Robeson's visit to Spain during the civil war also heightened his regard for the troops there, especially the African American volunteers in the Abraham Lincoln Brigade, and bolstered his resolve against fascism.

This chapter will focus on a few key episodes in the evolution of Robeson's posture as a politically engaged artist. First, the years in London were crucial in his political development. While there, Robeson read voraciously and studied world language families at the London School of Oriental Languages. This intense study influenced Robeson to expand his concert repertoire of African American spirituals to include folk songs from a variety of countries, including Scotland, England and Russia. Robeson's decision was well received by audiences and prompted one British reviewer to assert that "if he adheres to his stated policy of singing nothing in the future but the folk songs of the world, he should become the greatest of the interpreters of folk music...."[2] Moreover, in this period, Robeson also began to articulate his views on black culture in articles that were published in a number of periodicals. This section will examine a few of the major themes regarding African culture that he pursued in these essays.

Second, Robeson's interaction with the diverse community of West Indians, African Americans, and Africans in London was also vital to his intellectual development. For instance, Robeson met African American activist Max Yergan during these years in London. At that time, Yergan was affiliated with the Young Men's Christian Association (YMCA) and had been working in South Africa. He wanted to establish an organization to inform the African American public about contemporary issues in Africa. Together, in 1937, Yergan and Robeson founded the International Committee on African Affairs, which would later be known as the Council on African Affairs. Robeson was also involved with London coalitions such as Harold Moody's League of Coloured Peoples and the West African Students Union, who made him an honorary member in 1933. Through such groups, he networked with future African leaders like Jomo Kenyatta and Kwame Nkrumah. Robeson strove during this period to fuse his artistic work with his blossoming political engagement. The best example of his synthesizing of politics and art during this decade was as the lead in C. L. R. James's play on the Haitian revolution, *Toussaint Louverture*, though it only enjoyed a short run on London's West End in March of 1936. This section will focus on James's play as an important precursor to Robeson's Broadway *Othello*.

Finally, in the late 1930s, Robeson made his commitment to utilize art in the fight against fascism explicit in a famous 1937 speech at London's Albert Hall. This section will examine that speech along with Robeson's hiatus from film work and his visit to the front of the Spanish civil war to sing for the troops fighting against Franco's regime. These elements in Robeson's life were situated against the backdrop of fascist rule that was spreading across Europe and which meant, in Robeson's view, that "the artist must take sides" in the contemporary struggle.

"I Want to Be African": Robeson on Black Culture

During the 1930s, after his debut in *Othello*, Paul Robeson substantially honed his position regarding African American culture by maintaining that African Americans suffered from an inferiority complex because they were attempting to emulate white culture. Instead, he declared, "What he [the African American] should do is try for 'black greatness' and not an imitation of 'white greatness.'"[3] Robeson believed that it would be through their distinctive traits that African Americans would make their most valuable contribution to American culture. Significantly, these characteristics were directly linked to their African lineage. Robeson posited that the African American "believes himself to have broken away from his true origins; he has, he argues, nothing whatever in common with the inhabitant of Africa today—and that is where I believe he is wrong."[4]

Robeson theorized that a fundamental divide existed between Eastern (i.e., Africans, Asians, and other so-called "primitives") and Western cultures. This divide was exemplified by the overreliance on intellectualism exhibited in the West. Intellectualism has led to technological advancements in applied science, but these have been attained at a great price. Robeson explained, "[T]he cost of developing the kind of mind by which the discoveries of science were made has [come] . . . at the expense of his creative faculties." Additionally, "In the West it [creativity] remains healthy and active only amongst those sections of the community which have never fully subscribed to Western values—that is, the exploited sections, plus some rebels from the bourgeoisie."[5] Thus, Robeson postulated, in American culture, specifically, African Americans possessed a greater capacity for creativity because they had not fully assimilated.

In Robeson's view, creativity was also linked closely to emotional depth, which he found to be lacking among westerners and highly developed in the darker races. He proposed, "No matter in what part of the world you may find him the Negro has retained his direct emotional response to outside stimuli . . . the Negro feels rather than thinks, experiences emotions directly rather than interprets them by roundabout and devious abstractions...." As a result of this intuitive nature, "His soul contains riches which can come to fruition only if he retains intact the full spate of his emotional awareness, and uses unswervingly the artistic endowments which nature has given him."[6] In sum, "His immense emotional capacity is the Negro's great asset." Robeson ruminated, "Given guidance and an outlet who can say what it might not achieve?"[7]

These elemental differences between Eastern and Western culture, therefore, should not be shunned but embraced in the black community for, as Robeson proclaimed, "It is not as imitation Europeans but as Africans, that we have a value."[8] How might these African traits be employed? Robeson asserted, "Now, as to the most important part which, in my opinion, the Negro is qualified to play in the American scene. I would define it as 'cultural,' with emphasis upon the spiritual aspect of the culture."[9] Cultural forms, then, would be of particular importance when considering the contributions of African Americans to American society. For example, unique cultural manifestations, such as the spirituals, were created as a result of the vital emotional qualities preserved in the African American community even through the most oppressive circumstances. Robeson explicated the emotional characteristics of black Americans: "They have been unhappy and badly treated, but they have retained (though they have not been fully able to express) their best and most characteristic qualities: a deep simplicity, a sense of mystery, a capacity for religious feeling, a spontaneous and entirely individual cheerfulness; and these have found expression in the only culture which Americans can point to as truly belonging to their country."[10] Spirituals, then, were manifested out of a deep reserve of emotion which emerged from the slave experience in the United States. This music was a uniquely American creation because it was not a musical form that emulated European art but was organic to the particular condition of African enslavement in the United States.

Robeson's analysis was illuminating for several reasons. First, he was addressing African American traits that were commonly exploited by the white community as evidence of inferiority. Yet, Robeson did not subscribe to the inferiority theory because, he argued, the white community perceived these traits through the lens of a Western worldview. Because they were preoccupied by the logic of scientific thought and out of touch with emotion or creativity, the white community misinterpreted the gifts of African Americans. Sterling Stuckey has contended that Robeson's thesis was evidence of his African nationalism. Stuckey pointed out, "Robeson, remarkably, did not hesitate to affirm without a trace of shame, in fact with great pride, some of the very qualities which whites thought stamped blacks as inferior: with pleasure he referred to the African's rich emotional heritage, his genius for music, his religiosity—traits from which many black intellectuals recoiled."[11] Richard Dyer has also argued, "Robeson represents the idea of blackness as a positive quality, often explicitly set over against whiteness and its inadequacies."[12] Robeson's perspective, then, privileged the emotional capacity of blackness as an antidote to the inherently reserved quality of Western art.

C. L. R. James has noted that during the production of *Toussaint Louverture* in 1936 Robeson "used to speak to me quite often about this type of what I may call the psychological personality of the Black man." Robeson, then, did not merely pursue his cultural analysis in essay form but continued to subject it to further explication in discussion with members of the Pan-African community such as James. When recollecting Robeson's cultural argument, James raised an important point. He observed that "while Paul was insisting that the Black man had special qualities which were the result of his past in Africa and his centuries of experience in the Western world, he was equally aware of the fact that this Black man was able to participate fully and completely in the distinctively Western arts of Western civilization."[13] Thus, Robeson maintained that the unique characteristics of people with African heritage did not preclude their ability to fully participate in Western art in a meaningful way. Robeson's own success in cherished Western art forms, such as Shakespeare, reinforced this idea. Robeson did not want to be excluded from Western art but believed that his cultural heritage could add emotional depth and enhance existing forms. An actor who was not black, for example, could not interpret Othello with the same qualities of emotional expression as Robeson.

Robeson's analysis, though primarily developed in England in the 1930s, underscored many of the ideals of the New Negro Renaissance (also known as the Harlem Renaissance) in the United States in the 1920s. African American art and social thought flourished during this cultural movement. For example, Alain Locke's foundational 1925 collection, *The New Negro*, paid tribute to the significance of African American cultural forms. Locke observed in his opening essay, "Recall how suddenly the Negro spirituals revealed themselves; suppressed for generations under the stereotypes of Wesleyan hymn harmony, secretive, half-ashamed, until the courage of being natural brought them out—and behold, there was folk music."[14] Similarly, in his essay "Negro Art and America," Albert Barnes postulated, "That there should have developed a distinctively Negro art in America was natural and inevitable." He continued, "It is a great art because it embodies the Negroes' individual traits and reflects their suffering, aspirations and joys during a period of acute oppression and distress."[15]

These ideas resembled Robeson's position pretty closely. Yet, it was not surprising that Robeson's views on black culture overlapped with those of the New Negro Renaissance since he came of age as a performer in Harlem in the 1920s. He gave his first recital of spirituals in 1925 when that music was in vogue and critically acclaimed. During that time, other vocalists, such as Roland Hayes, were also performing programs entirely of spirituals. Interestingly, African American spirituals remained essential to Robeson's repertoire for the next three and a half decades long after their heyday in the Harlem cultural scene. By maintaining his repertoire of folk music, which expanded to include folk songs from around the world, Robeson's vocal career helped demonstrate Barnes's conception that "[t]hrough the compelling powers of his poetry and music the American Negro is revealing to the rest of the world the essential oneness of all human beings."[16]

In addition, W. E. B. Du Bois theorized analogous ideas on black culture, especially concerning the spirituals. Du Bois, like Robeson, regarded the spirituals as a unique example of a truly American cultural form. In chapter fourteen of his landmark 1903 text, *The Souls of Black Folk*, Du Bois considered the spirituals to be evidence of "a gift of story and song" contributed by African Americans. One cannot avoid being moved by his heartfelt query: "Our song, our toil, our cheer, and warning have been given to this nation in blood brotherhood. Are not these gifts worth giving? Is not this work and striving? Would America have been America without her Negro people?"[17] Du Bois expanded on the notion of gifts advanced by the black community in his 1924 volume, *The Gift of Black Folk*. After outlining African American contributions in many fields of endeavor, Du Bois concluded that black Americans brought a "peculiar spiritual quality" to American civilization. This quality "though hard to define" possessed a "certain spiritual joyousness; a sensuous, tropical love of life" as well as an "intense sensitiveness to spiritual values." Indeed, such a characteristic revealed "the imprint of Africa on Europe in America."[18] Du Bois's and Robeson's theses were quite similar, especially when one considers Robeson as a practitioner of the spirituals and Du Bois a scholarly proponent of them. However, it did not appear that Du Bois's work was a direct influence on Robeson. Sterling Stuckey deduced, "Though both men were concerned with problems of cultural transmission, and though both respected each other long before eventually joining forces in the same organization, they appear to have arrived at their cultural positions, as closely related as they are, independently."[19]

Other artists and intellectuals developed similarly nuanced positions on culture during the Harlem Renaissance. Author Claude McKay, a West Indian, emphasized a common African heritage and was "keenly conscious of being a child of the diaspora" as articulated by St. Clair Drake in the introduction to McKay's autobiography *A Long Way From Home*.[20] McKay noted in his autobiography that while the white community had given the Negro race the benefits of modern civilization, they could not "give Negroes the gift of a soul."[21] He was, however, critical of the black middle class whom he viewed as a pitiable imitation of the white middle class because they lacked wealth and property. In his novels *Home to Harlem* and *Banjo*, McKay focused on the experience of the lower classes who still "enjoyed a more direct, vital, and realistic relationship to life" because they had not lost their "spontaneity" and "happiness" as had their middle-class counterparts in their attempt at assimilating to Western culture.[22] Interestingly, in 1937, Robeson starred in a film adaptation of McKay's *Banjo* titled *Big Fella*. Robeson's cultural theory was somewhat akin to McKay's although Robeson did not emphasize a class analysis in his writing on African culture in the 1930s. His class analysis, later in his *Freedom* column in the early 1950s, underscored the need for interracial unity among the working classes.

Robeson's essays on the centrality of black cultural forms were vital to examining his artistic career because Robeson took his inheritance of African identity to heart. In 1935, he decreed that "for the rest of my life I am going to think and feel as an African—not as a white man."[23] Furthermore, this commitment directly impacted his artistic productivity. The following year he announced, "Meanwhile, in my music, my plays, my films, I want to carry always this central idea—to be African. Multitudes of men have died for less worthy ideals; it is even more eminently worth living for."[24]

How then did Robeson's perception of African culture relate to *Othello*? First, and perhaps most obviously, playing Othello fulfilled Robeson's ambition to maintain ties to African culture since Othello was an African character. This also spoke to the question of why Robeson returned to this particular role more than any other in his career. In addition to being an African role, it was a Shakespearean role that was respected in the Western canon, the combination of which was extremely rare. Despite his critique of much of Western culture, Robeson felt an affinity for Shakespeare's English.

In the same article where he proclaimed that he would think and feel as an African, he also wrote, "I found that I, who lacked feeling for the English language later than Shakespeare, met Pushkin . . . on common ground."[25] Shakespeare's English probably felt familiar to him because it was the language of the King James Bible to which Robeson was exposed from an early age in the A.M.E. Zion church. It was through Shakespeare that Robeson also had his introduction to oratory in high school. Thus, Robeson was attracted to the role of Othello because he felt comfortable with Shakespeare's language and because it was an African character.

Robeson's analysis of African culture was also vital to understanding why he would not be offended by the qualities that Shakespeare endowed in the Moor of Venice. In fact, the traits which some might read as demeaning stereotypes, especially in the twenty-first century, would have been embraced by Robeson as highlighting Othello's African sensibilities. For example, Othello clearly possessed a deep reserve of emotion, especially regarding his love of Desdemona. Othello remarked, in act III, scene 3, "Perdition catch my soul, / But I do love thee! And when I love thee not, / Chaos is come again." His love was so encompassing that if anything were to impinge on it, it would throw Othello's entire world into chaos. This, of course, was exactly what happened in the play. Moreover, several of Robeson's postulates on African traits were directly applicable to Othello. First, Robeson wrote that the African "feels rather than thinks," which perfectly described Othello's jealousy. Next, he maintained that the African "experiences emotions directly rather than interprets them," which demonstrated how Othello played precisely into Iago's scheme. Third, Robeson felt that the African possessed a "deep simplicity," which illustrated how Othello could trust Desdemona's love so implicitly one moment and yet immediately believe Iago's suspicions the next moment. Finally, according to Robeson, the African embodied a "sense of mystery," which was one of the primary reasons Desdemona fell in love with Othello in the first place.

Thus, Robeson did not perceive Othello's character traits as inherently negative or inferior but as African. Locke evocatively described coming to such a realization as "shaking off the psychology of imitation and implied inferiority."[26] Robeson did not aim to imitate a white interpretation of Othello onstage but to explore his uniquely African character traits. These characteristics which, some might claim, exemplified Othello's inferiority actually made him, according to Robeson's analysis, more authentically African. In this way, Othello was Robeson's consummate opportunity to "be African" onstage.

With this in mind, the appraisals of Robeson as Othello can be interpreted in a completely new manner. The reviews from all three of Robeson's productions were replete with references to his "simplicity" or "naturalness" as Othello. Such comments can be construed, especially in hindsight, as degrading to Robeson, and some very well may have been written in that spirit. However, according to Robeson's analysis, such reviews were not essentially negative. If he came across onstage as simple and natural, then he had portrayed Othello effectively, since Robeson viewed such as traits as intrinsically African. Robeson might have thought to himself, "Of course I look natural portraying an African because I am an African!"

One important question remained: if Robeson did most of his theorizing on African culture in the 1930s, did he change his position later? The centrality of the Afro-American and African freedom struggles to all of his endeavors, artistic and political, from the late 1930s to the end of the 1950s demonstrated that he maintained his commitment to "think and feel as an African." Furthermore, *Othello* was probably the best example that he did not alter his view of African culture. It was the only role he played onstage from 1943 to 1959. He could have accepted other parts, especially in the 1940s when his popularity was at its height. However, Robeson must not have been offered any other roles that met his expectations for portraying African culture with dignity. That was why he left the film industry in 1942. The most compelling evidence, however, was Robeson's landmark comeback concert at Carnegie Hall in May of 1959, just a few months prior to his final production of *Othello*. Before reciting Othello's final monologue, Robeson firmly emphasized Othello's African heritage: "Othello came from a culture as great as that of ancient Venice. He came from an Africa of equal stature. . . ."[27] The conviction in Robeson's commanding baritone when underscoring the term "equal" was unmistakable that night. Othello's African origin remained central to his assessment of the character through the late 1950s. Furthermore, the opportunity to portray Shakespeare's Moor in the mid-1940s and again in the late 1950s allowed Robeson to sustain the connection between his cultural theory and his artistic career.

Robeson in C. L. R. James's *Toussaint Louverture*

"I 'discovered' Africa in London," recalled Paul Robeson in a 1953 article in *Freedom* newspaper.[28] London's diversity stemmed primarily from immigrants who left British colonies for jobs and education in the metropolis.

During the 1930s, Robeson interacted with future leaders of Africa, and he became acquainted with C. L. R. James, a scholar from the West Indies. In 1932, James had sailed from his home in Trinidad to the United Kingdom. While there, he ghostwrote an autobiography of the famous cricketer Learie Constantine. The prolific Trotskyist remained busy throughout the thirties, publishing several more volumes during that decade including *The Case for West Indian Self Government*, *Minty Alley* (a novel), and *World Revolution 1917–1936*. James also met with Leon Trotsky in Mexico, and the exiled leader regarded James as a leading expert on the "Negro question." In addition, James completed the archival research for his groundbreaking monograph on the San Domingo revolution of 1791–1804, *The Black Jacobins*, published in 1938. Audiences, however, got a sample of James's scholarship on Haiti in 1936 when he fashioned the historical data into a play, *Toussaint Louverture*, starring Paul Robeson as the black revolutionary hero.

In 1926, Robeson disclosed to an interviewer that he dreamed of doing "a great play about Haiti, a play about Negroes, written by a Negro, and acted by Negroes."[29] Then, in 1934 while visiting Russia, Robeson had discussed making a film about Haiti and Toussaint L'Ouverture with Soviet film director Sergei Eisenstein. This film was never produced so it was C. L. R. James's interpretation of Toussaint onstage that ultimately fulfilled Robeson's desire. James's play was most definitely "a play about Negroes, written by a Negro, and acted by Negroes." It embraced the black man as a dramatic hero while inserting him directly into the current political discourse. *Toussaint* was an important precursor to Robeson's Broadway *Othello* on several levels. First, it gave Robeson the opportunity to portray another dignified black leading character. In doing so, Robeson also challenged James's conception of black masculinity and had a lasting impact on James's view of black leadership. Second, the *Toussaint* play offered vital commentary on the current political climate, including the Italian invasion of Ethiopia, just as *Othello* on Broadway was produced against the critical backdrop of World War II. Arguably, more than any other piece prior to Robeson's New York debut in *Othello*, *Toussaint Louverture* in 1936 reflected his progression toward becoming a more politically astute performer and provided a vehicle that merged a growing radical Left sensibility with an anticolonial consciousness.

Why did James choose to present the narrative of the Haitian revolution as a play prior to its release as a historical monograph? A talented writer, James produced a novel, literary criticism, history, social commentary, political theory, and an array of letters over the course of his lifetime. Why, then, choose to tell the specific story of Toussaint in the theater? In part, James wanted to ensure that this particular narrative was accessible to the general public. James believed that two of the great periods of classic drama occurred in ancient Greece when Sophocles, Euripides, and Aeschylus produced their great works and in Elizabethan England when Shakespearean drama was at its height. The medium of drama, according to James, aimed to "attract the attention of the masses." He explained, "As among the Greeks, the whole nation from the highest to the lowest was represented in the Shakespearean audience."[30] James viewed the theater as a means of expression that could attract a mass audience. People who might not have access to or be inclined to read a history like *The Black Jacobins* might take advantage of an opportunity to see a dramatization of historical events. James felt strongly about conveying this narrative to the broadest possible audience. Also, the impact of drama could be greater than that of a monograph. James elucidated this idea when discussing the pace of Shakespeare's plots. He observed that drama opened a "new world of movement" that could bring to life "the clash of social forces."[31]

How better to convey the drama of Haiti's revolution to a mass audience than by having Paul Robeson, star of stage, films and concert hall, portray the hero? In fact, James later recalled that the Stage Society in London agreed to mount the production if Robeson could be cast as the lead.[32] In one of his letters to literary critics, James offered a definition of a great artist as "an individual who embodies in himself some mighty social current of thought and feeling."[33] James must have sensed Robeson's greatness coming to fruition for, in 1936, Robeson was on the cusp of embodying the social currents of his era. This idea was not lost on the reviewers of *Toussaint*, for several of them noticed that the dignified revolutionary leader was a character after Robeson's own heart. It was not until the late 1930s that Robeson forthrightly proclaimed his political views. At that point, he became a great artist according to James's conceptualization. For the rest of his career, Robeson's art embodied some contemporary social current, whether it was antifascism, peace with the Soviets, or self-determination for African colonies.

Robeson's and James's interaction was significant to Robeson's career because *Toussaint* provided him with a unique opportunity to play a dignified black hero as written by a black playwright. Getting to know Robeson also impacted James greatly. For example, Robeson's physical presence made a lasting impression on James. In 1970, James still recalled with detail

Robeson's "magnificent self," from his height and proportions to his obvious strength and the "litheness of a great athlete" which Robeson possessed.[34] Robert Hill has commented on the effect which working with Robeson had on James, saying that "at a very fundamental level, Robeson as a man *shattered* James's colonial conception of the Black Physique."[35] Robeson's dignified carriage, his larger-than-life bearing coupled with supreme self-possession forced James to rethink the inheritance of British colonialism which decreed the inferiority of black masculinity.

The *Toussaint* project also afforded James the chance to build a friendship with a man whom he later described as "one of the most remarkable men of the twentieth century." Because Robeson and James migrated to opposing ends of the socialist spectrum, their direct interaction did not last long beyond the play's production. However, Robeson's character and charisma clearly had a long-term influence on James. He came to believe that Robeson could have personally led a social movement for black civil rights. He surmised that "if Paul had wanted to he would have built a movement in the United States that would have been the natural successor to the Garvey movement." Instead, Robeson committed himself to the possibility of a world revolution led by the Communist Party that could "save society from the evils of imperialism and capitalism . . . and could assist Black people in the United States to gain freedom and equality. . . ."[36] To James, Robeson could have been an important leader of black people in the tradition of West Indians like Marcus Garvey and Toussaint L'Ouverture. It was powerful, then, for James to have had the opportunity to cast Robeson as Toussaint, a historical figure who helped begin and lead a revolution. However, though he was a significant force for the revolutionary movement, Toussaint was not present for the formation of the independent black republic. It was Dessalines who ultimately established the independent black government in Haiti. As Michelle Stephens has posited, it was Toussaint's absence in this final step toward freedom that manifested the tragedy in James's drama.[37] Similarly, reflecting in 1970, James conceived of Robeson's absence from the consciousness of the contemporary civil rights leadership as tragic. He lamented, "The present generation of militant young Blacks have not merely forgotten him. It is worse. They never knew him. . . ."[38] The legacy of Robeson's foundational activism went largely unacknowledged by the generation which took the reins of the freedom struggle in the 1960s.

While James aimed to reach the masses through the medium of drama, he also intended that the play express his commentary on the current political circumstances of the Pan-African world. James once asserted that in order to assess a noncontemporary author, a critic "must get into his own head what were the social and political assumptions of the work he is studying."[39] What, then, was the political premise which James was addressing through *Toussaint* in the 1930s? James was exploring the possibilities for resisting colonization and pursuing self-government in a postcolonial context. There existed a clear link between the timing of the 1936 production of James's play and the invasion of Ethiopia by Mussolini's fascist troops the previous year. One perceptive theater critic summed up the political context of *Toussaint*, saying that "it is a great romance that at a time when Italy is crushing out Abyssinia with gas bombs and aeroplanes [sic] and tanks, there has been produced in London . . . a play by a coloured man in which he pleads for his people."[40]

Anna Grimshaw explicated this connection further in her introduction to *The C. L. R. James Reader*. She pointed out that *Toussaint* had been planned as a response to the debates concerning intervention in the Ethiopian crisis. Grimshaw noted that James "hoped to make his audience aware that the colonial populations were not dependent upon leadership from Europe in their struggle for freedom, that they already had a revolutionary tradition of their own."[41] She asserted in another essay that the play "had considerable impact in left wing circles."[42] One of James's primary concerns as a theorist was the form that the world revolution would take, and he proposed that it could begin in Africa. James believed that "the future is not born all at once. It exists in the present." The key was to "know where to look."[43] By demonstrating the revolutionary tradition of Haiti through *Toussaint* and later the monograph *The Black Jacobins*, James hoped to illustrate "how the African revolution would develop."[44] Thus, out of the present circumstance of crisis in Africa the future anticolonial struggle could be born.

Through this play, James implored the current and future leaders of anticolonial revolutions in Africa (several of whom he knew personally) not to make the same misjudgment as Toussaint, who had not relied on the instincts of the masses once the revolution was in motion. Toussaint misplaced his hope on the idea of fraternity with the French. However, his aspiration of inclusion in the French empire was erroneous. Michelle Stephens observed that a vision of fraternity on equal terms with the French was not possible because of Toussaint's race and his previous condition of enslavement.[45] James was suggesting through the illustration of Toussaint's miscalculation that future anticolonial leaders, instead, should aim for self-determination within a theoretical Pan-African empire rather than looking to Europe and the United States for alliances. Black self-government in a postcolonial context would be most successful within the framework of a black empire so that black leaders would not feel compelled to rely on fraternal relationships with their former colonizers. Stephens explained that James invoked the trope of the black empire because "[t]he dream of a black empire is a necessary fiction for the maintenance of an internationalist vision of black freedom embodied in the autonomous black state."[46] Thus, whether or not the notion of a black empire was feasible, the timing of James's play was intended to provide an analysis of the contemporary battle against fascist forces in Ethiopia and the wider question of independence for all African colonies. James must have been heartened if he read the theater review that remarked, "During a meeting of Negroes which I attended as a protest against Italy's invasion of Abyssinia, I heard speakers refer with pride to the inspiring life of Toussaint, a great man of color."[47]

For Robeson, the opportunity to portray Toussaint fulfilled his commitment to work on projects that presented African characters and themes with dignity. Additionally, the political implications of *Toussaint Louverture* foreshadowed the Broadway *Othello*. The stand against segregation taken by the New York *Othello* cast was part of the larger framework of activism during World War II that included the double victory campaign waged in the black community for victory over discrimination at home after the victory over fascism abroad. The political context of *Toussaint* also corresponded well with Robeson's growing antifascism and anticolonialism. Not until he broke the color barrier on Broadway in *Othello* would Robeson again have the chance to perform in a production which fully animated both his artistic and his political aims. The potency of *Othello* would be much greater, however, due to its unprecedented success, the fact that it was performed in his native land, and because Robeson had made his commitment to being a politically engaged artist more explicit in the late thirties.

The critical reception of *Toussaint* also predicted that of the Broadway *Othello*. Reporters emphasized traits like "dignity," "nobility," and "naturalism" that were also underscored in the commentary on Robeson's Othello portrayals. These were characteristics that Robeson highlighted in his essays on African culture. Thus, like Othello, Toussaint was a role that animated Robeson because it illuminated his theoretical vision of African characteristics. His excitement was certainly reflected in his stage performance, given the glowing reviews. Robeson's embrace of the role was observed by M. Willson Disher: "Mr. Paul Robeson found a hero after his own heart." He added that "it was good to see Mr. Robeson's wholehearted response to his part...."[48] General accolades for Robeson were not in short supply. For example, one reviewer summarized that Robeson "is one of the most impressive actors alive."[49] A writer for *Drama* noted that "Robeson moves through [the play] with that easy grace and sincere conviction that belong to anything he does."[50]

However, it was the reviewer for the organ of the League of Coloured Peoples, *The Keys*, who captured the particular context of *Toussaint*. This black periodical in London had been especially critical of Robeson's 1934 film *Sanders of the River* and, thus, found *Toussaint* to be a refreshing addition to Robeson's repertoire. The reviewer of *Toussaint* was most pleased to finally see Robeson in a play "worthy of his powers" and asserted that Robeson "does not fail to show what a great Negro actor can do, given the scope."[51] The scope, in this case, was portraying a dignified, heroic black lead character written by a black playwright, who specifically aimed to reach a broad audience and illuminate the future implications of the current Ethiopian crisis.

The Late 1930s: "The Artist Must Take Sides"

In 1937, Paul Robeson inaugurated a fund to aid African Americans fighting for democracy in the Spanish civil war. The *Negro Worker* reported, "In making his contribution of $250, Mr. Robeson said that he believed that there were hundreds of Negroes in the theatre and musical life who would understand that a hunger for equality for all oppressed mankind impelled him to take this step." Robeson commented on the severity of the Spanish crisis: "The freedom of all Peoples of the world is at stake in the conflict in Spain."[52] This action was indicative of Robeson's public stand against fascism in the late 1930s. Two significant events near the close of this decade demonstrated that Robeson's political conscience was increasingly influencing his artistic life. First, he took a hiatus from film work because he could not control the demeaning images of people of color that were continually projected through this medium. Second, his public stand as an artist against fascism culminated in one of his most celebrated speeches in London in June of 1937. The next year, Robeson confirmed his commitment by singing to the troops at the front in Spain. Thus, when Robeson returned to the United States in 1939, it was after having witnessed the proliferation of fascism across Europe and having made a pledge, as an artist, to support the cause of freedom and democracy. When, in 1942, his *Othello* premiered in the United States, Robeson's fame was based not solely on his artistic merit but also on his being a politically engaged performer.

❖ ❖ ❖

In a 1937 interview with the London *Daily Worker*, Robeson explained his current position regarding the film industry: "I shan't do any more films after the two that are being made now. . . . I thought I could do something for the Negro race on the films: show the truth about them—and about other people too. I used to do my part and go away feeling satisfied. . . . [However] [t]hings were twisted and changed—distorted. . . . That made me think things out. It made me more conscious politically. One man can't face the film companies. They represent about the biggest aggregate of finance capital in the world: that's why they make their films that way. So no more films for me."[53] *The Keys* celebrated Robeson's choice: "We congratulate Mr. Paul Robeson on his decision not to act in any more films until he can get a 'cast-iron' story—one that can't be distorted in the making."[54] Actually, Robeson did not break from the film industry permanently until 1942, but he stated similar reasons for doing so at that point. Still, this hiatus from film work in the late 1930s underscored his growing mistrust of and frustration with capitalist-driven art production. Robeson's attempts to fuse his political convictions with his artistic work were successful on the concert stage as a solo vocalist because within that framework he had total control of the presentation. His disappointment with film as a progressive medium meant that the stage would become a crucial vehicle for his artistic expression. This was especially true with Othello because it would be, as it turned out, the only character he played onstage from 1942 to 1959.

In his 1958 memoir, Robeson reflected upon Europe in the 1930s. He ruminated, "The years that I lived abroad witnessed the rise of fascism: the crash of martial music and the sound of marching jackboots drowned out the songs of peace and brotherhood." He was discouraged that Western nations had failed to act decisively against Franco and Mussolini. Robeson charged, "The Western powers were calm and unmoving in the face of the agony of Ethiopia and Spain." It was significant that Robeson linked Ethiopia, an important symbol for African nationalists, and Spain, an icon for the Left. This illustrated that the antifascist struggle, in Robeson's view, was a global, interracial movement. Robeson had also observed trade unions and coalitions within the British middle class mobilize against fascism. He then concluded, "And so it was that I, as an artist, was drawn into that movement and I came to see that the struggle against fascism must take first place over every other interest."⁵⁵

In joining this broad-based campaign against fascism, Robeson elucidated his position at a rally sponsored by the National Joint Committee for Spanish Relief of the Basque Refugee Children at the Royal Albert Hall on June 24, 1937.⁵⁶ Robeson was initially scheduled to broadcast a radio address from Moscow but, when asked by the committee, he traveled to speak in London personally. This accentuated his commitment to the message he delivered that night. He began by highlighting his belief that art should be rendered in service to the people. Robeson opened by saying, "Like every true artist, I have longed to see my talent contributing in an unmistakably clear manner to the Cause of Humanity. I feel that tonight I am doing so." He stressed that every person "must decide *now* [his emphasis] where he stands" with regard to the antifascist cause. No matter what one's profession might be, one must support the opposition because "through the propagation of false ideas of racial and national superiority, the artist, the scientist, the writer is challenged." Specifically, Robeson emphasized the role of the artist and his personal commitment to stand against fascism. He forthrightly affirmed the role of the artist in a time of political crisis: "The artist must take sides. He must elect to fight for Freedom or for Slavery. I have made my choice. . . . Not through blind faith or coercion, but conscious of my course, I take my place with you. I stand with you in unalterable support of the Government of Spain . . . because the liberation of Spain from the oppression of Fascist reactionaries is not a private matter . . . but the common cause of all advanced and progressive Humanity." Robeson stressed that he reached this decision "not through blind faith or coercion" but through careful rumination that made him conscious of his course. His pledge was thoughtful and certainly not a decision that he had reached overnight. This statement represented the culmination of years of study, observation, and dialogue throughout the 1930s. Robeson's deliberate pronouncement to stand, as an artist, with the forces of democracy against fascism influenced the path of his political and artistic career for the rest of his public life. Robeson believed passionately that there would be no progress toward full citizenship for African Americans or independence for colonized and oppressed people if fascism was allowed to spread unabated. On these grounds, he classified himself as antifascist throughout World War II and into the cold war era.

This decision compelled Robeson to visit the Spanish front in 1938 and it was, as he remembered later, "a major turning point in my life." There, he saw firsthand "that it was the working men and women of Spain who were heroically giving 'their last full measure of devotion' to the cause of democracy in that bloody conflict. . . ." Moreover, Robeson was impressed that the working classes from other countries responded to the call to aid the Spanish freedom fighters. Included in these forces were the American volunteers serving in the Abraham Lincoln Brigade, which was an interracial group organized through the Communist Left at a time when the armed forces in the United States were still strictly segregated. Robeson encountered these troops and recalled feeling "a sense of great pride in my own people when I saw that there were Negroes, too, in the ranks of the Lincoln [Brigade]. . . ." Ultimately, Robeson asserted, "Spain—the antifascist struggle and all that I learned in it—brought me back to America."[57] Upon returning to the United States, Robeson immediately became identified with progressive and antifascist coalitions. He continually strove to wed his political beliefs with his artistic endeavors. Nowhere would those two forces in Robeson's life be more successfully conjoined than during the run of the *Othello* from its debut in 1942 until its final curtain in New York in 1945.

◆ ◆ ◆

CHAPTER FOUR

Robeson's Othello on Broadway

In his book *Creating a Role*, the influential theorist of dramaturgy Constantin Stanislavsky created a framework through which an actor could approach a new role. He maintained the fundamental importance of understanding the play in its entirety in order to place the character one was portraying into the broader context of the play itself. Stanislavsky suggested that the outer trappings of plot and circumstance would lead the actor to discover the true inner mysteries of the character. He posited, "There is a direct bond between the internal and external circumstances of a play. . . . It is difficult to assess them separately. If you penetrate through the external facts of a play and its plot to their inner essence, going from periphery to center, from form to substance, you inevitably enter the inner life of the play."[1] Though Stanislavsky's basis for this analysis was to aid the actor who needed to conceptualize an unfamiliar role, his framework can also be useful in analyzing the historic Broadway production of *Othello* that starred Paul Robeson. As Stanislavsky suggested, the external circumstances were inextricably linked to uncovering the "inner life" of the production.

What, then, were the "external facts" surrounding the periphery of this celebrated Broadway revival? First, the historical and political context of the Second World War was paramount. The continued discrimination against African Americans through segregation and disenfranchisement was also crucial to the context of the production. In the summer of 1942, when *Othello* premiered, the United States was still reeling from the surprise attack on Hawaii the previous December and was in the throes of a tremendous mobilization, the scope of which was staggering and unprecedented. Early naval defeats in the Pacific meant that a victorious outcome for the United States was far from certain. The war effort was inevitably on the minds of the audience members who flocked to see Paul Robeson's American debut as Othello. African Americans who enthusiastically purchased tickets for the show had undoubtedly considered the importance of harnessing the antifascist spirit of the war to also defeat discrimination in the United States for a "double victory" against fascism abroad and the manifestations of domestic fascism. They knew that de facto and de jure segregation on the home front was mirrored by strict segregation of African Americans in the armed forces including the blood supplies provided by the Red Cross.

How do these external circumstances help uncover the "inner essence" of this Broadway production? The inner essence or import of this revival was not simply that Robeson was the first African American to portray Shakespeare's Othello on Broadway. The significance of the production lay in the calculated vision of the production team which emerged from the context of the historical circumstances of the war and contemporary racial segregation. The profundity of Robeson breaking the color barrier was considerably strengthened by the deliberate methodology behind Robeson's and director Margaret Webster's vision for a revival with a black lead actor. Both publicly argued in favor of a black actor playing Othello. Insisting on an interracial cast in segregated America meant that they faced obstacles in mounting the initial summer stock production. The cast further supported Robeson's stand against performing in segregated theaters when the troupe embarked on a U.S. tour. The wartime context was consciously invoked in a program note which linked Othello's service for Venice with the interracial fight against fascism. Robeson also alluded to the circumstances of the war in his commentary on the play. The historic nature of this production, then, was born directly out of the external conditions of the contemporary moment. The revival purposefully made a statement concerning the present circumstances of both the war and segregation through the vehicle of Shakespeare's *Othello*.

Additionally, the inner essence of the production was indelibly marked by Robeson's presence as the lead actor. His interpretation of Othello had developed since his professional debut in the role in 1930. The perspective that he brought to the play in the 1940s was no doubt influenced by the evolution of his antifascist political thought that had blossomed throughout the previous decade. Perhaps most important, the actor playing the title character exuded a towering stage presence that did not simply convey the character of Othello but also radiated his personal charisma with a sense of purpose that undergirded each performance. Paul Robeson was one of the world's most recognized celebrities in the early 1940s, and this fame was inextricably linked to his involvement in the worldwide struggle against injustice and fascism. Paul Robeson on Broadway meant more than merely subverting the color bar in New York. He was ever mindful of the importance of locating openings in which to advocate for the dignity of his people. This conscious effort to use his celebrity for a social purpose infused the production with political undertones.

Nathaniel Buchwald, writing in the *Morning Freiheit* newspaper, drew an illustrative parallel between Robeson's offstage persona and his portrayal of Shakespeare's Moor. He cited one example: "As Othello proudly describes his courtship of Desdemona, you cannot help but hear the proud son of the Negro people, Paul Robeson, denounce the American Brabantios of his own day who also maintain that normal social relationships between Negroes and whites are 'against all rules of nature.'" Buchwald continued with another illustration: "You get the impression that Othello attains his high station despite his black skin . . . even as Paul Robeson does in his own field of endeavor." Moreover, he summarized the distinctiveness of Robeson's stage interpretation: "Yes, the great, the original, the compelling, the revealing element in Paul Robeson's Othello is Paul Robeson."[2] Robeson's own charisma and unique position as a political advocate added texture and power to his stage persona. Without Robeson's singular presence, the production would have been markedly different, lacking in political implications, and quite possibly never would have occurred at all. It was Robeson who approached Margaret Webster when he felt his acting had sufficiently matured to again take on the role of the Moor of Venice. Yet it was not only his theatrical ability that had taken shape in the twelve years between the London production and the Cambridge premiere, Robeson's political analysis was also more fully realized. This enabled the Broadway production to offer an incisive vision that was grounded in the contemporary historical reality.

Robeson's and Webster's Vision for *Othello* on Broadway

This production of *Othello*, directed by Margaret Webster, has been chronicled not only by theater historians and biographers, but by Robeson in various speeches and articles and especially by Webster who wrote copious letters and essays. A word about Webster's theater background will help illuminate her approach to directing Shakespeare. Webster was the only daughter of two British theater legends, Dame May Whitty (1865–1948) and Ben Webster (1864–1947). Thus, she was baptized into a life in the theater from the beginning. Though she became most famous as a director, she began her theatrical career as an actor working with contemporary luminaries such as Sybil Thorndike, John Gielgud, and Laurence Olivier.

In the late 1920s, Webster was a member of the Ben Greet Players who performed Shakespeare in repertoire at outdoor venues around Britain. This experience helped engrain in her the idea that Shakespeare was intended to be performed for the masses and should not be held to impossible standards or made elitist and inaccessible. Webster came to believe that Shakespeare could only be truly revealed on stage because "plays do not come totally alive without the human element of incarnation." As a result, "stage people tend to find their academic counterparts either baffling or exasperating."[3]

By the time *Othello* debuted as a summer stock production in Cambridge, Massachusetts, in 1942, Webster was an accomplished director of playwrights such as Henrik Ibsen and Tennessee Williams, though she was primarily associated with her interpretations of Shakespeare in the United States, which included *Richard II*, *Twelfth Night*, and *Macbeth*. Brooks Atkinson, the seasoned theater critic for the *New York Times*, pronounced Webster to be "the finest director of Shakespeare this town ever had."[4] Webster maintained an extremely full work load all of her life through acting, directing, writing about the theater, adapting plays, and starting a repertory company. For example, in 1942 just a few months prior to the *Othello* opening, she published *Shakespeare Without Tears*, a book of Shakespearean commentary. Webster also gave lectures on the Bard while maintaining a live radio broadcast reading Charlotte Bronte's *Jane Eyre* five mornings a week. Uta Hagen, who portrayed Desdemona in the Broadway *Othello*, remarked that while Webster was "a brilliant woman," she "belonged in a university."[5] Indeed, Webster did end up as a Regents Professor of Theater at the University of California, Berkeley, in the early 1960s.

Webster argued in *Shakespeare Without Tears* that *Othello* involved "a sweep of movement which, in the theater, overwhelms all theoretical debate as to the motivation of its principal characters."[6] As a result, Webster did not trouble herself over the question of Iago's motivation or the somewhat bewildering fact that the basis of the plot hinged almost entirely on a missing handkerchief. She did assert, however, that Iago's motivation was no mystery, for the audience must simply accept his explicit confession that "I hate the Moor."[7] The "sweep of movement" that she imagined in

Shakespeare Without Tears was brought to life onstage in her production of *Othello*. Several critics commented on the whirlwind pace of Webster's direction in their reviews. She condensed the play down to two acts, each with four scenes. In this way, the play was presented with such swiftness so as not to give the audience time to question the plot. This framework immediately differentiated the Broadway *Othello* from the lengthy 1930 London production, with its three intervals and extraneous flourishes like the dancing women.

In addition, Webster viewed Othello's status as an outsider from the Venetian ruling class to be of principal importance to the plot. She addressed this issue not only in *Shakespeare Without Tears* but also in several articles. As if to assuage any doubt as to Othello's racial orientation, her essay in the souvenir program for the Broadway revival was titled "The Black Othello." In it, she outlined a brief history of the play since the Elizabethan era as evidence for her position on Othello's race. Webster unequivocally stated, "The difference in race between Othello and every other character in the play is, indeed, the heart of the matter." The program for the Princeton performance in 1942 included a note to clarify Othello's racial origin as a dark-skinned African and concluded that "[t]he traditional concept of Othello as a North African Mohammedan Moor is a historical inaccuracy." To further underscore her position, Webster asserted clearly in a piece in the *New York Times* that Othello's race distanced him from Venetian society to such an extent that it "throws into the sharpest relief all the emotional conflicts of the play [and it is] the essential vulnerable point on which Iago fastens [and it] gives depth and poignancy to the tempest which he arouses in Othello's soul and leads directly to tragedy and destruction."[8]

Webster's writing, however, was not devoid of racial stereotyping. Although she advocated casting a black actor to play Othello, the racialized language she utilized was at times revealing. Some of her writing seemed to affirm that the only way to effectively portray Othello was to cast a black actor because he would be closer to Othello's savageness. In *Shakespeare Without Tears*, she noted that Othello's race was "close to the jungle" and that Othello was "not of our breed." She concluded that there can be no tolerance of infidelity in the "tribal world to which [Othello] belongs." Furthermore, because of Desdemona's alleged grievance, Othello "owes expiation to the gods.... The shedding of her blood is not revenge or murder. It is a terrible sacrifice offered by the Priest-King to the primal gods, ordained and ineluctable."[9] Though Othello was familiar with the conventions of Western civilization, Webster seemed to be conceptualizing Othello as a primitive who reverted to tribalism when his world began to crumble. Had she forgotten that Othello converted to Christianity? Or was Webster simply influenced by contemporary discourses on the barbarity of the Dark Continent? Her writing represented an example of the subtle differentiations between white and black interpretations of the idea of primitivism. According to his writing in the 1930s, Robeson viewed so-called primitive African traits as positive accompaniments to Western culture because of their emotional and spiritual depth. He viewed Othello's racial difference or foreignness not as negative or inferior but as having something singular to contribute to society. On the other hand, Webster's conception of Othello seemed to indicate that Othello's unique characteristics were unassimilable and the ultimate cause of his tragic demise. Still, Webster understood that the scope of Shakespeare's plot worked most believably and efficiently with a black Othello. Webster's participation in the project was crucial to setting the stage for Robeson's historic portrayal.

How, then, did Robeson articulate his interpretation of *Othello* in the 1940s? At this point, in contrast to 1930, he concentrated less on the characterization of the lead role and more on the political implications of the play as a whole. His writing in the 1940s revealed a more fully conceived assessment of the politics of the play than Robeson expounded in 1930. In September 1943, an interview with Robeson on *Othello* was printed in *PM* magazine. In it, he declared that he enjoyed *Othello* because with it he was "killing two birds with one stone." He elaborated, "I'm acting . . . and I'm talking for the Negroes in the way only Shakespeare can. This play is about the problem of minority groups. It concerns a blackamoor, who tried to find equality among whites. It's right up my alley."[10] However, Robeson thought the published article had not accurately portrayed his position, and he felt compelled to write a letter to the editor that further elucidated his perception of race in the play. In it he explained, "Concerning Shakespeare's *Othello*, it is an interesting point that the great dramatist as far back as 1600 [1604] posed the question of the acceptance by a society of one of alien culture and race. And therefore this is a play which is of great interest to us moderns today as we face the whole problem of relations of peoples between different races and cultures. Also, of course, it is a play of love, jealousy, pride and honor—emotions common to all men."[11] Robeson, then, was underscoring the universal themes in the play and connecting them to present social circumstances.

In several of his letters to literary critics, C. L. R. James made a similar point that the historical moment in which Shakespeare lived was crucial to the insights offered in his writing. James suggested, "It was Shakespeare's good fortune to live in an age when the whole economic and social structure was in the throes of revolutionary change on a colossal scale." These systemic changes allowed Shakespeare to explore human nature acutely. James commented, "He lived at a time when these new social forces were expressing themselves in a million ways . . . and he saw these things and wrote."[12] Robeson offered an analogous insight in an article titled "Some Reflections on *Othello* and the Nature of Our Time" in 1945. Robeson observed that in the early 1600s Othello, like Shakespeare, was standing on the cusp of a new society, for he lived at a time when "[m]edievalism was ending, and the new world of the Renaissance [was] beginning."[13] Robeson took the analysis one step further by metaphorically linking Othello's circumstances with the present moment. The Second World War had only just reached its explosive conclusion as Robeson observed, "So now, interestingly enough, we stand at the end of one period in human history and before the entrance of a new. All our tenets and tried beliefs are challenged." While Shakespeare had created an African character that helped defend the promise of this new world of the Renaissance by thwarting an incursion of the Turks into Christian Venice, Robeson understood that the interracial stand against fascism in World War II was an important turning point in global history. He continued on an optimistic note, "We have been engaged in a global war. . . . This can be the final war. It is possible to solve once and for all the problems of human poverty, to attain a speedy freedom and equality for all peoples." As the world emerged from the theaters of war, there was an opportunity to ensure a lasting peace by working toward full freedom for his people in the United States and for those in colonized nations.

The souvenir program for the Broadway production also made an important statement connecting this revival directly to the wartime context. Significantly, the progression of the war mirrored the development of the Broadway revival: the production premiered in Cambridge and played briefly at Princeton in the summer of 1942 as the United States was ramping up the mobilization effort, then opened on Broadway in the autumn of 1943 around the time of the Allied landing in Italy and toured the United States from late 1944 to the spring of 1945 while the decisive battles in Europe certified victory against the Germans. This statement in the program, then, was salient to audiences who would have immediately recognized the importance of being united for a common cause. It read, "As this production of 'Othello' begins, we are in the middle of a year and in the middle of a war; and when at war, it may not be out of place to keep other wars, of other times in mind.... We are now engaged in a war to protect a way of life which we feel offers the greatest benefit to the greatest number of people. Venice in the Sixteenth Century was fighting too; her wars were to protect Christianity in the Eastern Mediterranean. In our conflict, all races are allied to fight for common ideals. The Negro pilot of the Army Air Corps may fly under the command of Chiang in China; just as soldiers of other races fought with Venice for the protection of Christianity." Thus, the cooperation of all races in the fight against fascism during World War II was as essential as Othello commanding the troops for Venice. The conscious intent of this production of *Othello*, then, was undoubtedly to present not only a Shakespearean play but to make a statement about the contemporary racial and political climate.

How did this production coalesce? Margaret Webster had seen Robeson in the 1930 London production. She recalled in her autobiography, *Don't Put Your Daughter on the Stage*, that Robeson first approached her about directing *Othello* in 1938 after he had seen her production of *Hamlet*.[14] In an article from 1944, Webster put the date at 1937 and underscored the fact that Robeson had had "an American production on his mind ever since... 1930."[15] She remembered having seen him at the Savoy in 1930 and "thought him very bad."[16] Yet, she decided to direct a new revival because Robeson agreed that his performance in London had not been strong, but since then he had "studied and restudied the role and he thought he was ready to play it."[17] Webster also saw potential in Robeson since "the London production did almost nothing to help him deal with the problems peculiar to him, nor to bring out the tremendous new values which his playing of the part gives the play."[18] The 1930 production had, of course, been hampered by a number of deficiencies including the mutilated script and poor direction. No one on the 1930 production team had supported Robeson by consistently advocating the importance of casting a black actor in the lead role as Webster did for the Broadway production.

Still, with a black actor cast in the role of Othello, the project was immediately met with resistance. For example, Webster first approached her friend actor Maurice Evans about playing Iago to Robeson's Othello. He flatly refused on the grounds that the "public would never go for it."[19] Ultimately, the husband and wife team of José Ferrer and Uta Hagen were selected to portray Iago and Desdemona. Both were young and relative novices in the theater world. Ferrer had been praised in a recent production of *Charley's Aunt* though he had never performed any Shakespeare. Hagen already had undergone her rite of passage into Shakespeare as Ophelia in Eva Le Gallienne's production of *Hamlet*. She had also just made her Broadway debut as Nina in Anton Chekhov's *The Seagull*. Webster opted to play the other principal role, Emilia, herself to simplify matters since the initial rehearsal schedule was only two weeks long.[20] Webster did not relish wearing so many hats for one production: director, coproducer, actor, and fundraiser. She worried that stretching herself in this way would adversely affect her acting. Yet, unlike the case of producer Maurice Browne, whose acting definitely suffered when he played Iago in the 1930 London production, Webster's hectic schedule did not inhibit her stage performance. The critics were, for the most part, very complimentary of her portrayal. After the Broadway run, however, Webster chose not to accompany the troupe on the U.S. tour, so Edith King played Iago's wife with the traveling cast.

The Summer Premiere in Cambridge, 1942

Although securing a venue and the requisite financial backing had been challenging, the revival was scheduled to premiere in August 1942 at the Brattle Theatre in Cambridge, Massachusetts, under the auspices of the Theatre Guild. The Brattle was selected since no theater in New York would agree, at that time, to take on a production with an interracial cast. This represented a contrast to race relations in England during the 1930 production. Of course, not all critics had been pleased to see Robeson play Othello, but there did not seem to be any particular difficulty reserving a venue.

Webster arranged the script for the production and condensed the action to eight scenes in two acts from Shakespeare's five-act play. The scenes for act I were simplified to a street in Venice (Shakespeare's act I, scene 1); the Senate (I, 2 and 3); a seaport in Cyprus (II, 1–3, and III, 1–2); and the castle (III, 3). Webster's act II was similarly concentrated into a room in the castle (Shakespeare's III, 4, and IV, 1–3); the castle (IV, 3); the street (V, 1) and a bedroom in the castle (V, 2).[21] The part of the Clown was removed, and most of the other cuts affected the speeches since, unlike many of Shakespeare's dramas, there were no subplots in *Othello*. Iago's lengthy soliloquies, in particular, were shortened, though Othello's vital speech before the Senate was also slightly reduced.[22] It was slated in the script for Othello to kiss Desdemona once on each cheek upon their meeting at Cyprus. Such demonstrative affection was one of the chief concerns in staging *Othello* with a black male and a white female given the historical paranoia about miscegenation in the United States. Perhaps two kisses on the cheek would

4.1 Scene from *Othello* on Broadway with Robeson and Uta Hagen as Desdemona. Library of Congress, Prints & Photographs Division, FSA/OWI Collection, LC-USW331-054945-ZC.

be viewed with less antipathy than kissing on the mouth as Robeson and Peggy Ashcroft had done onstage in London in 1930. According to Webster's script, Othello would kiss Desdemona twice more, once before killing her and once after the deed had been done (figure 4.1).

The sets remained uncomplicated and were brought to life by set designer Robert Edmond Jones. Webster commented on his approach to *Othello* in a speech in 1944: "I do believe that Jones's idea of using color and costume and richness of texture, to suggest the background he wants, is the way to handle Shakespeare, rather than elaborate reproductions of the Council Chamber in the Doge's Palace or the Castle . . . in Cyprus."[23]

4.2 Robeson as Othello on Broadway. Library of Congress, Prints & Photographs Division, FSA/OWI Collection, LC-USW331-054944-ZC.

This methodology resembled the way in which Shakespeare's plays were presented in his day. The emphasis then was less on staging than character and poetry. Playgoers used their imaginations and the rich descriptions of Shakespeare's blank verse to set the scene. Jones's set was versatile so it could easily serve the swiftly moving action from scene to scene. There would, then, be no problem with ostentatious displays of bulky sets that distracted during clumsy scene shifting in this production, unlike the 1930 revival. Moreover, for this production, Robeson was not decked out in tights and puffy sleeves but, rather, in more dignified flowing robes including the beige corded silk robe with the brown leather belt which became the quintessential vision of Robeson as Othello (figure 4.2).[24]

4.3 Scene from *Othello* on Broadway with Robeson and José Ferrer as Iago. Library of Congress, Prints & Photographs Division, FSA/OWI Collection, LC-USW331-054941-ZC.

Webster elucidated the methodology behind her casting of the tall, majestic Robeson with the smaller, more lithe Ferrer. She described Robeson as "an enormous man with a wonderful voice, moving rather slowly, and having a great quality of gentleness and dignity, but having much less passion than the Othello of Salvini." Therefore, she continued, "Against Robeson I thought it would be wise to handle Iago as a swift, a mercurial, in a sense a volatile creature . . . [that] would provide the speed and the lightness to complement Robeson's slowly moving tragic weight."[25] Robeson also commented on the successful contrast between himself and Ferrer in an interview in 1944: "The way I play it, I'm calm, I'm quiet, through all the early part. I don't make an unnecessary move. And I think that's right. Of course, if I didn't have a mighty active Iago I couldn't get away with that massive calmness, perhaps, but with Joe [Ferrer] . . . all over the stage . . . it is an effective contrast."[26] Ferrer's Iago, then, was effectively employed as a foil to Robeson's Othello. Iago behaved as a kind of shape shifter as he maneuvered through his various incarnations as abettor to Roderigo, advisor to Cassio and confidant to Othello. Robeson's Othello, on the other hand, remained sturdy and dignified throughout the course of the play (figure 4.3). This formula served the actors and plot well and was noticed by several reviewers.

As the production came together, Margaret Webster remained in close contact with her parents in Britain by writing myriad letters to them from the United States. These letters appeared to be a frank and honest assessment of her life in the theater world. During the summer rehearsals in 1942, her initial reaction to directing Robeson was positive. On July 9 she penned of Robeson, "He has improved out of all knowledge in technical command and freedom, and is ENORMOUSLY [her emphasis] exciting to work with. He seizes onto an idea like lightning and it blossoms instantly like a flower."[27] Several weeks later, just before the premier, Webster remained hopeful: "The OTHELLO rehearsals shape very well, and Paul works wonderfully; he curiously lacks the quality of real rage though! . . . But he's getting over it extraordinarily well, and the clothes are excellent and will help him."[28] By the time the show was on Broadway, Robeson had developed a method to invoke the necessary rage onstage. By recalling the racism he had experienced on the football field as a young man, he used the technique of emotion memory to channel his outrage as Othello.

The show debuted on Monday, August 10, 1942, at the Brattle Theatre in Cambridge to rave reviews. Uta Hagen recalled the media coverage of the revival: "I don't remember a lot of talk until we arrived in Cambridge and were going to play, and suddenly the word went around that this was going to be a major event, because for the first time, a black man and a white woman [were playing] in Shakespeare."[29] Webster detected that once a steady stream of glowing reviews starting flowing, producers in New York "who for four years refused to touch the idea with a twenty-foot pole are begging to be allowed a 'piece of the show', & have us come to their theatre. . . ."[30] The *New York Times* observed that the Brattle had been selected because of its proximity to Harvard University and that in such a venue the production "would get a fair hearing."[31] Several reviewers noted the capacity crowd at the theater. The *Boston Evening American* proclaimed that hundreds were turned away for the opening.[32] Margaret Williamson wrote a charming piece for the *Christian Science Monitor* describing the festive spirit surrounding the lengthy column of people hoping for tickets outside the theater. The show was so popular that people waited in the blazing August sun for hours on the slight chance that a standing ticket might become available. She noted, "The line was [as] heterogeneous as any queue outside a theater or concert hall," and it included everyone from southerners, Frenchmen, and several black soldiers in uniform to young girls and white-haired women. Fortuitously, there was a cancellation and Williamson purchased the last coveted ticket in the house. Despite the ordeal of waiting in the summer heat and forgetting to pack a lunch, she "sat spell-bound" through the show and concluded that "it was something worth remembering."[33] The diverse crowds that Williamson witnessed even at this early date became a hallmark of this production, especially when it toured in the United States.

Turning to the critical reception of the revival, many reviewers praised Webster's direction. The reviewer for the *Boston Daily Globe* reported that Webster "possesses a special faculty for presenting Shakespeare to modern audiences in terms of vivid theater."[34] Another reviewer asserted that Webster's production represented "Shakespeare as we rarely have seen it."[35] The reporter for the *Harvard Crimson* felt, "It is through the directing that the play becomes a living thing."[36] Elinor Hughes appreciated Jones's set design because it allowed the play to run just under three hours "thanks to the use of a semi-permanent set and the quickest scene changing on record."[37] Still, not all critics agreed with the pace that Webster employed. The critic writing for *The Christian* observed that the "telescoping of the play" had "certain disadvantages" including "the rapidity with which Othello was taken in by Iago's machinations."[38] However, this reviewer consented that a black man as Othello "underlines the sense of division between him and the Venetians and lends credibility to the intensity of his passions." Rudolph Elie, Jr., writing for *Variety*, agreed that "Robeson playing opposite a white girl" was "electric" and that "no white man should ever dare presume to play [Othello] again...."[39] A reporter for the *Pittsburgh Courier*, an African American newspaper, noticed that "a short time ago the whites would have advanced a thousand objections" to the interracial romance in *Othello*. This at first "bewildered" the reviewer, who then concluded optimistically that "in one leap Negro artistry had gone from the bottom to the highest pinnacle of this profession."[40]

Most of the accolades went to Robeson, who was undoubtedly the star of the show. *Variety* asserted that his performance was "a revelation." The *New York Times* found Robeson's portrayal to be "heroic and convincing."[41] Reviewers never ceased to be mesmerized by his voice, as with one reporter who likened it to a cello.[42] The writer for *The Christian* felt sure that Robeson "would be an impressive Othello" no matter what the color of his skin was.[43] Owen Dodson, head of the drama department at the historically black Hampton Institute, exclaimed, "This was an occasion!" but worried that although Robeson inhabited the role, "there is an over-restrained quality . . . a fear of overacting when Othello cannot be too overacted."[44] Elliot Norton, writing for the *Boston Sunday Post*, posited, "This huge, handsome colored man, with his fine dignity and his sonorous voice, brought power and sympathy to the character of the tragic Moor and complete conviction to the play."[45] Louis Kronenberger anticipated in *PM* that "after further polishing" the revival would "come to Broadway this winter."[46] Kronenberger was correct in his prediction; however, the revival would not premier on Broadway until the 1943 season.

Ralph Warner, writing for the *Sunday Worker*, characterized the political impact of the production even in this initial incarnation. He reinforced the historic implications of a black actor performing in Shakespeare on the professional stage. Warner related the "thrill of surcharged excitement as one discovers that this 'Othello' is no theatre makeshift, but a universally valuable work, in which a man of black skin fights nobly . . . in the unceasing struggle for equality."[47] He concluded with a keen observation: "'Othello' starring Paul Robeson, is more than a mere play. It is a significant cultural event in American life, a long step forward to the higher democratization of our theatre." Such a democratization of the theater was illustrated by the diversity of the crowd who clamored for tickets. It was not surprising that such an insight would come from the *Sunday Worker*, the organ of the U.S. Communist Party, which consistently reported on Robeson's activities through the 1940s and 1950s. But it was with considerable foresight that already in 1942, with just one performance to its credit, Warner classified this production as pathbreaking even before it appeared on Broadway, broke the record for Shakespearean performances, or set out on a historic U.S. tour.

Elliot Norton commented that the rapt audience had sat "without rattling chairs or rustling programs" despite the sticky heat. Margaret Webster believed the night of the premiere in Cambridge to be "about the hottest I ever remember" and that Robeson's "robes had to be wrung out between scenes." Nonetheless, the final curtain was accompanied by applause and an unusual stamping of feet. Webster asked a local actor what was going on. He replied enthusiastically, "Boy, that's the best you could get" at Harvard![48] She then excitedly conveyed to her parents that "it's really fantastic, the proportions the thing is assuming! . . . [I]t's practically a national issue!"[49] Robeson's wife, Eslanda, also wrote to Webster's mother, Dame May Whitty, to express their enthusiasm about the reception of *Othello*. She offered ebullient praise for Whitty's daughter as she effused, "But you have no idea of the days of intensive work which Peggy put them all through, and which actually felt like fascinating, sometimes even gay conferences, which everybody enjoyed enormously. Paul and I will always be grateful to her for what she has done for him in 'Othello.' This happy and successful experiment is a milestone in his career, and entirely so because of the privilege of working with Peggy."[50] This was a remarkable contrast to the anxiety chronicled in Essie's diary concerning the opening of the London production twelve years earlier. Unfortunately, relations backstage did not remain so convivial when the Webster production made the transition from summer stock to Broadway.

The Broadway Opening, October 1943

It was not until the autumn of 1943 that *Othello* opened in New York on Broadway. This was due, in part, to Robeson's hectic concert schedule which had already been booked for the season.[51] In the summer of that year, problems arose between Webster, the Theatre Guild, and the other principal actors. New actors were considered for the roles of Iago and Desdemona because some members of the Theatre Guild felt Ferrer and Hagen were too expensive.[52] This was frustrating for Webster, as coproducer and director, because her relationship backstage with Hagen, Ferrer, and Robeson was becoming increasingly strained. She mentioned to her parents that Hagen and Ferrer had been "very difficult for a long time" and were "over-rating their financial worth to . . . a ridiculous extent" since Robeson was the true box office draw for the show.[53] Cast changes were made public, and the *New York Times* reported that Hagen and Ferrer had quit the revival.[54] Robeson subsequently jumped into the fray and threatened to leave the show if Ferrer and Hagen were not reinstated. Webster, now exasperated, scribbled in a frantic note to her parents, "Paul arrived this morning at the costumer's

& announced that he had finally decided he wouldn't play Othello without the Ferrers & . . . that was that!!! Against his inarticulate but immovable resolve . . . reason broke in vain. No Ferrers, no Robeson, no Robeson, no show. And I, as usual, [was] left to straighten it out."[55] Two days later, the *Times* noted that Hagen and Ferrer were back on the program and their momentary replacements (Stephan Schnabel and Virginia Gilmore) were leaving voluntarily. The explanation offered for Hagen's and Ferrer's return was in order that the production "may be presented as closely as possible to the original" that was performed in Cambridge.[56] By August 29, Webster related to her parents that "[t]hings seem to have straightened out; the Ferrers are in [a] chastened mood & working well & I am getting back to my own centre [sic] tho [sic] still a bit sick & weary."[57] This row foreshadowed another argument that arose just prior to the U.S. tour and resulted in Webster leaving the cast. It also underscored the tension between Webster and the other leads. Robeson clearly understood that the revival could not be mounted in his absence, and he was not afraid to use this leverage in shaping the production.

Around this time, Webster also began to complain in her letters about directing Robeson. This could be due partially to the stress of the recent upheaval in the cast, but, nevertheless, from this point forward, her view of Robeson was more critical, especially with regard to his acting technique. She lamented, "He's very hard to direct in that he has not only no technique (which he knows) but no conception of impersonation. He can only do it if I can get a kind of electric motor going inside himself & this has to be started by some feeling—not Othello's feeling, but Robeson's. Fortunately, his tremendous vocal resource protects him on the technical end; & my job is to jockey Robeson into some approximation to Othello . . . All very difficult!" By September 12, a few short weeks before the Broadway opening, Webster reported that "[r]ehearsals look pretty good—Paul & Jo [Ferrer] both enormously improved. Paul is so disarming it's impossible to stay angry with him!! But it's like pushing a truck uphill to make him act, yet, when he catches fire . . . he goes careening off at eighty miles an hour & . . . is, in his own way, quite magnificent. But so undependable!" Eight days later, she conceded, "Paul's Othello [although] , , , still crudely & even in places clumsily executed, has undoubtedly the stature of great tragedy." At this moment, she found Ferrer to be "enormously improved" and Hagen to be "very nearly <u>very</u> good [her emphasis]."

On the other hand, Uta Hagen, who was a confidant of Robeson's during this period, recalled that he and Webster shared a tense relationship.

"He was not crazy about her, which is no secret," Hagen remarked in an interview in the 1990s. She further characterized Webster's interaction with Robeson as displaying "a terrible kind of chauvinism." Hagen pointed out that Robeson looked for input on his acting from others in the cast, as he had during the 1930 London production, "And I remember he asked Joe Ferrer a lot of questions, and he asked me a lot of questions.... But he was like most genius people, unbelievably curious and was dying to absorb something he wasn't familiar with." Furthermore, "Webster didn't help him at all, except externally kind of, for outer shape and form. But [in] the real craft of acting, she was of no help at all."[58] Robeson and Hagen engaged in a love affair during the run of *Othello*, so Hagen might have been inclined to relate to Robeson's perspective more closely than Webster's. Still, Hagen's assessment of the dynamics backstage was important not only as a cast member, but her reflection on this period was enhanced by a legendary forty-year career as a stage actress and acting teacher. Hagen was in her early twenties in *Othello*, but went on to win two Tony awards for best actress and a Tony lifetime achievement award. Additionally, in 1948 she joined Herbert Berghof as artistic partner at HB Studio in New York. Berghof, who later married Hagen, had opened the studio in 1945. Here, Hagen mentored generations of students in the craft of acting during her distinguished career as a master teacher. Hagen also wrote two respected books on acting technique: *A Challenge for the Actor* (1991) and *Respect for Acting* (1973) in which she emphasized her interpretation of Constantin Stanislavsky's method approach to acting.

Hagen observed in retrospect that Webster's "treatment of the play was an ordinary, academic approach to Shakespeare." Indeed, it was the "other elements [that] came into it, that fired the production, in spite of her." Thus, in her letters Webster admitted her frustration directing Robeson, and Hagen has corroborated Webster's struggles. Webster's background and approach to Shakespeare was more traditional, and she probably did not identify with Stanislavsky's methods, which Robeson utilized. In fact, she articulated this in the letter where she stated with aggravation that Robeson "has to be started by some feeling—not Othello's feeling, but Robeson's." Here she was describing perfectly, but clearly not relating to, Stanislavsky's idea of emotion memory in which an actor called upon a personal memory to help unleash the emotion necessary for a particular scene. Though Robeson's portrayal undoubtedly improved between 1930 and 1942, it appeared that once again, he did not receive the kind of direction that could have further enhanced his performance. It was with a tinge of irony and, perhaps, regret that Hagen reflected years later, "I could have helped him now, [with] what I know about teaching [laugh]. I suddenly thought, [gasp], I could have . . . turned him into the genius actor [laugh]."[59]

The *Othello* revival opened on Broadway at the Sam Shubert Theatre on Tuesday, October 19, 1943, under the auspices of the Theatre Guild. The Theatre Guild, which had been on the cutting edge of theater since the 1920s, had also sponsored the highly acclaimed production of *Oklahoma* that spring which was considered a turning point in musical theater in the United States. The *Othello* engagement was unquestionably a success on many levels. The ten curtain calls opening night, the record number of performances, and the extended U.S. tour all demonstrated its popularity among theatergoers. In addition, Robeson was awarded numerous honors including a medal from the American Academy of Arts and Letters for good diction on stage and an award from *Billboard* for an outstanding lead performance. For Webster, this was the only production with which she was ever associated that "made real money."[60] An article later synthesizing the history of the Theatre Guild noted that with this revival of Shakespeare's *Othello* "what was deemed as his least profitable tragedy became his most successful."[61]

And there were scores of admiring reviews. In his dissertation on Webster's directing, Ely Silverman remarked that he found only one review of *Othello* that was fundamentally negative.[62] This was a slight underestimate as more than one critical review was uncovered for this study. However, Silverman's point remained relevant: the essentially negative reviews were definitely in the minority. Several noteworthy themes emerged from the contemporary reviews of the Broadway *Othello*. One conclusion can be certainly drawn: most of the reviewers who were critical of Robeson did not cite his dark skin as a chief liability. This was not to say that racial language was not employed in many reviews. Indeed, phrases like "simplicity of mind," "simple savage," and "simple black barbarian" recurred in characterizations of Robeson as the Moor and of Shakespeare's Moor. Yet, most reviewers who were critical of Robeson referred to his unpolished technical skill rather than his skin tone. This represented a departure from the 1930 reviews in which the Arab vs. Ethiopian debate was hotly contested. Overall, this trend perhaps reflected some progress in race relations. Although it was, at first, difficult to secure a venue for an *Othello* revival with a black lead in New York, once Robeson graced the stage, reviewers and audiences by and large responded favorably to this dark-skinned Othello.

Before delving into the reviews by theater critics, one should note a survey in Harlem that provided a rare glimpse into public opinion on Robeson's

Othello. When one is examining historic productions, often the only data available are observations of newspaper critics and the recollections of cast members. Yet, thanks to a poll conducted by the *People's Voice* newspaper, opinions from the African American community in New York were also preserved. Each week, the *People's Voice*, a progressive African American paper started by Adam Clayton Powell, Jr., conducted a poll on various topics and published a selection of responses. In early May 1944, the question posed was "Do you think the roles given to the Negro actors in the theatre and on the screen are improving?"[63] Seven responses were published and, of those, four pointed to Robeson's *Othello* as evidence of progress. Interestingly, three of these four respondents were employed in the arts. A music teacher from New York was not optimistic but maintained that Robeson was the only exception to a dismal trend. A private in the army stated simply, "Yes. Doesn't Paul Robeson in *Othello* mean anything?" Hall Johnson, a conductor and composer, believed that "Paul Robeson raises his people to the point unbelievably near the ideal by his role in Othello." Finally, an orchestra leader thoughtfully connected Robeson's political advocacy to his Othello role and emphasized the gravity of not simply waiting for handouts: "Paul Robeson gets what he gets, not as a favor handed down, but because he is way ahead of most Negroes in his political and economic understanding. He allys [sic] himself with progressive and liberal labor and political forces that believe in democracy and believes they should live their beliefs." Robeson's politics were well known in Harlem and resonated in the community along with his celebrity as an actor. Even though the survey was conducted over six months after the Broadway opening, Robeson's Othello continued to stand out in the minds of these African Americans as an important challenge to segregated cultural institutions.

Regarding the response to opening night, Webster attempted to explain the unique magnetism with which the revival held the audience. She confided to her parents that she had experienced exhilarating opening nights before but "nothing . . . like last night." Webster continued to describe the scene: "They yelled at us through a long succession of calls & fairly screamed at Paul & finally I had to make a speech to finish it up. . . . The notices are better than we are—it was just one of those nights. Magic happened—not so much the performance which . . . was very good but not more so than it had been before, but to the audience, who just got drunk."[64]

The contemporary reviews helped uncover the various elements which merged to enable magic to happen that night. Many reviewers noted approvingly of Robeson's and Webster's ambition to utilize a black actor in the role of Othello. For example, John Chapman asserted that the production was a "bold artistic experiment" and that "it seems not only natural but also absolutely right that Shakespeare's black man should be [played by] a black man."[65] Louis Kronenberger, writing for *PM*, observed that the production recorded a "victory . . . for democracy" because "a great Negro is playing a great role that no Negro ever performed on Broadway."[66] One reviewer corroborated Webster's view of the plot in writing that Robeson's blackness "helped explain why he was so ready to believe that Desdemona could be unfaithful to him. He was different than the men around him."[67] The *New York Herald Tribune* declared that the revival was a "tribute to the art that transcends racial boundaries." The reviewer ruminated that "[it is] a sign of hope for the future when a Negro actor . . . is so enthusiastically welcomed into the great tradition of the English-speaking stage. . . ."[68] Rosamond Gilder, writing in *Theatre Arts*, contemplated, "There is every reason why a Negro should act the part, and . . . Paul Robeson's appearance in it is long overdue."[69]

Several reviewers focused their praise on Webster's direction. Robert Garland regarded Webster's skill playfully: "[S]he is not afraid of William. In the privacy of her own room, she probably calls him Bill. And . . . she walks right up to his manuscript and makes the most of it."[70] Another critic, Ward Morehouse, acclaimed Webster's direction as "quick and inventive and the pace of the performance is thus heightened."[71] Webster was even venerated as "the high priestess of Shakespeare in our day"[72] Wilella Waldorf concluded, "Since she came over from London . . . Miss Webster has been breathing new life into the Shakespearean revival business."[73]

Robeson's improvement since the 1930 production in London was commented upon by several reporters. One reviewer believed that "what Mr. Robeson needed, apparently, was a director like Margaret Webster and time to grow into the part. . . ."[74] The *New York Times* reviewer, Lewis Nichols, perceived that Robeson "had grown and developed from just a good interpretation of the Moor to one that approaches magnificence."[75] Rosamond Gilder noted that Robeson's performance had "grown in authority and sweep since the try-out in the summer theatre [in Cambridge in 1942]." The dynamic between Robeson and Ferrer onstage was often recognized by reviewers. Ward Morehouse described the effect as "an agile Iago . . . in contrast with the towering Robeson" and observed that these scenes "contribute a great deal to the speed and force of the production." Lewis Nichols extolled Ferrer's adroitness: "[H]is Iago is a sort of half dancing, half strutting Mephistopheles . . . ," while "he and Mr. Robeson are excellent foils for one another."⁷⁶ Reviewers also enjoyed contrasting Uta Hagen's Desdemona with Robeson's Othello; as one critic put it, "her fair slenderness is a striking analogy to the Robeson hugeness."⁷⁷

Conversely, reviewers were divided over Robeson's baritone voice. Some believed his concert career highlighted his vocal ability and enhanced the lyrical nature of his delivery. Yet, other reviewers felt that he depended too much on intonation and that made his lines sound monotonous. For instance, Burton Rascoe asserted, "Mr. Robeson's magnificent and tremendous voice is in perfect character with his fine portrayal of Othello. . . ."⁷⁸ However, E. C. Sherburne felt that although "his powerful, resonant voice . . . was notable . . . ," still, "Mr. Robeson often seems to be chanting rather than speaking his lines."⁷⁹ However, whether it enhanced or impeded his performance, one conclusion seemed clear: Robeson's voice was a prominent aspect of his portrayal of Othello.

Thus, the majority of reviewers in the mainstream press agreed on the overall success of the production. Robert Garland summarized, "Shakespeare gave Paul Robeson his great opportunity." Similarly, Burton Rascoe observed that the audience was spellbound: "Never in my life have I seen an audience sit so still, so tense, so under the spell of what was taking place on the stage. . . ." One reviewer stressed the importance of the production for the reputation of the Theatre Guild: "If it does nothing else this season or next, The Theatre Guild will have revived through *Othello* much of its former prestige. . . ."⁸⁰ John Chapman posited of *Othello*, "We now have one classic on Broadway and it is a good thing. A very good thing. We could use more." Finally, one reviewer summarized, "Unquestionably 'Othello' in this rendition has notable social significance, as well as dramatic appeal."⁸¹

How did the African American press respond to Robeson's Othello? Carl Diton, reporting for the *Chicago Defender*, stressed the importance of Robeson defying a racial barrier: "Whatever silly, racial prejudices New Yorkers may have had in the past were swept aside Tuesday night as they vociferously applauded the first performance of Shakespeare's 'Othello' with Paul Robeson in the leading role." He further postulated, "Viewing the play from a purely racial angle, there is nothing to offend either race."⁸² Another article in the *Defender* by Ruth Rolen, one of the few women to review the production, asserted, "The majority of both white and colored [people] . . . were so entranced in Paul Robeson's superb characterization of the leading role that all else save his fine acting was forgotten."⁸³

The reviewer for the *Pittsburgh Courier* complimented Webster's directing but concentrated on the fine performance by Robeson, who "commands all eyes and ears." The review closed by pronouncing that Robeson "acquitted himself in such a manner as to make both himself and members of his race proud."[84] An editorial by the eminent W. E. B. Du Bois doubted if a white actor would ever again take on the role of the Shakespeare's Moorish general. He "watched the audience as much as the stage" and concluded that "the listeners thrilled to Robeson's mighty voice and stature."[85] J. A. Rogers, a self-educated scholar who emigrated from Jamaica, had attacked the idea of African inferiority in his books. In light of the Broadway production, Rogers felt compelled to argue in an editorial in the *Pittsburgh Courier* that Shakespeare intended Othello to be a black man. He likened Shakespeare's use of the word "Moor" to the contemporary locution "colored" or "Aframerican" [*sic*]. Rogers also thoughtfully maintained that the argument questioning the race of Othello would continue "until there is no longer a color line."[86]

Dan Burley of the *Amsterdam News* in New York also focused on the racial implications of the revival. The title of the review revealed his conclusion: "Paul Robeson as 'Othello' Strikes Big Blow at Intolerance." His observations are worth quoting at some length, for they emphasized how the black press perceived very clearly what appeared only sporadically in the mainstream press: Robeson was on stage to make a statement about American racism. Burley explained, "'Othello' on Broadway with Paul Robeson in the leading role represents the most concrete step to date taken by the Negro on the American stage. In fact, it is of far greater significance that the ability of a Negro has finally been judged more important than his color and the consequences are exciting, [and] thrilling to contemplate." He concluded, "The Theatre Guild strikes a sledge hammer blow at those proponents of lilywhite theories based on the inability of minority races to absorb the culture of the groups in power."[87] Thus, in the mainstream press, the production was viewed as a success mostly in theatrical terms, while the black press praised Robeson's acting but, more fervently, articulated the political implications of the production. Benjamin Mays, president of Morehouse College in Atlanta, conferred an honorary doctorate on Robeson in 1943. In his speech, he praised Robeson: "You have rendered the world a great service in Othello by demonstrating that Negroes are capable of great and enduring interpretations in the realm of the theatre. . . ."[88] Notice that Mays stressed that Robeson had done the *world* a great service. Robeson's performance, then, was significant not only in the American theater but also in terms of international perceptions of the United States. This statement harmonized beautifully with Robeson's involvement in international politics and his emphasis on utilizing the struggle of his people to symbolize the fight for human rights around the world.

The left-wing press, particularly the *Daily Worker*, also highlighted the political importance of the Broadway *Othello*. Mike Gold's consideration of the audience which "consisted of a ... universal humanity" corroborated the comments made by Margaret Williamson about the diverse ticket queue at the Cambridge premiere.[89] Gold's remarks also confirmed Ralph Warner's thesis from the summer opening that the revival was a step toward the democratization of the American theater. Robeson's presence in *Othello* clearly attracted an unusually heterogeneous theater crowd. Gold believed this phenomenon confirmed "that this Paul Robeson is the greatest personality in America today, the richest force for American democracy and art."

Just as Robeson had noted in 1930 that Othello had been portrayed with dark skin in Shakespeare's day and the tradition had changed with the rise of the African slave trade, Samuel Sillen wrote an article that emphasized the historic context of race and Shakespeare's play. He ruminated, "The further we get away from Shakespeare the more intense becomes the problem of Negro national oppression . . . [and] the more emphatic becomes the insistence that the Moor was descended from the Caucasian race." Thus, he cogently affirmed that Robeson's dark-skinned portrayal had not "created a new Othello but . . . has brilliantly restored the Othello that Shakespeare conceived. . . ."[90] Samuel Putnam focused on Robeson's power onstage and his singular presence. Putnam admitted that he had difficulty separating his "social-political impressions . . . from the aesthetic ones" but decided, in the end, that they should not be divided anyway. He inquired, "What would 'Othello' be without Robeson?" and responded that with a "giant" in the role against the backdrop of troubled times, "Robeson . . . in more senses than one, IS the play" [his emphasis].[91] These journalists from the Left, then, recognized that the Broadway *Othello* was meaningful not solely because any black actor was playing Othello, but it was Robeson specifically who drew diverse crowds to the theater and reinforced the political significance of the production. Robeson's antifascist politics imparted the wartime context of the play with a particular substance of which the production would have been deprived in his absence.

One final theme emerging from media coverage of the play, concomitant with the political implications of the revival, was the importance of dignity to Robeson's performance. The struggle to recapture recognition of civil rights and human dignity had long been imperative to African American intellectuals and artists. The practice of racism attacked a person's innate sense of dignity and self-respect. Why was dignity so vital to one's self-image and very existence? Bernard Boxill pointed out in his article "Self-Respect" that the natural rights outlined in the Declaration of Independence were proclaimed to be "self-evident" in order "to secure for each of us a minimum of dignity." Because these rights were characterized in this way, Boxill explained, it meant that "it is evident without proof . . . that people have human rights."[92]

However, recognition of shared humanity and basic rights, although intrinsic to the founding documents of this society, had historically been denied African Americans. This occurred through the dehumanization of slavery and the subsequent refusal to enforce the protection of citizenship rights supposedly guaranteed by the Fourteenth Amendment of the Constitution. The African American community was forced to fight to proclaim their humanity and reclaim legal recognition of their civil rights. In doing so, they faced profound obstacles in light of the powerful theories of racial inferiority constructed by and maintained through the system of Jim Crow segregation and various forms of terrorism (e.g., lynching and the Klan), as well as economic subjugation and disenfranchisement.

Thus, one strategy of the black community in response to oppression and pseudoscientific claims of the inhumanity of black people was to assert their dignity in the hopes that their humanity would then be acknowledged by the larger society. Frederick Douglass scathingly asserted in 1854, "Now, presuming that what is evident to beast and bird, cannot need elaborate argument to be made plain to men, . . . that the Negro is a man."[93] In 1926, W. E. B. Du Bois pointedly contended the specific importance of art to this struggle: "[T]he point today is that until the art of the black folk compels recognition they will not be rated as human."[94] This fight for recognition of the humanity and dignity of African Americans was imperative to the crusades for citizenship protection and voting rights. Robeson was cognizant of this battle and sought roles which conveyed the dignity of his people. The actor and friend of Robeson's Ossie Davis explained Robeson's approach to acting: "But to thoroughly understand him is to understand his acting as a part of the struggle in which he was engaged. To vindicate the dignity of his people. And to establish wider parameters for what we mean when we say human being. All of this he consciously assumed as his responsibility."[95] Playing the role of Othello was crucial to Robeson not only as an actor but also as a political advocate who realized the importance of portraying the dignity of his people in order to counter vicious and demeaning stereotypes. Robeson maintained, "It's one of the few roles in which a

Negro appears with great dignity and for that reason I'm doubly glad to be doing it."[96] Thus, Robeson utilized Othello as his most significant opportunity as an actor to express the dignity of his people. Whether or not one considered Shakespeare's character to be innately dignified, it was clear in many of the reviews and Robeson's acting philosophy that he emphasized Othello's dignity in his interpretation.

Boxill further observed, "The sense which the person with dignity conveys is the sense that his rights are so plain . . . as to tacitly, but unmistakenly and eloquently, call shame on all who refuse to acknowledge them."[97] Robeson's Othello must have radiated an eloquent statement of dignity, for it compelled comments from many of the reviewers, especially in the left-wing and black newspapers. In the notices examined for this study, the word dignity appeared to describe Robeson in almost one third of the articles. Analogous phraseology such as "majesty," "nobility," and "commanding respect" occurred many times as well. Comparable themes like "performance of stature" and "human quality" also appeared. For example, critic Joyce Dana felt that Robeson's dignity made the character of Othello for once appear sympathetic: "The beautiful sonority of his speaking voice, the dignity of his bearing, his believable transformation . . . makes the multiple murders of 'Othello' bring to that final scene of death not only nobility but understanding."[98] The reviewer for the *New York Herald Tribune* insightfully summarized, "The important thing is not that Mr. Robeson increases the dignity of his people by his performance . . . but that he has won recognition for that dignity from those who were either blinded by prejudice or far too casual in their assumptions concerning inter-racial relationships."[99]

Dignity, then, was clearly fundamental to Robeson's portrayal of the role and, according to the reviews, he successfully communicated this idea onstage. Because it was a conscious decision of Robeson's to, in Ossie Davis's words, "vindicate the dignity of his people," this was a political act. Robeson established not only that there was a space for African American actors on Broadway in a classic play of the Western canon but did so while defying the debasing images of his people and eliciting acknowledgment of African American dignity. He helped set a precedent for a black presence in Shakespeare on the professional stage. Robeson's presence onstage implicitly declared that black actors deserved a place on Broadway and that their contribution would begin to engender new interpretations of Shakespeare. More broadly, his human dignity was publicly recognized. As the critic above implied, this enabled some people who viewed the play to more readily accept the humanity of African Americans. This recognition could, in turn, challenge them to reevaluate their assumptions about natural or intrinsic rights.

Richard Dyer concluded in his chapter on Robeson in *Heavenly Bodies* that Robeson's body while in some arenas was "correlative of manly power" ultimately "does nothing" because he was "contained by frames, montage, narrative, direction, vocal restraint."[100] However, at least in *Othello*, Robeson's comportment might have come across as restrained because he was so focused on offering a dignified interpretation. To argue that Robeson "does nothing" was to view his work purely in aesthetic terms and overlook his advocacy offstage as well as his political objectives as an artist. Robeson commented generally in a 1944 interview, "I like to feel . . . that my work has a farther reach than its artistic appeal. I consider art a social weapon."[101] An article by P. L. Prattis, editor of the *Pittsburgh Courier*, quoted Robeson more specifically on the political implications of *Othello*: "Not simply for art's sake do I try to excel in 'Othello' . . . but more to prove the capacity of the people from whom I've sprung and of all such peoples, of whatever color, erroneously regarded as backward."[102] Like Dyer, several of Robeson's critics found his performance to be overly reserved. This may be a valid observation given his size and Webster's strategy of playing Robeson and Ferrer as foils for one another. Still, Robeson's overall ambition to portray a dignified Othello and his political aim to demonstrate the humanity of his people should be balanced with the aesthetic critiques of his acting. More was at stake in *Othello* than solely histrionic technique and aesthetic virtue. Robeson's artistry contained a consciously applied political dimension that was equally, if not more, vital to his stagecraft.

Critics of Robeson

The major critics of Robeson's performance included some unfavorable reviewers and a few colleagues who knew and worked with him. Of the critical reviews analyzed, three concerned the Chicago leg of the U.S. tour. Ashton Stevens, who did not enjoy the show, reviewed it twice and found Robeson to be "dull and heavy" while he displayed "very little inner power."[103] The *Chicago Times* reviewer characterized Robeson's Othello as "lacking in nuance" and posited that "it carries conviction by sheer weight rather than by any display of theatrical genius." This critic did, however, reflect upon Robeson's dignity, sincerity and potency due to his dual role as an actor and an American leader of stature.[104] It should be noted that the Chicago engagement at the Erlanger Theatre came at the end of a seven-month U.S. tour, so the cast was probably worn out and Robeson might not have been at the height of his powers. Actor Laurence Olivier once described Othello as "a monstrous, monstrous burden for the actor."[105] On several occasions, Robeson declared how exhausting he found the role of Othello to be, and he was often performing up to eight times a week. Robeson remarked on this in interviews in October 1944, January 1945, and at a speech in April 1945, the same month as the Chicago run.[106] Moreover, Robeson was maintaining an intense schedule while on tour as he continued to give speeches and make political appearances between *Othello* shows. An FBI informant observed that, in April 1945, Robeson often made two or three appearances in addition to theater performances some days.[107] That same month, President Franklin Roosevelt unexpectedly died after having just taken the oath of office for the fourth time in January. The notion of Harry Truman, an untested national leader, negotiating peace terms was unsettling at such a critical juncture in the war. Roosevelt's death was a blow to many progressives, like Robeson, who had espoused the New Deal. Thus, national events coupled with a rigorous itinerary were likely taking a toll on Robeson's acting in Chicago.

The one critic of Robeson's performance that Ely Silverman noticed for his dissertation was Margaret Marshall writing in *The Nation*. Marshall asserted that the hero of this revival was Ferrer's Iago and not Othello. She then commented on the racial implications of her observation: "A friend to whom I mentioned this wondered if the sympathy for Iago was an expression of prejudice against a Negro Othello. The answer is no. It was rather the expression of a secret admiration for the man who exercises power. . . ." She went on to state that the curtain calls for Robeson on the opening night were "sentimental" and "far more self conscious than the wry sympathy accorded to Iago. . . ." Thus, Marshall took the position that the ovations for Robeson were more about sentiment for him as the first black actor to play Othello on Broadway than his actual performance. This was perhaps a legitimate observation, since African Americans have often been feted when they are "the first" to represent their people in an important arena. But Marshall continued, "Both Mr. Robeson and Miss Webster have tried to prove that Othello is a Negro; they have attempted also to prove that 'Othello' is a play about race. Both theories seem to me false and foolish." Marshall also critiqued specific aspects of Robeson's performance as she alluded to his inertness and lack of agility. She concluded that the play was "not a tragedy since Iago runs the show."[108] Thus, Marshall did not believe that Othello was black or that the play was about race, recalling the disputes that appeared in a number of the 1930 reviews. Marshall's perspective, however, was shared by few of those who reviewed the Broadway show, making her comments more a personal viewpoint and less illustrative of the overall trends in the notices. Marshall effectively demonstrated that the *Othello* revival with a black lead, though generally praised, was not unanimously accepted.

Miles Jefferson wrote a survey of the "Negro on Broadway in 1944" for *Phylon*, an interdisciplinary journal started by W. E. B. Du Bois at Atlanta University in 1940. Jefferson first gave Robeson the benefit of any doubt by alerting the reader that he viewed the production early in its New York run when Robeson, perhaps, had not yet settled into the role. But Jefferson agreed with Marshall that Iago "took the show" and felt that Robeson was "largely reading his speeches." Jefferson went on to state that Robeson seemed "static and stiff except on occasion when he resorted to sensational tricks to cover up an inner insufficiency." He then pointed out how Robeson revealed his naked chest in the final act to the delight of the audience. These criticisms were thought provoking since they were not tinged with the racial bias disclosed in Marshall's review. It was significant, however, that while Jefferson agreed with some of Marshall's observations, he reached a completely different conclusion. Jefferson remarked that Robeson would surely grow into the role and broadly considered the consequences of Robeson's appearance on Broadway. Jefferson ruminated that "his assumption of [the role] marked a step forward (or let us say should, in fear of being too optimistic!) in the identification of the modern American Negro actor with a play offering lofty and limitless scope." He then called for more roles for other black actors of "established ability" to be given such opportunities.[109] Thus, Jefferson, while critical of Robeson technically, firmly believed in the importance of his performing in a leading dramatic role on Broadway. He still viewed Robeson as a trailblazer and hoped his appearance would become a precedent for other, perhaps more technically accomplished, black actors.

A noteworthy analysis of Robeson in *Othello* was formulated by Langston Hughes as a Simple Story. These brief narratives chronicled the exploits of one of Hughes's most famous and enduring characters, Jesse B. Semple or just Simple, the streetwise commentator from Harlem. In "Simple sees 'Othello,'" published in the *Chicago Defender* in June of 1944, Simple philosophized that the role of Othello was beneath Robeson, much to the dismay of the companion with whom he parlayed.[110] Simple complained that when his girlfriend, Joyce, took him to the theater, it was always to see a drama about a Negro playing the fool. He cited *Native Son* and *Othello* as examples and was disturbed that "every time white folks see Art . . . it is about a colored man choking a white woman to death." Simple alleged that such art is "not good for the Race" and made him feel ashamed. He was particularly troubled because he felt that Robeson "is a great man, and a race man [and] also a leader." Simple's acquaintance maintained that Othello was just a man who has his weaknesses like anyone else, and, besides, it was a play and Simple should not regard the content so literally. However, Simple remained adamant that Othello was not just a man; he was Paul Robeson.

This exchange offered an important counterpoint that did not appear in much of the documentation of the Broadway *Othello*. Through this piece, Hughes wondered if the subject matter of *Othello* was worthy of Robeson's talent, which was a justifiable question. Why would a role in which he, as Simple put it, walks "around in a bathrobe slapping his wife all over the stage" be a priority for Robeson's acting career? By this time, he had given up film work because he found it to be too demeaning. Yet, he returned to *Othello*. Why? The issue to which Robeson was responding was not whether black artistic talent existed but the racist denial of that talent. Othello was valuable because, first, it was a leading role, which was extremely rare for black stage actors. Second, it was in a Shakespearean play, which garnered respect from the theater establishment. In the nineteenth century, Ira Aldridge proved that African Americans could excel in Shakespearean theater. But he was deprived of the opportunity to ever perform in the United States. Thus, Robeson's Othello was vital because it signified that a black actor had been accepted on Broadway in a classic play, and this had the potential to open other venues for African American performers. Robeson also emphasized Othello's dignity in order to contradict degrading stereotypes of people of African descent, and he used the production as a platform from which to speak out against segregation. Because of its political significance, Robeson's assumption of the role transcended Simple's concerns about the content of the play. Simple's disquiet about the role highlighted Robeson's stature, as an actor and a leader, in the African American community and for this reason was a unique and constructive addition to the historical record of the Broadway *Othello*.

C. L. R. James, who had worked with Robeson on his play about Toussaint L'Ouverture in London in 1936, was also critical of Robeson's Othello. James, a Marxist theorist and historian, was also an astute observer of culture. James wrote literary criticism including an article titled "'Othello' and 'The Merchant of Venice'" in which he argued that race was not the central issue of the play but rather Othello's foreignness.[111] However, Robeson viewed these issues to be indivisible since Othello was an outsider to Venetian society primarily because of his race. James, who was raised under the British colonial system, held Shakespeare in the highest regard. Thus, when he saw Robeson on Broadway as Othello, he felt moved to articulate his conclusions in a series of letters.

Constance Webb, whom James was courting at the time, was the recipient of this correspondence, which tended to offer candid glimpses into James's views on a wide variety of subjects. Concerning *Othello*, James insisted that Robeson lacked the proper rhythm of the Shakespearean language and complained that Robeson sometimes simply "stood in one spot and *said* the lines, just said them [his emphasis]."[112] He was obviously passionate about Shakespeare and had little patience when he believed the Bard had been violated. This particular letter went on for several pages as James explored the revolutionary tendencies of Desdemona's behavior that Uta Hagen failed to capture on stage.

References to Robeson appeared in ensuing letters when James waxed about Elizabethan stage conventions and the central elements of playwriting. Thus, as Shakespeare was near and dear to James, he had little tolerance for what he felt was a "lousy" aesthetic performance from Robeson. Nevertheless, James did confirm the political importance of the production. He attested, "The mess that colour [sic] can cause in a happy married life was particularly clear and the whole American Negro question was highlighted by the play. *Politically* it is a great event [his emphasis]." James's remark concerning the potential "mess" that race could cause in an interracial marriage was particularly revealing, as he would later marry Webb, a white American. Significantly, James subsequently declared of the revival, "I could see it often again."[113] Despite his criticism of Robeson's acting, James believed the production was of great consequence as political and social commentary and judged it worth seeing even multiple times. Therefore, a pattern was discernable within the critiques of Robeson. Critics such as Margaret Marshall, though in the minority, criticized Robeson and could not reconcile a black Othello. Conversely, black reviewers, such as C. L. R. James and Miles Jefferson, were disapproving of Robeson's acting but still deemed the production as vital and worth viewing on political grounds. Langston Hughes similarly admired Robeson but stood out by voicing objections about the content of the play.

One final critic of Robeson must be examined: Margaret Webster, the director of the Broadway production. As previously mentioned, there was tension backstage between Webster and the cast prior to the Broadway opening. Another argument erupted while preparations were being made for the U.S. tour. This time the disagreement concerned the placement of Hagen's and Ferrer's names in the billing of the show. Webster scrawled to her parents, "Paul is insisting on starring the Ferrers in smaller than his own name but in a star position above the title." And she was "bitterly opposed" to this idea since Ferrer and Hagen did not possess the status for such prominent placement in the advertising. Two days later, Webster reported that Robeson had refused to sign his contract for the tour unless the new billing was instated. The following week, Webster decided to leave the cast since she was "so sick & disgusted with it all." Through this turbulence, Webster experienced the intransigent side of Robeson that would enable him to maintain his political posture through the repression of the cold war. She noticed, "But actually no one can control Paul . . . once he really digs his feet in the ground."[114] Uta Hagen recalled of this squabble that "there was a tremendous crisis with the Theatre Guild and Paul insisted that we have this billing. That was kind of, one of those ugly things that are not meaningful." She also surmised that Webster might have just been "miffed because she wasn't included."[115] The part of Emilia, then, was played by Edith King on the U.S. tour.

Within the context of backstage conflict before and after the Broadway engagement, Webster was increasingly critical in her letters of Robeson's acting. She inquired rhetorically in one letter, "Can you imagine that anyone can be a great Othello without being a good Othello?"[116] This question spoke to the larger issue of Robeson's technical skill as an actor. Webster also addressed this issue in an article in 1944: "Technically, from the standpoint of the expert in histrionics, he was not, and still in places is not, an especially good Othello; spiritually, he is a great one." Webster then cited his political maturity since 1930 as a chief asset. She explicated his growth: "Experience deepened and enriched him; it strengthened him in the passion and patience which he has given to the struggle for his race. . . ."[117] Uta Hagen confirmed Webster's concerns about Robeson's technique but believed that it "didn't seem to bother anybody" because his stage presence was so powerful. She reminisced, "In the play . . . he had . . . charisma. . . . And a human— I can only say vibration that was so overpowering that when he stepped on stage [gasps]—I mean you could only gasp. Just the presence. He had it."[118] Another cast member, Louis Lytton, who played the Duke, recalled of Robeson onstage, "One felt the man's great heart: he inspired and lifted the scenes to the heights."[119]

The question of Robeson's technical skill was raised in several critiques of his acting. When Robeson began acting in New York in the 1920s, the cultural heritage of African Americans was celebrated as being natural, intrinsic, and unblemished by Western structures or conventions. In his writing in the 1930s, Robeson resolutely emphasized that African Americans should not imitate European art forms but draw inspiration from their innate connection to Africa. Training in Western techniques, then, could tarnish the African American artist's instinctive ability. Eslanda Robeson's 1930 biography underscored the idea that it was Robeson's "precious instinct which always guided him" in his acting.[120]

Robeson continued to allude to this instinctual approach in the 1940s. A 1944 article in *Theatre Arts* asserted that although Robeson had given what is "quite likely the most acclaimed performance [of Othello] . . . within living memory, he never had thought of his own acting in terms of technique." It continued, "[H]e [Robeson] will tell you that by instinct he is really not an actor at all, that his methods and thought-processes are not those of a deliberate craftsman like his friend José Ferrer. . . ."[121] This explained some of Webster's frustration directing Robeson; they were approaching their craft from completely different angles. Hers was in the mold of traditional British stage customs, whereas Robeson came from a world steeped in folk song and preaching. He made a living primarily as a vocalist of African American spirituals. In fact, she once bemoaned the fact that Robeson sounded as if he "never got out of the pulpit."[122] Yet, Robeson had stated unmistakably, "Oratory was the basis of my approach to the theatre."[123] His interpretation was clearly tied to the tradition of the black church, where he was raised, which emphasized oratorical skills and even staged plays and dramatic readings. In his memoir, Robeson described how he relished "the rhythmic eloquence of our preachers" who were "masters of poetic speech."[124] Robeson also utilized Constantin Stanislavsky's strategies, but because Webster was unfamiliar or uncomfortable with this methodology her direction was not as effective as it could have been in guiding Robeson's performance. Webster sensed this impasse and, as biographer Millie Barranger noted, "Webster faulted herself for not being a Method director. . . ."[125] This, no doubt, contributed to the strain in Robeson and Webster's working relationship.

Even though he did not characterize himself as a technician, Robeson was using several of Stanislavsky's methods in his interpretation of Othello. Around the turn of the twentieth century, Stanislavsky's fresh style of dramaturgy broke theater away from the external trappings of the nineteenth century. His strategies were based not on physicality or melodrama as were popular in the 1800s. Stanislavsky pointed the way toward more nuanced performance based on the internal psychology of the actor. He believed it was important to present a subtle interpretation that was believable to the audience. His approach was pioneered in the United States by the Group Theatre in New York in the 1930s, making these ideas still relatively new at the time of the Broadway *Othello*. One of Stanislavsky's modes that Robeson utilized was analysis. In his book *Creating a Role*, Stanislavsky emphasized the importance of analysis when preparing for a new role. He theorized, "Through analysis the actor becomes further acquainted with his role. Analysis is also a method of becoming familiar with the play through the study of its parts."[126] Robeson had definitely analyzed Shakespeare's *Othello* as evidenced by his thoughtful commentary on the play in 1930 and his articles in the 1940s such as "Some Reflections on *Othello* and the Nature of Our Time."

Stanislavsky also encouraged the actor to search for personal memories that would help conjure the emotion necessary for a role. He suggested, "The material considered here consists of living, personal memories related to the five senses, which have been stored up in an actor's emotion memory . . . which are analogous to feelings in his role."[127] Robeson also employed this technique of emotion memory. In a 1943 interview, he explained, "I took Othello apart bit by bit . . . to find out what each word meant. I listened carefully to directors and Shakespearean authorities, but in some cases their Othello didn't think and act exactly as I believed a great Negro warrior would do, and in those cases, I played it my way. . . . All I do is feel the part. I make myself believe I am Othello and I act as he would act."[128] He further elucidated in an interview in 1944, "The rage—that rage he [Othello] feels is maddening, he is out of his head. And I know what that is like because I felt it once myself. One time I went out of my head in a rage and night after night out there on the stage I remember it."[129] Robeson's rage stemmed from the racism he experienced as a college athlete on the football field, and he used this memory as a conduit for Othello's anger. Moreover, being the sole black competitor on the Rutgers football team was analogous to being the only black actor in the *Othello* cast. In both situations Robeson was a focal point "onstage" and he utilized the memory of discrimination as a football player to help channel the emotions necessary to push past the racial assumptions of theater segregation.

Several critics lamented Robeson's lack of overt action when interpreting Othello. It was possible that Robeson, in his attempt to maintain a dignified composure, came across to some as overly restrained. Interestingly, Stanislavsky recommended that movement be minimized and that the only action from the actor should stem from deliberate internal motivations. He warned, "External action on the stage when ... not called forth by inner activity, is entertaining only for the eyes and ears; it does not penetrate the heart...."[130] In *Building a Character*, Stanislavsky similarly cautioned, "Unrestrained movements, natural though they may be to the actor himself, only blur the design of his part, make his performance unclear, monotonous and uncontrolled."[131] Robeson's interpretation of Othello was influenced by the motivation to portray African Americans with dignity. His inner impulse was, in part, to defy the stereotype of black people as buffoons and uninhibited caricatures. Stanislavsky advised actors to take a subtle approach; however, Robeson's interpretation might have been too understated for some critics. Still, self-restraint was probably necessary for an actor who was challenging the color barrier on the New York stage. In order to be accepted, Robeson could not appear to be dangerous to audiences even though his character murdered his white wife at the close of the play. Perhaps he veered too far toward one extreme and became overly restrained because of his focus on being dignified. In fact, Stark Young alluded to this idea in his review in *The New Republic*. He wrote that at times Robeson "gives us the wearing sense of an overworked diaphragm where only the relaxation of dignity and strength are required."[132] Yet, Robeson seemed to believe that he could not risk relaxing his dignity. Though Robeson's interpretation did not please a few critics, the gravity of his Othello went much deeper than technique. Numerous reviewers, even some who were more critical of Robeson's acting, agreed that this significance was political.

The Politics of Robeson's Broadway *Othello*

Certainly, the production was exceptional in that the two male leads were from minority groups: Robeson, an African American, and Ferrer, who was born in Puerto Rico. The most overt political stand taken by the *Othello* cast was the refusal to perform in any segregated theaters. This position was initiated by Robeson but supported by the rest of the troupe and directly impacted the U.S. tour. The stance against segregation was clarified in the *People's Voice* newspaper: "Through the insistence of Paul Robeson, clauses have been inserted into all contracts with road theatres to set aside a certain number of orchestra seats for Negroes for the production of Othello. . . ."[133] Not only did Robeson insist that the theaters not be segregated, but he specified that if he detected any segregation after arriving, then he would not perform. The *People's Voice* further articulated the historic nature of Robeson's antisegregation posture: "Paul Robeson . . . recently signed a contract . . . stipulating that if he detects segregation . . . in any part of the theatre, he can walk right off the stage. . . . And he made history, too, with the signing of the contract, for never before in the annals of the theatre has any such amazing clause ever been written." Marvel Cooke, who wrote that piece, also hoped that Robeson's stand would signal "the start of a movement in the entertainment industry to put an end to discrimination in the theatre once and for all."[134] This was a prime example of Robeson's stubbornness in the face of discrimination. Thus, the production was historic not only because it starred the first African American actor in Shakespeare on Broadway but because Robeson's insistence against segregation contested other barriers as well.

Robeson's strict standards against segregation obviously constrained the U.S. tour schedule. The tour ran from early September 1944 to early April 1945 beginning in Trenton, New Jersey, and traveling north and westward, including dates in Canada. It wound its way to California and ended with a two-week engagement in Chicago before returning to New York to officially close the show. Clearly, there were no engagements for *Othello* in the South. However, theater segregation was not confined to the South, as Uta Hagen recalled. She pointed out, "We broke the precedent of playing to segregated audiences. . . . And by segregated houses, I mean in the north. We never played south of Saint Louis, and [were] confronted in Indianapolis, in Minneapolis, in Buffalo, in Sacramento, in Seattle [where] segregated houses were the norm." Hagen remembered, in particular, the reaction in Detroit: "People from Grosse Point and all the auto manufacturers, and all the multi-rich, were sitting next to very elegantly dressed black people. They shocked them [laughs] so much that they went crazy and just froze in the audience. And what happened on stage did not ever seem to alarm anyone, as much as what happened in the audience [laughs]."[135] The Detroit opening made quite an impression, as Robeson also recalled the impact of that diverse crowd: "On the opening night of *Othello* there were very few rich folks in the audience. Nobody quite knew what had happened, but I saw that the Ford workers, Negro and white, had most of the seats, and it was a memorable opening."[136] The U.S. tour, in addition to defying racial segregation, further confirmed Ralph Warner's thesis that the *Othello* revival encouraged a unique democratization of theater audiences.

It was not surprising that Robeson would take such a stance against theater discrimination, because his political views were increasingly influencing his artistic career during this period. For example, an article in the *Amsterdam News* in 1943 announced that Robeson would perform a scene from *Othello* at a rally for the election of Ben Davis to New York City Council.[137] Robeson again emphasized the stand against segregation in the *Othello* tour and noted how fervently he believed that "art is tied up with the political background" in a 1949 interview.[138] However, did the political nature of this production influence other members of the company? The resounding answer was yes.

One of the most significant legacies of the Broadway production, besides the record-breaking 296 performances, was its impact in the struggle against discrimination. Robeson publicly asserted in 1943 that the positive reception for *Othello* was indicative of progress in the fight against racial discrimination.[139] An interview with Ferrer and Hagen in 1944 declared that "Othello has made one change in them—it fanned the quiet disapproval they always felt for race discrimination into flaming crusading anger."[140] For instance, José Ferrer made plans to produce Lillian Smith's *Strange Fruit* for the stage in 1945 and the following year, he publicly "called on actors 'who are stars'... to refuse to appear in theatres where Negroes are refused admission."[141] In 1946, Ferrer also contributed to a dialogue on the role of the theater in society when he chaired a symposium called "The Artist as Citizen" at a meeting of the Independent Citizens Committee of the Arts, Sciences and Professions. Robeson also spoke at this event, where he declared that the United States had but two choices for its political future: proceeding "back to fascism or on to socialism."[142]

Margaret Webster received an award of recognition from the Interracial Councils of New Jersey "for her contribution to interracial understanding."[143] She continued to work with African American actors in Shakespeare as demonstrated by her critically acclaimed production of *The Tempest* in 1945 which starred Canada Lee as Caliban. That same year she wrote an article in the *New York Times* pleading for a "rebirth of the theatre." In it, Webster explained the dissatisfaction she felt because a social quality had been lost in the theatre and held up her production of *Othello* as an example of the potential power of the stage. She reflected on the Broadway debut, "It obliterated time and distance, welding into one entity actors and audience ... fusing together the great poet-dramatist of 1600, the Negro actor lifting a standard for his race, the fictional Othello and Iago, [and] the Broadway first-nighters of 1943. At the end there were, I think, few members of the audience who did not leave the theatre shaken and aware and not an actor on the stage who did not feel humble and glorified."[144] After some months of reflection, Webster did not sound at all resentful about her experience with the *Othello* revival. Regardless of the friction occurring behind the scenes, that opening night possessed a beauty and dignity which made it a powerful and unforgettable occasion.

All in all, this production challenged both artistic and racial barriers in the United States. Of course, it presented a black actor as Othello, but it also defied the idea that Shakespeare could not succeed in a long-term Broadway run. Additionally, the production opposed the political boundaries of theater segregation. The *Seattle Times* critic ruminated that the production was a "monumental achievement" with "epochal" stature because it demonstrated that "great art knows no racial barriers."[145] John K. Hutchens, writing in *Theatre Arts*, determined of Robeson, "His race, and the American stage, have moved forward a little because of him."[146] Many who saw the revival reached a similar conclusion, but one of the most memorable assessments came from a Russian journal. A translation of "Othello in the American Theatre" from *Literatura i Iskustvo* unmistakably situated Robeson's performance within the tradition of Ira Aldridge and the historical context of the Second World War. Russia was an important antifascist ally to the United States in 1944 when this article was penned. The author, V. Rogov, asserted, "The acting of Aldridge in serf-ridden Russia (season of 1858) sounded a clarion call. The acting of Paul Robeson during these years of war with humanity-hating fascism also goes far beyond the accustomed limits of theatrical activities." He further illuminated the political significance of the production: "Many American writers and journalists whom I happened to meet in Hollywood and New York consider the 19th of October 1943—the day when Othello opened—as the date upon which the doors of the American theatre opened for the Negro people.... This is a most significant victory for democratic America against the dark forces of Jim Crow—a species of fascist ideology in our days."[147] This insight connected well with Ralph Warner's idea that the *Othello* production democratized the theater. The revival helped open the doors of the theater to African American stage actors because of Robeson's presence on Broadway; however, it also invited the black community to be audience members and to view the play without the indignity of segregation. Robeson had also ruminated on the connection between Aldridge and Shakespearean performance. He emphasized the significance of Ira Aldridge's performing in Russia during the tsarist era in a preface that he wrote for a biography of Aldridge. He pronounced that

"Aldridge brought more than Shakespeare to the people. As a descendant of slaves, himself, a victim of prejudice and oppression, he understood and was especially sensitive to the serfdom of Tsarist society and the oppression of national minorities. . . ."[148] Indeed, all of these observations can also be applied to Robeson, who was the son of a slave and a victim of prejudice, and who was acutely aware of the oppression of national minorities. And it can be said most emphatically that Robeson "brought more than Shakespeare to the people."

CHAPTER FIVE

"I Give of My Talents to the People"
Robeson's Politics in the 1940s

"Robeson... in more senses than one, IS the play," Samuel Putnam asserted in his review of *Othello* on Broadway. Similarly, Mike Gold believed that "Paul Robeson is the greatest personality in America today, the richest force for American democracy and art." Nathaniel Buchwald also suggested, "Yes, the great, the original, the compelling, the revealing element in Paul Robeson's Othello is Paul Robeson." These writers all signaled an important theme emerging from that record-breaking production. It was Robeson: his charisma, his persona, his countenance and physical comportment that coalesced onstage brilliantly and powerfully as Othello. These elements, however, were present not only when Robeson was portraying Shakespeare's Moor but whenever he stood before a crowd to denounce fascism or led a delegation to demand antilynching legislation. In the 1940s, Robeson was in the spotlight for his most celebrated acting role, but he was also increasingly in the public eye as an activist. Thumbing through the newspapers of the era, one found that media coverage of Robeson did not distinguish between Robeson's artistic pursuits and his political activities. If Paul Robeson, the star, was engaged in any endeavor then it was worth covering. It was during this period that the symbiosis between Robeson the actor and Robeson the activist began taking shape. The politics of his performance as Othello was only half of the story of Robeson in the forties, for there was also beauty and power in the performances of his politics.

African American writer Zora Neale Hurston once noticed, "Every phase of Negro life is highly dramatized.... Everything is acted out."[1] This was certainly true of Robeson since much of his life was acted out in the public domain. As a youth, he stood out as a bright and talented African American in a largely white high school. He was known in the community because his father ministered to the people through the church. In college, Robeson was recognized as a scholar, gifted debater, and, especially, as an accomplished athlete. At this young age, Robeson made headlines for his impressive performances on the football field and was respected as a potential leader for his moving orations such as his Rutgers commencement address. In the 1920s, the sight of Robeson simply walking down the street in Harlem became a public event as passersby eagerly crowded around to shake hands with the blossoming artist. Robeson's charisma took Europe by storm through the 1930s in the concert halls of Russia, the theaters of London's West End, and the frontlines of war-torn Spain. By the 1940s, clearly identifying the demarcation between Robeson the artist and Robeson the political advocate was becoming more complicated. When was Robeson performing without making a political statement? When could his activism be separated from his artistry? Robeson's recitals were exceptionally indistinct as either art or politics because audiences got a taste of his singing, political commentary, and frequently even a measure of Shakespeare's *Othello* at these events. The political activist's dignified carriage and deep love for his people radiated through his performances on the theater stage. Likewise, the studied movement and diction of the artist were present at political functions. Robeson's resonant baritone in word and song undergirded all of his appearances.

A brief sidebar in *New Africa*, the organ of the Council on African Affairs, an organization Robeson cofounded, illustrated this seamlessness between Robeson's political activism and artistic career. Next to a photo of the actor, the editor asserted, "Superlatives were exhausted by New York dramatic critics in their praise of Paul Robeson's acting in 'Othello.' Since its opening on October 19, this splendid production of Shakespeare's play has been making history."[2] By itself, this short piece was by no means remarkable. Accolades for Robeson as Othello proliferated in the autumn of 1943. Yet, the next sentence made an important connection between Robeson's success in Shakespeare's play and his political advocacy during the 1940s. "On Tuesday, November 16th, Paul Robeson also contributed to history of another type when, as Chairman of the Council on African Affairs, he addressed the 12th New York Herald Tribune Forum on Current Problems." Just as the Broadway *Othello* had emphasized the wartime context of all races being allied against fascism, Robeson's performance at the Herald Tribune forum underscored the sacrifices of the war effort. He pointed out, "Thanks to the blood of our boys . . . the hitherto oppressed will have this liberty, opportunity and dignity."[3] The theme of dignity in Robeson's speech also mirrored the prominence of dignity in his Othello portrayal. An audience member at either of these events, *Othello* or the Herald Tribune forum, came away with a comparable message: all people should be able to join the fight against fascism on an equal basis to insure full freedom for all races.

Because the distinction between Robeson's onstage position as an artist and his offstage role as an activist was increasingly obscure in the 1940s, his political endeavors can be conceptualized as acts or performances within the public sphere. Was Robeson ever really "offstage"? In his writing on African American culture and his reflections upon *Othello*, Robeson emphasized an intuitive approach to art in general and acting specifically. Since being an actor came naturally to Robeson, this innate talent was part of his performing, whether he was "onstage" in a formal theater or not. For his performances in the political arena, Robeson utilized a range of vehicles: a radio microphone, a platform at Madison Square Garden, a press conference. For example, when he was walking in a picket line, the press covered the story and brought often international attention to the issue with which he was engaged. His break from the film industry was widely publicized and highlighted Robeson's distaste with the corporate interests of Hollywood. Robeson's celebrity and impassioned speeches against injustice helped raise money for causes such as famine relief in South Africa. The simple act of stating that African Americans preferred peace to war with Russia brought an avalanche of fury upon Robeson and made him, along with his supporters, a target for right-wing vigilantes. Langston Hughes wrote in 1926 that Paul Robeson singing "Water Boy" had the potential to inspire "the smug Negro middle class to turn from their white, respectable, ordinary books and papers to catch a glimpse of their own beauty."[4] By the 1940s, any Robeson appearance had the power to compel an observer, black or white, to stop and catch a glimpse of the beauty of an African American performer advocating for his people.

Early 1940s: Prior to *Othello* on Broadway

In his article "Criteria for Negro Art," W. E. B. Du Bois steadfastly argued, "Thus all Art is propaganda and ever must be, despite the wailing of purists. . . . I do not care a damn for any art that is not used for propaganda.

But I do care when propaganda is confined to one side while the other side is stripped silent." He concluded, "[T]he point today is that until the art of black folk compels recognition they will not be rated as human."[5] Robeson undoubtedly concurred with Du Bois's assertion. In his artistic career, Robeson strove to portray the humanity of his people by focusing on singing black folk music and trying to concentrate on acting roles that conveyed the dignity of African Americans. If, in Du Bois's words, all art was propaganda for the race, then could propaganda, or political activities, be artistic when performed by an actor like Robeson? If the singular Robeson persona could infuse his art with a political message, then why not view his politics as also possessing his unique artistic sensibility? He was still an artist, was still performing when striding up to the lectern at a political rally. Examples of the performative nature of his political endeavors abound in the 1940s.

Though Robeson had been abroad for much of the decade of the thirties, he wasted no time getting involved with progressive campaigns in the United States upon his return in 1939. A legendary Robeson performance that year "came to stand for" what Michael Denning characterized as "the aesthetic forms and ideologies of the Popular Front."[6] "Ballad for Americans," music by Earl Robinson and lyrics by John La Touche, offered Robeson a distinctive opportunity to meld art and politics in an unparalleled performance. Robeson presented the anthem live on CBS radio November 5, with a repeat performance on December 31, 1939, to much acclaim. This patriotic hymn celebrated the ideas of Life ("Yes sir!") and Liberty ("That's right!") and American heroes like Crispus Attucks, Tom Jefferson, Abe Lincoln, and Tom Paine. The final stanzas underscored the importance of the general laborer and his contribution to the economy ("I'm the everybody who's nobody and the nobody who's everybody"). The chorus queried, "Am I an American?" and Robeson replied, in the call and response pattern, with an array of answers emphasizing tolerance for people from all religions and ethnic backgrounds.

It was, perhaps, ironic that Robeson, a black performer, was the messenger of a song which could surely be characterized as sentimental at a time when many African Americans lived under Jim Crow subjugation and were disenfranchised. Robeson recognized this underlying reality but must have believed that the image of him singing about inclusiveness and American ideals could be a powerful symbol. A black performer who publicly identified with the working class intoning a ballad about economic and ethnic differentiations within the scope of U.S. history implied a need for class and racial unity that would have been lost without Robeson's presence.

Importantly, Robeson's interpretation of the song definitely appealed to the general laboring public. Following the initial broadcast, "the sustained roar of applause in the studio has had no counterpart in the history of radio. It was so tumultuous and genuine that the program couldn't continue for nearly four minutes."[7] The song had piqued the imagination of a country that was just emerging from the depths of the depression and was on the brink of a war against fascism. "Ballad for Americans" was imbued with the spirit of the Popular Front, and the lyrics pointed to an optimism which Robeson shared that a new, more egalitarian society could be forged in the wake of the fight against fascism. Robeson also performed the ballad at stadium concerts to much commendation. Other vocalists attempted alternative versions. Yet, a *New York Times* article in August 1940 asserted, "Since it took the nation by storm last winter, the rise in popularity of 'Ballad for Americans' has been undiminished. Several recordings have appeared, of which the one with Paul Robeson . . . remains the best."[8]

Robeson maintained his characteristically hectic schedule through the early 1940s as he embarked on concert tours across the United States while concurrently speaking at union rallies and, after the United States officially entered the war, appearing at mass meetings for Soviet-American friendship and war bond rallies. He also remained actively involved with the Council on African Affairs and spoke before other civil rights groups such as the National Negro Congress. Robeson's popularity was not hampered by wartime bans as illustrated by a concert in New Jersey in early 1943. Pleasure driving was outlawed at this time, but undismayed concertgoers performed creative feats of transportation to attend the show. Some walked up to five miles, and one resourceful fan ice-skated a mile and a half across a frozen lake to hear Robeson sing![9] Robeson's performances, encompassing music and politics, were, in the words of Denning, "an embodiment" of the "Popular Front vision."[10] His political commentary emanated at all public appearances. An editor at the *People's Voice* declared that Robeson, who possessed "democracy's greatest voice" was "the only man in the world who can turn a concert into a rally for the rights of minority groups. . . ."[11]

The performative nature of Robeson's political appearances was illustrated well at a rally of twenty thousand people for the Congress of Soviet-American Friendship in November 1942. At this mass meeting, Vice President Henry A. Wallace announced the inauguration of a second front in North Africa and promised continued friendship with Russia following the war. Robeson, who also spoke to the crowd assembled, was introduced in a very theatrical fashion. According to an FBI informant, at a prescribed moment, the hall was suddenly engulfed in total darkness. The audience was then assured that the next voice they would hear would be that of an antifascist. They must have waited breathlessly until the spotlights dramatically illuminated Robeson on the stage to thunderous applause. Surely, this introduction and reception rivaled any that Robeson received in a theater setting. Robeson's remarks that evening emphasized his political posture: "I have been called an anti-fascist. I am exactly that. Because I am an American and because I am a Negro."[12] This introduction of Robeson, not as an actor or singer but as an antifascist, exemplified his position as a commentator on American culture and politics. Indeed, he had shared the rostrum that day with the vice president, an army general and the Soviet ambassador. The staged effects which heightened his entrance, however, highlighted an element of drama in a Robeson performance even if it was at a political rally. For Robeson, whose warmth and charisma radiated in any setting, such an entrance was only fitting.

In 1942, the same year as his debut in the summer stock production of *Othello* at Cambridge, Robeson's political consciousness forced him to break completely from the film industry. He had previously taken a hiatus from film work because of his frustration with the lack of control he had over the final product and the debasing images of African Americans that proliferated in the industry. His past film projects had sometimes been criticized in the black press, as with *Sanders of the River* in 1934. This movie had celebrated British imperialism rather than African cultural forms, as Robeson had initially hoped. In an interview from 1938, a disenchanted Robeson noted that films were just another investment for corporate interests: "[T]he film industry is the clearest example of the workings of capitalism. . . . 'You've only got to ask who controls United States Steel, who controls Chase National Bank. And then you find the same guys control the film industry.'"[13]

Tales of Manhattan, with Robeson and Ethel Waters, was released in the autumn of 1942. The film presented a loose string of vignettes connected by an overcoat that impacted several disparate lives as it traveled from person to person. In the final sketch, Robeson and Waters, playing rural sharecroppers in the South, happen upon the coat, which fell from an airplane, and find its pockets mysteriously brimming with cash. This fortuitous discovery induced Waters and Robeson into a chorus of hallelujahs. The *Wall Street Journal* reviewer believed that the pair of African Americans "perform their offices to good effect" but was disappointed that Robeson did not sing until the very end.[14] Additionally, the *New York Times* pointed out that

Hollywood had *Tales* "stamped as a box office winner."[15] The black press told a different story, however. Nell Dodson, writing for the *People's Voice*, admonished the "corny" direction and overwrought language portrayed by the tenant farmers. She offered, "When the [Robeson and Waters] characters ask the preacher for shoes . . . it is neither far-fetched nor ridiculous, but the dialect and the over-drawing of the types makes it so." Dodson attentively suggested that had the film been "[h]andled with feeling and understanding on the part of the director, the results might have been different."[16] Robeson's portrayal of a caricature in the film can be juxtaposed with his politically charged performance in response to the film.

Robeson was disappointed with the film and felt compelled to explain his reasons for signing on to the project at a press conference. He emphasized that he had hoped he could get the producer to change the script but was told that too much money had been invested in the project and to alter any of it might risk alienating the southern market. Thus, "they continued to show the Negro in time-honored Hollywood fashion." Robeson stressed that he had since turned down several film offers due to his disillusionment with *Tales* and even "confirmed the report that he would picket the picture himself."[17] Subsequently, in September 1942, the *New York Times* reported that Robeson had unabashedly announced he was "through with Hollywood until movie magnates found some other way to portray the Negro." He vented his frustration: "But in the end it [*Tales*] turned out to be the same old thing—the Negro solving his problem by singing his way to glory. This is very offensive to my people. It makes the Negro child-like and innocent and is in the old plantation tradition."[18] Except for his narration of the labor documentary *Native Land* later that year, *Tales of Manhattan* was Robeson's final film appearance. Other movie projects were discussed later in his career, such as a Russian production of *Othello*, but never came to fruition due to his passport revocation in the 1950s. Robeson's clear public act of turning away from the movie magnates following *Tales* signaled a new direction in his career. In this case, it was Robeson's lack of performing in films that hammered away his point that credible roles for African Americans were far too rare. Refusing to act in movies, a medium in which he had little control, afforded Robeson the time to perform his art and politics in venues where he could be in charge of the final product.

It was significant that this crucial turning point in Robeson's career came just after his summer debut as *Othello* in Cambridge. In the *People's Voice*, Nell Dodson astutely questioned why Robeson had not left the *Tales* project sooner: "Any man who did what Robeson did in Kansas City not so long ago—demand recognition of equal rights—surely could step out of a role he knew would bring public censure. If he had walked out of the film when he found what the circumstances were, it would have been as effective an act of protest as could have been made." She then effectively contrasted the *Tales* fiasco with the Cambridge premiere: "A man who plays Othello with the supreme talent he proved was his is big enough and influential enough to make his every action keenly felt in theatre circles."[19] It was remarkable that Dodson could premise this connection solely on the basis of the summer stock opening of *Othello*. Robeson had not yet even performed on Broadway, when his interpretation of Shakespeare's Moor had indisputably reached its pinnacle. Even the brief Cambridge run had demonstrated Robeson's eminence as Othello. Yet, Dodson also made explicit the relationship between *Othello* and Robeson's politics: *Othello* acted as a vehicle from which Robeson could perform his politics and his "every action" could be "keenly felt." Because of his ascendancy in that well-respected role, Robeson could now wield additional authority on political grounds. This was precisely what happened during the tour of the Broadway production, especially with regard to segregation. Robeson refused to perform in any segregated theaters and this public stand against injustice was successful because *Othello* had catapulted him to a higher, albeit short-lived, level of influence.

Political Performances During the Mid-1940s

During the mid-1940s, Paul Robeson's prominence reached its apex: glowing reviews indicated that his place in the history of Broadway and Shakespearean theater was secured, his popularity was reinforced through numerous awards and honorary degrees, and his left-wing political affiliations were not called into question as long as the United States and Russia were allied. Significantly, the Broadway *Othello* occurred during the war mobilization as well as a time of mounting civil rights protest. As political circumstances increasingly influenced the major theatrical production with which Robeson was employed, the relationship between Robeson the artist and Robeson the activist became ever more conflated.

The war effort engaged progressives and Communist Party members who pushed for a second European front after Germany invaded Russia in June of 1941. Following the attack on Pearl Harbor in December, most of the United States, except for small pockets of Socialists and conscientious objectors, rallied around the cause of antifascism. The World War II years also represented an important period of campaigning for civil rights by African Americans. Perhaps most famously, A. Philip Randolph, founder of the Brotherhood of Sleeping Car Porters and a leader in the National Negro Congress, planned a March on Washington Movement against employment discrimination. The notion of a mass protest during wartime roused President Roosevelt to pen Executive Order 8802. This law outlawed discrimination in the defense industries and formed the Fair Employment Practices Committee (FEPC). Although it did open jobs for African Americans in some wartime industries, the FEPC was largely impotent because it did not possess the power to enforce any of its recommendations. These jobs were often menial and many African Americans remained segregated in wartime boom towns. Moreover, the armed forces remained segregated through the war for the thousands of African Americans who served and were treated with segregated blood from the Red Cross when they were wounded. On the issue of separated blood supplies, Walter White of the NAACP wrote in the *People's Voice*, "How ironic must be the laughter today in Berlin and Tokyo as they listen to American assertions that the war is being fought . . . to wipe out totalitarianism based on racial bigotry!"[20] Meanwhile, the NAACP was continuing its long-term strategy in the courts that would climax with the 1954 *Brown* decision on school segregation.

In 1942, the *Pittsburgh Courier*, an African American newspaper, introduced the term "double v," which referred to the need for a double victory against fascism abroad as well as race discrimination in the United States. African Americans fought valiantly against fascism and, thus, also came home fighting for full citizenship rights. This idea was adopted widely in the black community during the war years. The spirit of the Double V campaign was evident at a rally of seventy-five hundred when Adam Clayton Powell Jr. backed Benjamin Davis, of the Communist Party, for city council and proclaimed, "The will of the anti-Fascists . . . and the anti-Ku Klux Klan will send Benjamin Davis, Jr. to the City Council on November 2nd."[21] W. E. B. Du Bois, who had initially been optimistic about the prospects for African Americans following World War I, warned in 1942, "We may sadly admit today that the First World War did not bring us democracy. Nor will the second." A few months later he was cautiously optimistic: "Is it for the freedom of Negroes in the Southern United States and Negroes in West Africa to vote? If this is the freedom we are fighting for, my gun is on my shoulder."[22]

Robeson was increasingly engaged in the push for civil rights during the World War II era. His visibility was at its peak on the political front (at rallies, conferences, mass meetings, and political campaigns), and the record number of Broadway shows, coupled with the extended U.S. tour, meant that thousands also saw him in *Othello*. Amiri Baraka has estimated that perhaps as many as five hundred thousand people around the country viewed Robeson's Othello.[23] Robeson's stand against segregated theaters should be considered against the backdrop of the broader momentum against discrimination including the March on Washington Movement, the NAACP's judicial strategy, and the Double V campaign. His historic appearance as a black actor breaking the color barrier in Shakespeare on Broadway also helped fuel this larger movement. His milestone represented further evidence of black dignity and success in a venue previously viewed as being for whites only. Robeson's politics were also evident in his performances in various civil rights campaigns.

In December 1943, shortly following his Broadway debut, Robeson spoke before a conference of club presidents, general managers, and the commissioner of baseball, Kennesaw Landis, to argue for the entry of African Americans into major league teams. Landis, who presided over the proceedings, underscored Robeson's unmitigated fame in his introduction: "It is unnecessary to introduce Paul Robeson. Everybody knows him or what he's done as an athlete or artist."[24] In his comments, Robeson argued for the admittance of African Americans into mainstream baseball on the basis of the current movement against segregation and his success as a black actor on Broadway. At a press conference following the meeting, Robeson stressed that "this was an excellent time to bring about an entry of Negro players into organized baseball." He noted that when he played for Rutgers the presence of an African American athlete "on a collegiate gridiron had been unheard of" but now was "commonplace." In a similar vein, "a Negro in a white cast long was considered incredible" but his appearance in *Othello* had become "the outstanding success of his career."[25] The spirit of his remarks was clear: the tenor of the country was changing with regard to segregation. Robeson could have chosen to utilize only sports metaphors from his days as a college sportsman, but he employed the Broadway *Othello* as an indicator of the approaching downfall of the color line. Four years later, Jackie Robinson joined the Brooklyn Dodgers as the first openly acknowledged African American to play in major league baseball since the turn of the twentieth century. Thus, Robeson's ground-breaking performance in *Othello* undergirded the case he made against segregation in other arenas. He had performed as the sole black player on the athletic field at Rutgers as well as on the Broadway stage, and could now submit these events as evidence in his appearance before Landis and the press. Whether performing as a ballplayer, actor, or activist, Robeson communicated the same antisegregation message.

Robeson's performances as Othello not only furthered the fight against segregation but supported other political causes as the production was touring the United States from late 1944 to early 1945. Two *Othello* performances in California were sponsored by the Council on African Affairs (CAA) along with other organizations. These events served as tributes to Robeson and raised funds for the sponsors. The first, in January 1945, was held in Los Angeles and jointly sponsored by the CAA and the Musicians Congress, which was formed "to further the ideals of democracy through music and to build lasting friendship among all races and nations by the exchange of cultures."[26] Numerous individuals and groups, including entertainers, organizers, and educators, purchased space in the program to send greetings to Robeson and acknowledge his artistry and advocacy. For example, sixteen professors from UCLA recognized Robeson as "an ambassador of the arts" who "has taught by living example the way to a better understanding among all peoples." The introductory notes to the program, written by Dalton Trumbo, honored Robeson's commitment to political activism: "Tonight an artist's organization . . . and an educational organization . . . have joined forces to pay tribute to an American who, within his own personality, uniquely combines the artist, the musician and the politically responsible citizen of America and the world." He concluded pointedly, "And yet his work as a citizen has not interfered with his growth as an artist. Rather, the artist has complemented the citizen, and vice versa. They have matured together, and now they cannot be separated." Thus, Trumbo shrewdly observed that by this point in his career, Robeson's artistry was indistinguishable from his political activities.

Another benefit performance sponsored by the CAA occurred the following month in San Francisco and was cohosted by the American-Russian Institute. The souvenir program similarly carried warm wishes to Robeson from many sources such as the *People's Daily World* and *California Eagle* newspapers as well as the International Longshoremen's and Warehousemen's Union, of which Robeson was an honorary member. The opening remarks of the program for this engagement reflected the note in the initial Broadway *Othello* program from 1943 that underscored the cooperation of all races in the fight against fascism. The 1945 benefit program emphasized the approaching close of the war and the need for an end to fascist tendencies in the United States. It read in part, "Just as it was necessary for the United Nations to become firmly welded in order to achieve victory, so is it necessary for Americans of all races, creeds and colors to unite for a free and democratic America with equal opportunity for all. Only such an America can guarantee a just and lasting peace."[27] This analysis echoed the spirit of the Double V campaign and again firmly grounded Robeson's Othello within the contemporary political context.

This program also included an essay reprinted from *New Masses* titled "From Aldridge to Robeson" that paralleled Ira Aldridge's social consciousness and fame as Othello with Robeson's. It mentioned how Aldridge, though he practiced his art abroad, donated part of his salary to the abolitionist cause and asserted that by "remembering Ira Aldridge we may better understand how truly historic is the triumph of Paul Robeson." Finally, the remarks by the American-Russian Institute summarized the ethos of both of these performances in California, which celebrated Robeson's Othello performances as an occasion to highlight contemporary political issues. The institute, whose work accentuated intercultural relations, extended "its warmest thanks . . . for making possible this benefit performance of a magnificent production which, in its own way, emphasizes cultural unity." Robeson's Othello and his political pursuits complemented well the missions of the Musicians Congress, the American-Russian Institute, and the CAA, which he served as chairman. Overall, his performances as Othello functioned, on a broad scale, as a conduit through which Robeson could represent the dignity of his people and speak out against segregation. Additionally, these particular engagements fused Robeson's art and politics by engaging a theatrical presentation in order to benefit specific political organizations that admired Robeson and shared his progressive goals.

Robeson's artistry and activism were also conjoined through his continuous political appearances during the *Othello* tour. The engagement at Chicago's Erlanger Theater happened to coincide with the death of President Roosevelt on April 12, 1945. Over the course of his unprecedented number of presidential terms, FDR's New Deal reforms had persuaded many African Americans, who had formerly been loyal to Lincoln's Republican Party, to vote Democratic. Additionally, Roosevelt had appointed Mary McLeod Bethune, a distinguished educator and founder of Bethune-Cookman College, to a cabinet position in the National Youth Administration, from which she advocated for black rights. Prominent African Americans, including Robeson, had supported Roosevelt's 1944 campaign against Thomas Dewey. FDR's death must have been an upsetting occasion for Robeson as it was for New Dealers and progressives around the country. The newspaper reviews of Robeson's Othello in Chicago were fairly critical as the strain of national events along with his hectic schedule was most likely taking a toll on him. It was his heartfelt appearance at an oratorical competition for young people the day Roosevelt died which perhaps best portrayed Robeson's response to the president's untimely death. In his speech, Robeson "paid tribute to the late President Roosevelt and urged the young orators competing to use their talents in keeping with the principles the great leader died for before the world."[28] Robeson continued to uphold those principles during the next election by actively campaigning for, not the Democratic candidate Harry Truman, but the Progressive Party candidate who had worked with Roosevelt: Henry A. Wallace.

Robeson persisted in the battle against segregation in 1945 when he embarked on a tour across Europe with the first interracial group of entertainers for the USO. The initial plan had been for the whole *Othello* troupe to make the USO engagement but this did not occur due to scheduling confusion. Robeson headed out, instead, as a solo vocalist accompanied by his long-time collaborator on the piano, Lawrence Brown.[29] These performances recalled his visit to the troops in Spain in the late 1930s and accentuated his commitment to supporting those who had fought against fascism. Robeson, unsurprisingly, was a big hit with the soldiers. One reviewer captured how the GIs in Germany were clearly moved by Robeson's performance, "There were rapt spellbound expressions on the faces of most of those in the audiences, and there were tears plainly to be seen in some eyes."[30]

Black troops, especially, were bolstered by Robeson's visit. A reporter for the Associated Negro Press observed, "Without a doubt, in the men's minds here, Mr. Robeson is one of the greatest champions for the integration of the colored millions in the United States into every phase of American life." Characteristically, Robeson's performances were punctuated by his analysis of the current political climate back in the States. In Paris he cautioned, "Negro troops returning to the U.S. will find an America not greatly altered in terms of their position although Negroes have made significant economic progress during the war."[31] Robeson's performances with the interracial USO tour anticipated the desegregation of the military by three years. This tour was important because he, again, publicly broke a historic color barrier and because it documented his popularity among the troops. Some of these soldiers would not remain Robeson fans, however, as the groups of vigilantes who lashed out against him in the late 1940s were partially composed of veterans from such organizations as the American Legion.

Throughout the 1940s, Robeson was bestowed with many honors, large and small, from honorary degrees to medals of achievement. A few of these were solely for his performance in *Othello*, while others recognized his art as well as his dedication to the struggle against fascism and injustice. For example, he was recognized by the Newspaper Guild of New York for his outstanding contribution to the theatre. The American Academy of Arts and Letters also honored Robeson with a medal for good diction on stage, and he was given the Donaldson Award for outstanding male lead performance by *Billboard* magazine. These all occurred in the space of just one year: 1944! In a testimony to his widespread popularity, high school students in New York City also recognized Robeson. The Abraham Lincoln School in Brooklyn voted for Robeson as the recipient of the Lincoln Award for being the "most outstanding American" of 1943. At the ceremony, Robeson sang for the students, much to their delight, and presented the principal with his newest album.[32]

Honorary doctorates were showered on Robeson from a number of institutions including Hamilton College (1940), Morehouse College (1943), and Howard University (1945). These citations not only celebrated Robeson for his artistic pursuits but acknowledged the marriage between his art and activism. The president of Hamilton asserted, "In honoring you today, we do not, however, express our enthusiasm for your histrionic and musical achievements alone . . . [but] as an exemplar of the humanity and the greatness of our democratic heritage."[33] Benjamin Mays, president of Morehouse, directly invoked the significance of Robeson's *Othello* as an important service to the African American race as testimony "against the typical cheap performances that Hollywood and Broadway too often insist on Negroes doing." Mays continued, "We are happy, therefore, to be the first Negro college in the world to place its stamp of approval upon the leadership of a man who embodies all the hopes and aspirations of the Negro race. . ."[34]

Probably the most prestigious award Robeson received during this period was the thirtieth Spingarn medal from the NAACP in October 1945. *Chicago Sun* publisher Marshall Field presented the award, which was given for the "highest or noblest achievement by an American Negro during the preceding year or years." In his speech, Field contrasted the obstacles faced by African Americans and whites in any field of endeavor: "But when a Negro achieves a similar pre-eminence in what is still a white man's social system, he requires all of these qualities and the additional courage and strength necessitated by our shameful caste system in this country." The citation for Robeson directly correlated his art with his political advocacy. It read, "For his distinguished achievements in the theatre and on the concert stage, as well as for his active concern for the rights of the Common man of every race, color, religion and nationality."

In his acceptance speech, Robeson's performance highlighted his regard for the Soviet Union, which had sacrificed, by far, the most lives in the recent war against fascism. Peaceful relations with the former ally were being called into question by late 1945, and the Truman administration's domestic initiatives ultimately heightened anticommunist reaction and isolated progressives. Robeson must have known that this was a pivotal moment if friendship with the Soviets was to continue. In his acceptance speech, he stressed the spirit of eliminating domestic fascism, as the Double V campaign had envisioned. Robeson lauded the progress toward eradicating discrimination and unemployment made in one generation by the Soviet people. He "urged the creation of a world where people, whether white, black, red or brown, can live in peace and harmony, and where resources can be used for the good of all. . . ." However, those present were not pleased by Robeson's acclaim for the Soviet people. The *Pittsburgh Courier* reported that his invocation of Soviet accomplishments had "shocked" the audience.[35] This award further underscored the alliance between Robeson's dual role as an artist and champion of civil rights. Yet, the negative reaction to this speech foreshadowed the fallout following Robeson's performance at the World Congress of Partisans of Peace in the spring of 1949.

What conclusions can be drawn from this array of awards, in particular the Spingarn medal? First, Robeson was publicly recognized in many quarters for his artistic merit and as a supporter of social justice and human rights. As pointed out by President Mays, *Othello* was a significant part of Robeson's larger political legacy. Biographer Martin Duberman observed that the Spingarn ceremony signaled "the apex of Robeson's public acclaim and the onset of his fall from official grace."[36] Indeed, the Spingarn medal represented a turning point in Robeson's career, for he would soon be attacked by NAACP leaders Walter White and Roy Wilkins, as well as disparaged in the NAACP's organ the *Crisis*, and the idea of Robeson as a "leader," as Mays remarked in 1943, would be denied by a number of African Americans, including Jackie Robinson, who testified against him before HUAC.[37]

As the political climate of the nation changed during the Truman administration, anticommunist politics cast suspicion on progressive causes. Even as early as 1945, Robeson events were cancelled due to his political views. For example, in Chicago that year, students at Northwestern University encountered opposition from the administration when they attempted to book a hall on campus for a Robeson appearance. The administrators queried whether Robeson would "sing, or talk too" and when students indicated he might speak also, they were informed that no venue on campus would be available.[38] The answer to the question posed by the Northwestern administration was a foregone conclusion, however, since Robeson was well known for presenting his political views while onstage. As one reviewer in Detroit described a Robeson concert: "As always, for all his gentility, Robeson made the crowd know that he has a gospel to deliver whenever he confronts an audience; the gospel which insists that the oppressed and down-trodden of this earth shall be suffered to rise."[39]

Immediately after World War II, the cause for peace with the Soviet Union became imperative in the wake of hardening cold war ideologies such as Winston Churchill's "Iron Curtain" speech in March of 1946. At this point, Robeson became even more involved with progressive causes through groups like the Council on African Affairs and the Civil Rights Congress, founded in 1946. That year, the Council launched the most visible campaign of its career for famine relief in Africa. Four million black South Africans were confined to plots of land that were wholly insufficient for their numbers. As a result, they were victims of chronic poverty and hunger. A drought had worsened conditions and relief from the British was entirely inadequate. While the United States was focused on rebuilding Europe, the CAA raised awareness about this acute situation in Africa through their monthly newsletter, *New Africa*, and hosted two rallies that raised money and collected food to ship to the continent. The mass meeting on January 7 at Adam Clayton Powell's Abyssinian Baptist Church in Harlem packed the house with four thousand people who donated over seventeen hundred dollars in funds and twenty million pounds of canned goods. The crowd listened to Council officers Max Yergan and W. Alpaeus Hunton speak. Marian Anderson's singing received a huge ovation. Yet, it was Robeson, the consummate performer, who "had the audience hanging on his every word."[40]

A rally six months later focused on famine relief and also emphasized the colonial struggle for freedom. Robeson utilized a variety of methods to communicate the acute circumstances on the continent. A message from Robeson published in the *Daily Worker* pointed out that the desperate plight of hunger in Africa "is practically unknown to the outside world." He continued, "We Americans . . . have the responsibility of providing something more than food for the people of Africa . . . . We must see that their demands for freedom are heard and answered by America and the United Nations."[41] Robeson was known for not mincing words. At a radio appearance covered by the *New York Post* Robeson sharply criticized the West's position regarding colonized people. "He charged that Anglo-American diplomacy now is aiding the most reactionary elements all over the world." He also deftly connected the African situation with that of African Americans: "Nobody knows, but the peoples of Africa may be free before those of Mississippi."[42]

The mass meeting on June 6 filled Madison Square Garden with fifteen thousand supporters and represented the apex of the Council's influence and notoriety. The rally enjoyed publicity from a range of mainstream publications such as *PM* and major New York papers including the *Herald Tribune*, the *Times*, and the *Post*.[43] Luminaries including W. E. B. Du Bois, Mary McLeod Bethune, Adam Clayton Powell, Jr., and Councilman Benjamin Davis graced the rostrum. At the rally, resolutions were passed on international cooperation, self-determination for all people, and admittance for colonial people into the U. N. Prime Minister Jan Smuts was condemned for his flagrant policies of discrimination and the state of disease and hunger plaguing the Union of South Africa. Still, it was Robeson who delighted the audience. His speech immediately enveloped the crowd into his magnetic aura. Robeson's unique charisma engendered a sense of intimacy between himself and this huge audience while the personal terms remained throughout his message. He began, "I think I can say that never before have I faced such an audience as this with the sense of responsibility, of urgency, of intimacy with you that I now feel."[44] He clarified that when he referred to "the Negro" he included all people of the Diaspora: "American Negroes, as well as West Indians and Africans." He further characterized those living in the underdeveloped world as "our brothers in colonial bondage." Thus, in the midst of troubled times, Robeson maintained an increasingly staunch activist posture, but the warmth and allure of the artist continued to infuse his political performances.

In 1946, as African Americans were questioning the strictures of segregation more and more, a spike in lynching occurrences indicated that the fight against discrimination was going to be a prolonged battle. Returning soldiers, especially, were targeted, as their behavior was perceived to be too liberated after returning from the more liberal continent of Europe. At a conference of the American Crusade Against Lynching, over which Robeson presided, Aubrey Williams testified to the catastrophic proportions of the lynching epidemic. He indicated that the current "reign of terror in the South . . . is the worst thing that has happened in the last forty years," and furthermore, "[f]ederal action to date amounts to nothing."[45] In September, the Crusade launched a hundred-day campaign against terrorism in the South that culminated in a mass meeting in Washington, D.C., and sent a delegation to discuss the issue with President Truman. This group was led by Robeson and the meeting with Truman represented one of Robeson's most powerful performances in the political arena.

The delegation's interaction with Truman was chronicled by numerous newspapers which interrogated the group at a press conference following the meeting. During their conversation with the president, Robeson first read a message requesting that Truman make a formal statement against lynching and inaugurate "a definite legislative and educational program" to eliminate mob violence. However, Truman demurred, claiming such action would not be politically expedient. Robeson, taking full advantage of his audience with Truman, pointed out the paradox of the United States condemning Nazis in the Nuremburg trials for the oppression of minorities while allowing African Americans to be lynched at home. Truman, however, refused to see the relevance of this parallel and maintained that domestic problems should not be mixed with foreign policy. While the president characterized the United States and Britain as "the last refuge for freedom in the world," Robeson sharply disagreed and pointed out that current British and American policy was "not supporting anti-fascism." Finally, Robeson attempted to convey to the president that the temperament in the black community was changing: "He said returning veterans are showing signs of restiveness and indicated that they are determined to get the justice here they have fought for abroad." Several papers reported that Robeson directly countered the commander-in-chief, citing that if the government failed to do something about lynching then "the Negroes will." Robeson's performance was clearly pushing Truman's buttons. The *Chicago Defender* noted that Truman "shook his fists," declaring that Robeson's observation sounded like a threat. Robeson, seeming very much in control of the situation, assured the president it was not a threat but "a statement of fact about the temper of the Negro." This performance illustrated that Robeson possessed the courage, the sharp intellect, the sheer presence, not to mention the dramatic flair, to stand toe-to-toe in a debate with one of the most powerful men in the world. (In stark contrast, around this time, another delegation met with Truman on the lynching issue. It was led by Walter White and was decidedly more conservative in tone; the president was, not surprisingly, more favorably disposed to their gradualist approach.)

Immediately following the meeting with the president, Robeson remained poised. A presidential assistant was spinning the meeting for a reporter, noting that the issue of lynching was important but insisting that the timing was wrong politically. Overhearing this, Robeson interjected, "This is an issue that cannot be ducked." Faced with a press conference at which he relayed the interaction with Truman, Robeson maintained his unswerving posture and clarity on the issue at hand. Louis Lautier, of the *Afro-American*, felt that the reporters "ganged up on Robeson" in a "no holds barred" question-and-answer session. Still, Robeson's composure was undeterred even when one reporter insisted on knowing whether Robeson was simply following the Communist Party line. After candidly underscoring that he remained "violently anti-fascist," Robeson persuasively retorted, "It depends what you mean by Communist party line. Right now the Communist party is against lynching. I'm against lynching." The give-and-take between Robeson and the reporters clearly took on a stagelike quality. The clamoring reporters scribbled in their notebooks and tried to catch Robeson off guard. This was juxtaposed with Robeson's sturdy comportment and clear delivery. He remained unintimidated by the public setting and intelligently, even artfully, responded to their queries. This led Lautier to incisively conclude, "Robeson showed that he was just as able to take care of himself in a rough-and-tumble session with the press as he was in playing a scene with the scene-stealing Jose Ferrer as Iago."[46]

The pinnacle of this eventful day was probably the mass meeting held that evening at the Lincoln Memorial. Four thousand people gathered despite the rainy conditions to hear Robeson sing and read a new version of the Emancipation Proclamation as he stood at the base of Lincoln's statue. Robeson questioned the meaning of freedom on the anniversary of Lincoln's famous pronouncement. "Citing the abolition of slavery nearly 100 years ago as the end of the slaveholding heritage only, Robeson stated that oppression of the Negro never ended in fact."[47] The staging of this occasion could have been as precise as that of any Broadway play. This was a poetic image: the darkened cloudy sky behind the larger-than-life sculpture of Lincoln, who represented for generations the idea of liberation from slavery. Yet, in front of Lincoln stood Robeson, in his own way towering and statuesque, probing the very idea of emancipation for a new, more militant generation and calling on all races to push, finally, for an end to mob violence.

Early in 1947, the issues of discrimination at home as well as poverty and self-determination in Africa moved Robeson to announce his retirement from the formal concert arena. After joining a picket line in St. Louis to protest theater segregation, Robeson remarked on his intention to "abandon the theatre and concert stage for the next two years to 'talk up and down the nation against race prejudice.'" He emphasized the critical juncture he had reached: "It seems that I must raise my voice, but not by singing pretty songs."[48] At a concert in Utah a couple of months later, Robeson made a more official pronouncement. He indicated to the "startled" audience, "You've heard my final formal concert for at least two years, and perhaps for many more. I'm retiring here and now from concert work—I shall sing, from now on, for my trade union and college friends; in other words, only at gatherings where I can sing what I please." Subsequently, during a radio interview, "he re-emphasized his firm intention to leave the concert stage, and his grim determination to work harder than ever for world peace and the betterment of the conditions of the Negro race."[49]

During a speech that April at a CAA rally, Robeson continued to underscore his departure from the formal concert arena but assured the audience that we was not abandoning his supporters. The content of his message focused on anti-imperialism. His warm relationship with the crowd was signaled by the continued interjections of "stormy applause" and "loud applause" in the transcript.[50] The closing of his performance climaxed in a prolonged ovation that highlighted his tremendous appeal to the people and the intimate relationship he established with the crowd. Robeson promised, "I will function as an artist, but no longer stand sort of, up there, doing just acting and concerting. I am going to sing, yes, as an artist.... But I give of my talents to the people.... I come from the people, and from the side of the people." This was met with resounding approval from the spectators. Yet, Robeson was not finished. He was building up to a calculated zenith and the crowd was following his lead. Robeson continued to embrace the audience: "I want nothing back but the kind of affection that comes to me tonight, the kind of feeling that you're there—that's what allows me to do what I do—because you are there!" This expression of affection mirrored the closeness he felt with the crowd at the 1946 famine relief rally. He concluded, "I stand here fighting only in my own way, as an artist, against fascism ... we fight it, you fight it, all of us fight it—to the death!!" The transcriber recorded that there was then "tremendous and enthusiastic applause, [a] stormy ovation." Thus, as political circumstances became acute, Robeson responded to the crisis by using his talents as an artist to publicly maintain his antifascist principles. However, Robeson's warmth and engaging charisma as a performer certainly were not going to be left behind even as he departed from the formal concert stage to concentrate on his political message, on being the people's artist.

Following these announcements, Robeson, while facing mounting controversy on the road, appeared more frequently at union halls and other supportive venues. He also traveled for the first time to perform in Hawaii and Panama in 1948. In its review of Robeson's performance, the *Honolulu Advertiser* asserted that "no one in the audience will forget the excerpt from Othello. . . ."[51] This was a particularly theatrical occasion when, after Robeson's recitation, "one could hear a pin drop. The wind howling outside gave atmosphere to the dramatic interlude." In Panama, an excerpt from *Othello* was "masterfully rendered at the end of each concert to the delight of the audiences."[52] Even as he became more politically motivated and temporarily retired from the formal concert arena, Robeson's artistic connection with *Othello* remained intact. A similar pattern unfolded in the 1950s. As the repression against Robeson mounted, impassioned recitations of Othello's final monologue symbolized his fighting spirit.

Paris, Peekskill, and the Aftermath

It was in the late 1940s, most precipitously in 1949, that the mainstream perception of Robeson radically changed from champion of the working man, as in "Ballad for Americans," and forerunner in the entertainment industry, as in *Othello*, to suspicious left-wing affiliate of Communist causes. Robeson had not dramatically altered his message of friendship with the Soviet Union, self-determination for colonized people, and civil rights for African Americans even as a bifurcated cold war ideology gripped the West. However, U.S. politics did change, particularly regarding the Soviet Union, which had been an ally during World War II. W. E. B. Du Bois characterized this period with acrimony: "The world staggered backward; guided by a southern slave-driver we 'got tough with Russia.'"[53] As Robeson often pointed out in speeches, no one had lost more soldiers to the cause of antifascism than the Soviets. Nevertheless, Robeson's message of friendship and peace became increasingly suspect as anticommunism took hold of the American imagination. The major fallout for Robeson began in the spring of 1949.

From April 20 to 25, 1949, the Congress of the World Partisans of Peace convened in Paris. Two thousand delegates from sixty countries converged to discuss the growing alarm over heightening cold war tensions caused by recent events such as the Berlin airlift, the formation of the North Atlantic

Treaty Organization (NATO), the pending victory of Communists in China, and the possibility of a nuclear arms race. Du Bois attended as a representative of the National Council of Arts, Sciences and Professions, which had recently sponsored a peace conference in New York. He was quite impressed with the proceedings, which he described in a detailed statement that was disseminated by the Council on African Affairs. Du Bois set the scene: "The Paris outpouring for Peace was extraordinary . . . because of the single-hearted earnestness, the deep determination, the unflagging interest which kept 2500 persons fastened to their seats for eleven sessions . . . and a sixth day devoted to the most impressive mass demonstration I ever dreamed of." Undoubtedly, for Du Bois, the march of one hundred thousand people was the most moving aspect of the conference. He wrote with characteristic poignancy, "I never before saw a hundred thousand human beings. . . . It was unforgettable. No lying distortion and twisting of our prostituted press can conceal or erase the heartbreaking significance of this spectacle. None who saw it will ever forget."[54]

Notables such as artist Pablo Picasso attended the conference. In the inaugural address, Frederic Joliet-Curie, the chemist who won the 1935 Nobel Prize and was currently serving as high commissioner of atomic energy for France, condemned the NATO alliance as an "economic blockade of East Europe."[55] When Paul Robeson strode forward merely to take a seat on the stage, the crowd's response was so enthusiastic that he made a short, extemporaneous speech. Few at the Salle Pleyel that day could have conceived the profound ramifications of Robeson's remarks. His comments were not substantially different from any of the sentiments expressed by the other speakers. However, Robeson was excoriated in the U.S. press and quickly denounced by a number of black leaders just days later.

What exactly did Robeson say from that platform in Paris? An unpublished translation from the French read in part, "We in America do not forget that it is on the backs of the poor whites of Europe . . . and on the backs of millions of black people that the wealth of America has been acquired—And we are resolved that it shall be distributed in an equitable manner among all of our children and we don't want any hysterical stupidity about our participating in a war against anybody no matter whom. We are determined to fight for Peace. [Applause.] We do not wish to fight the Soviet Union. [Applause.]"[56] Yet, the quotation distributed in the U.S. by the Associated Press read, "'It is unthinkable' that American Negroes 'would go to war on behalf of those who have oppressed us for generations' against a country 'which in one generation has raised our people to the full dignity of mankind.'"[57] Biographer Martin Duberman convincingly argued that Robeson was misquoted by the AP.[58] There also could have been trouble with translating the speech. However, the spirit of Robeson's speech and the AP quote were similar, with the implication of both being that war with Russia or any other nation should be avoided. Still, the AP quote made Robeson sound as if he claimed to represent all African Americans. Black leaders, speaking from various platforms, swiftly disabused anyone lingering under such a misapprehension.

Interestingly, while there was no shortage of malice directed at Robeson for his Paris comments, few seemed to respond to Du Bois's speech, which was actually a more severe indictment of the United States. He declared, "Leading this new colonial imperialism comes my own native land . . . Drunk with power, we are leading the world to hell in a new colonialism with the same old human slavery which once ruined us; and to a Third World War which will ruin the world."[59] Yet, African American leaders quickly denounced Robeson. Their haste in decrying Robeson, no doubt, stemmed from the charged political climate of the cold war. Adam Clayton Powell, Jr., who had allowed the Council on African Affairs to host a famine relief rally at his church in 1946, read a statement from his pulpit, which said in part, "'[B]y no stretch of the imagination' was Paul Robeson qualified to speak for all Negroes in the United States."[60] Roy Wilkins, of the NAACP, expressed a similar sentiment: "Paul Robeson does not represent any American Negroes. Not even ten of them have held a meeting and named him as their leader and spokesman."[61] Mary McLeod Bethune, who also participated in the Council's famine relief rallies, corroborated that Robeson "does not speak for the Negroes of America." She went on to emphasize African American loyalty to the United States as did Charles Houston (lawyer and architect of the NAACP's judicial strategy), who added, "We would fight any enemy of this country."[62] NAACP leader Walter White also repudiated the idea that Robeson represented black America and stressed that only a "miniscule" number of African Americans "share Mr. Robeson's opinions." White did, at least, have the acumen to point out that "white America, meanwhile, would be wise to abstain from denunciation of the Paul Robesons for extremist statements until it removes the causes of the lack of faith in the American system of government."[63]

It was ironic that these leaders in the black community who, just a few short years ago, had honored Robeson with awards including the NAACP's illustrious Spingarn medal and collaborated with him on campaigns such as South African famine relief, were now so swift to deny that his views in any way reflected those of the African American population. Perhaps most famously, and most ironically, baseball legend Jackie Robinson testified before HUAC that Robeson "has a right to his personal views, and if he wants to sound silly when he expresses them in public, that's his business and not mine." This statement was trumpeted on page one of the *New York Times* as further evidence against Robeson.[64] Robinson, who had been pressured to testify, was heralded in the mainstream press as an African American veteran and star athlete and, thus, capable of publicly countering Robeson's supposed assertion about the loyalty of black Americans. However, the *Daily Worker* was quick to remind readers of Robeson's advocacy for desegregation in sports, which contributed to the movement that enabled Robinson to enter major league baseball.[65] The *Afro-American* also offered a thoughtful editorial on Robinson's testimony that suggested, "When Jackie Robinson talks about the things he has gained, he is thinking only of himself. When Paul Robeson said he is not willing to fight against Russia, he is not thinking of himself. . . . He is thinking about millions of colored people in the South who can't vote . . . and cannot get a decent job or education."[66] Years later in his memoir, Robinson noted that his respect for Robeson had grown and that he would "reject such an offer [to testify] if offered now."[67] Robeson quickly responded to the negative press upon his arrival back in the U.S. that summer.

Despite the prevailing attitude against Robeson in the media, a crowd of five thousand attended a welcome home rally sponsored by the Council on African Affairs at Rockland Palace in June 1949. There, Robeson did not back down from his Paris comments. His performance in Harlem that night revealed his unwavering commitment for civil rights and hinted at his personal intransigence. "At the Paris Peace Conference I said it was unthinkable that the Negro people . . . could be drawn into a war with the Soviet Union. I repeat it with hundred-fold emphasis. THEY WILL NOT." He closed by highlighting domestic civil rights: "We do not want to die in vain any more on foreign battlefields for . . . the supporters of domestic fascism. If we must die, let it be in Mississippi or Georgia! Let it be wherever we are lynched and deprived of our rights as human beings."[68] Robeson was adamant and his message unswerving. Here was the resolve of Othello on the frontline leading his troops into battle. Even still, Robeson's detractors were becoming more dangerous, as illustrated outside a small town in upstate New York that August.

The violence perpetrated against Robeson concertgoers outside Peekskill, New York, in the summer of 1949 has been well documented. A brief outline of the events will be drawn partially from Louise Thompson Patterson's firsthand account.[69] Right-wing groups like the American Legion could only view Robeson through the lens of cold war reactionism, and these violent attacks revealed their vehemence toward him. It was this event, probably more than any other, which set the tone for the dark repressive years of the early 1950s. Louise Thompson Patterson, who was active in the International Workers Order in the 1940s and married to Communist Party leader William Patterson, had been traveling with Robeson in the summer of 1949 to help arrange benefits that raised money for the Council on African Affairs. At this time, it was Robeson's custom to give an annual benefit concert for the Civil Rights Congress's (CRC) Harlem chapter. The concert that was scheduled for Saturday, August 27, never occurred, as it was prevented by groups of vigilantes. Howard Fast, who was chairman of the concert, described how around 7:00 p.m., about an hour before the concert was scheduled to begin, the "fascist mob" had gathered and erected a blockade to prevent more cars from entering the outdoor concert grounds. Those, including Fast and other CRC members and their families, who had arrived early were left at the mercy of the rabble, which had "worked themselves into a screaming alcoholic frenzy."[70] As concertgoers arrived, they were caught in a traffic jam and became victims of taunts, physical violence, rock throwing, and injuries from broken glass until the police intervened around 10:00 p.m.[71] The chaotic scene left scores injured and many cars overturned. Fast's article emphasized the racist intent of the mob: "It should be noted that the majority of the threats—and violence too—was directed against the Negro men in our ranks." The smell of charred wood that emanated from a giant twelve-foot cross illustrated clearly that the perpetrators, none of whom were prosecuted, were motivated not solely by zealous anticommunism.

Fortunately, the car carrying Robeson was delayed in the traffic jam and able to escape safely. On the evening of August 30, Robeson promised three thousand people gathered at Harlem's Golden Gate Ballroom that another concert would be held the next Sunday in answer to the previous violence. The performer vowed, "I want my friends to know, in the South, in Mississippi, all over the United States, that I'll be there with my concerts, and I'll be in Peekskill too."[72] Thompson Patterson stressed in her account that supporters were also determined to hold another concert. Indeed, the *Daily Worker* estimated that twenty-five thousand people mobilized in response to the call for the second concert. Hollow Brooks Grounds was protected by a ring of trade unionists that also surrounded the stage to guard Robeson.[73]

This concert remained peaceful until the crowd dispersed. At that point, about a thousand vigilantes who had gathered to protest the concert began throwing rocks and assaulting concertgoers. Thompson Patterson and other eyewitnesses confirmed that state troopers failed to protect the peaceful concert attendees.[74]

These violent attacks and the media slanders, which portrayed Peekskill concertgoers as having provoked the vigilantes, spurred Robeson's characteristic fortitude. He underlined the connection between Peekskill and the fight for African American rights by asking, "Where will the next Peekskill be? . . . Where will they demonstrate further the 'old Southern custom' of beating in the heads of Negroes and all those identified with the struggle . . . ?" Just as Robeson recalled the injury of a past racist attack to conjure his onstage rage as Othello, he was incensed after Peekskill and declared, "This thing burns in me and it is not my nature or inclination to be scared off."[75] A civil suit and a grand jury investigation were drawn out for months. Yet, Robeson and the Council on African Affairs responded immediately with the most obvious tactic for a performer: a concert tour.

Louise Thompson Patterson helped arrange the shows in Detroit, Chicago, Los Angeles, Cleveland, Philadelphia and Washington, D.C. She noted that the media contrived an atmosphere of fear by blaming the Peekskill violence on the organizers of that concert and, thus, city officials "made situations as difficult as possible" to try to discourage the follow-up concerts.[76] Nevertheless, supporters packed houses to hear Robeson. For example, an overflow crowd of four thousand with two thousand standing outside attended the show in Chicago. During his performance, he again emphasized the importance of dignity. Robeson assured the audience that he would not be silenced until "every black man in America can walk with dignity in his own country."[77] Thompson Patterson remarked that African American police in each city "took care of Paul" and described the tour as a "great success" because it "showed that the people throughout the country were ready to accept a challenge to support Paul."[78] Peekskill was, however, a harsh turning point for Robeson. It demonstrated the depth of the animosity directed toward him by a portion of the U.S. public. After 1949, the coverage of Robeson in the mainstream and some of the black newspapers would be primarily disparaging. On the other hand, for progressives, Peekskill became a potent symbol of fascism in the United States. The image of Robeson's venerable posture, surrounded by proud union men as he sang on the stage erected for the second concert at Peekskill, also fueled a fighting spirit on the Left in the face of racism and red-baiting.

A reporter covering Robeson's concert in Chicago astutely observed in an article for the Associated Negro Press that "Paul Robeson received his greatest Chicago ovation since Shakespeare's 'Othello' here Saturday night on Chicago's southside." This was an apt parallel. In *Othello*, Robeson rendered a moving artistic portrayal with dignity. After Peekskill, Robeson stood tall, not against the Turks for the Venetians, but against violence, racism, and red-baiting. Along with demonstrating dignity through his art, he spoke out for it explicitly in his singular baritone. His Othello had once been described as "sturdy as an oak." As the political situation became more acute, Robeson's activist posture also remained "sturdy as an oak," and his performances in the 1950s illustrated the deep wells of his stamina. Fortunately, the triumph of *Othello* was not erased from the public consciousness as Robeson was increasingly besieged by cold war repression. By maintaining Othello's final monologue in his repertoire, Robeson demonstrated his fortitude and made certain that his greatest success was not lost behind the specter of an iron curtain.

CHAPTER SIX

Robeson, *Othello*, and the Politics of the Cold War

"My Pop's influence is still present in the struggles that face me today. I know he would say, 'Stand firm, son; stand by your beliefs, your principles.' You bet I will, Pop—as long as there is a breath in my body."[1] This avowal, which appeared in his monthly column in *Freedom* newspaper, was indicative of Robeson's steadfast posture throughout the most repressive period of his career. The metaphor of Robeson being as solid as a majestic oak had appeared in the reviews of his Othello on Broadway and was evoked again in 1951 when cold war politics were jeopardizing his career. A writer in *The Worker Magazine* poetically compared Robeson's own quality of serenity, which was his "mark of confidence," to a towering oak. The reporter observed of Robeson that "amidst the gale's worst fury, he has stood fast and ever defiant." How did this oak remain stalwart? Look and "see how wide are Robeson's roots and how deep they go amongst the people of this land—specially the Negro people!"[2] In the early fifties, Robeson's political posture remained as secure as had been his celebrated interpretation of Shakespeare's Moor. How was Robeson's career affected by the political climate and how did he react? Two key themes emerged in this period: confinement and creative strategies to circumvent confinement. The attempts to confine Robeson grew directly out of the bifurcated "us-versus-them" politics of the era.

Robeson's cold war political analysis focused on antifascism, peace after World War II, maintaining the Soviet Union as an ally, and independence for all colonized people. Antifascism had rallied almost all political groups during the war. However, when anticommunism became a prime motivator behind American foreign and domestic policy under Truman, Robeson's politics were now out of alignment with the general tenor of the country. Radicals and progressives were now suspects. There was a litany of legislation that targeted suspected communists. For instance, federal employees were required to take loyalty oaths in 1947, and the Taft-Hartley Act mandated that union leaders proclaim their loyalty to the United States. The McCarran Act of 1950 required members of organizations labeled "subversive" to register with the federal government. During World War I, the Espionage Act had famously outlawed dissent against the government during times of war. The Smith Act, which extended the provisions of the Espionage Act, was used to indict leaders of the Communist Party in 1947. Hundreds of U.S. citizens were deprived of the right to travel internationally due to their political views until the Supreme Court ruled this unconstitutional in 1958. Untold numbers of citizens had their careers destroyed and were publicly maligned as a result of the red-baiting tactics and, in many cases, scurrilous testimony before the House Un-American Activities Committee (HUAC) and Joseph McCarthy's infamous committee in the Senate.

The red scare which enveloped the domestic front also seeped into foreign policy, most notably through the Truman Doctrine. This agenda promised aid to countries that renounced communism and supported brutal regimes in underdeveloped countries in the name of anticommunism. The Marshall Plan helped rebuild and stabilize the economies of Western Europe at the expense of countries that desired to free themselves from the yoke of colonialism. The question of alliances was nowhere more explosive than on the Korean peninsula from 1950 to 1953 when millions of Korean lives were lost in a contest of power between the Communist-supported North and the South, buttressed by the United States.

Within this environment, several strategies were employed to confine Robeson, who was viewed as an outspoken radical. His passport was revoked on the grounds that his public defense of African independence was not in the best interests of U.S. foreign policy. Venues refused to book Robeson events, and music companies declined to record his singing. The threat of violence hung like a specter over his public appearances post-Peekskill. Robeson was vilified by the media, who often distorted his political views. The FBI followed him, tapped his phones, read his mail, and utilized informants to obtain information about his endeavors. HUAC subpoenaed him in 1956. And government pressure led to the dissolution of many of the organizations with which Robeson worked, including *Freedom* newspaper, the Council on African Affairs, and the Civil Rights Congress.

What was his role as an artist during this time of crisis? Resolute as an oak, Robeson remained undeterred. He and his supporters utilized creative strategies to defy the confinement of the performer. When the media slandered him, Robeson started his own newspaper. Until it was disbanded, Robeson used the apparatus of the CAA to continue to speak out in favor of self-determination for Africa and to support the 1955 nonalignment meeting in Bandung, Indonesia. When concert halls closed their doors, he found available stages in black churches and union halls. When recording companies chagrined working with him, Robeson started his own company to distribute his music and, later, publish his memoir which clarified his political outlook. When the federal government withdrew his passport, he filed a lawsuit and argued convincingly that one's right to travel was protected by the Constitution. When the winds of anticommunist hysteria gripped the nation, Robeson dug in his heels and faced the maelstrom.

Robeson's performances on the cold war stage were some of the most powerful of his career. Othello's final monologue occupied a significant position in Robeson's repertoire during the 1950s. It recalled his great success on the New York stage, the pinnacle of his career only a few short years ago. This speech also signified the contemporary battle for the return of his passport, because the invitation to play Othello in England figured prominently as evidence in Robeson's case to travel abroad. *Othello* now became an important symbol not only of a past achievement but also of a future goal. His performances during this difficult period evoked the traits that had brought him success on Broadway: composure under pressure, dignity, and the controlled posture of his imposing physical presence. Robeson was an image of strength, of one not easily damaged. When his passport was returned in 1958, he left the United States almost immediately, and chief among his appointments abroad was another *Othello*.

The Struggle to Be Heard in the United States

In the early 1950s, Robeson was increasingly besieged by news stories that misrepresented his views and actions. He noted this trend with frustration in a 1954 press release: "I feel I must address myself to a few of the irresponsible, fantastic and absurd items which have appeared recently concerning my work, my outlook and my family."[3] In response to the hostile attitude in much of the mainstream press, Robeson and other progressives created the United Freedom Fund. One of the most important projects of this group was *Freedom* newspaper, which ran with some interruptions from November 1950 to 1955. As the name implied, this paper created a space in which Robeson could articulate his political analysis freely. Events in which Robeson participated could also be advertised and reported upon without distortion. Collaborators included progressives and Communist Party members such as Esther and James Jackson and historian Herbert Aptheker. Robeson was not involved in the day-to-day management of the paper; therefore Louis Burnham, who had been executive secretary of the Southern Negro Youth Congress and southern director of the Progressive Party, was recruited to edit the paper.

The paper emphasized international issues in the underdeveloped world, the domestic labor struggle, civil rights cases, and local reports from New York City. African and African American history and culture also figured prominently in the paper. Regular contributors included such luminaries as W. E. B. Du Bois, Eslanda Robeson, the up-and-coming Lorraine Hansberry, Alice Childress, whose column "Conversations from Life" was later compiled into the volume *Like One of the Family*, Howard Fast, John Henrik Clarke, W. Alphaeus Hunton, and Lloyd Brown. A list of the activists who wrote articles in *Freedom* read like a who's who of the contemporary civil rights and independence struggles around the world. For example, African National Congress leader Walter Sisulu sent a message from South Africa. A young Robert F. Williams penned a piece calling for a new militant student movement in the United States. Janet Jagan, the wife of Cheddi Jagan, who became prime minister of Guiana, provided an article on the people's movement in that nation.

Most important, *Freedom* supplied a platform from which Robeson's views could be portrayed accurately. Several retrospectives on Robeson's life and accomplishments were published in the paper. He also maintained a regular column titled "Here's My Story" that was included in almost every issue. As the name connoted, Robeson's editorials presented his appraisals of politics and culture, as well as anecdotes on his past and current activities, from his own point of view. This was *his* story, as opposed to the narratives in the mainstream press. These columns were written in collaboration with author Lloyd Brown. Brown, an African American writer who edited *Masses and Mainstream*, was perhaps best known for his novel *Iron City*. He contributed to Robeson's memoir, *Here I Stand*, and later wrote the volume *The Young Paul Robeson: On My Journey Now*. Several themes emerged from Robeson's columns that illustrated his main concerns in foreign and domestic politics. One issue that dominated was the battle for peace against the backdrop of the Korean War. Robeson believed fervently that money and time spent on a war meant there would be little progress on civil rights issues at home and the anticolonial struggles abroad. Another recurring theme was Africa, particularly South Africa, and the fight to end colonialism wherever it existed. He also underscored his belief that African Americans needed to unite and join forces with the labor movement in order to push for civil rights. Significantly, Robeson viewed the anticolonial and anti-imperialist battles abroad as inextricably linked to the fight for full citizenship for African Americans. Robeson's internationalist perspective was reflected in *Freedom*'s coverage of civil rights issues such as school segregation and lynching. Reading *Freedom*, one could not fail to see the struggle of African Americans within the broader context of self-determination for the developing world. The organization had difficulty raising funds throughout its brief career, and *Freedom* finally had to disband in 1955. Yet, it left behind an important record of Robeson's political commentary and activities as well as progressive African American journalism and literary and cultural criticism.

Whereas some civil rights organizations, such as the NAACP, opted to focus primarily on domestic issues during the 1950s, the Council on African Affairs, chaired by Robeson, maintained its global approach to the African Diaspora during this trying period. Advocating for African independence, however, was considered seditious in the cold war framework of foreign policy, as Robeson found out when the State Department refused to renew his passport. The Council had provided a vital apparatus for Robeson's writing in their bulletin and for his political advocacy through campaigns such as famine relief for South Africa in 1946. The Council leaders, however, learned that their organization had been put on the government's list of subversive groups in 1950. This made continuing its various campaigns much more difficult. For example, the CAA was banned from reserving Madison Square Garden for a rally to protest the denial of Robeson's passport in the summer of 1950 even though they had used the venue previously for functions. In 1953, the Council faced a hearing before the Subversive Activities Control Board (SACB). Attorney General Herbert Brownell petitioned the SACB to force the Council to register with the government as an agent of a foreign country as per the Internal Security Act of 1950, also known as the McCarran Act. To defend the Council, Alphaeus Hunton penned an eight-page response detailing the work of the organization and vehemently denying that the CAA was a "Communist front" group. He argued that "the single and consistent purpose for which the Council on African Affairs has existed . . . has been to provide accurate information on the conditions and struggles of the people of Africa and to promote and support their welfare and efforts toward liberation." Hunton concluded that the McCarran Act "is an instrument of censorship, of suppression and fear."[4] The existence of the group was tenuous at this point, and it was probably only through the tireless effort of Hunton that the Council survived until 1955.

Despite the government's attempts to confine the Council's work, the organization continued its activism as long as possible, producing its newsletter and keeping in touch with leaders in Africa. One of its most important campaigns was to monitor and publish United Nations votes concerning Africa and the question of trusteeship. From these documents it was apparent that the United States consistently supported the position of the European colonizers rather than U.N. trusteeship or self-determination for African people.[5] The Council also dedicated two of its final issues of *Spotlight on Africa* to covering and reviewing the Bandung Conference. Yet, in June of that year, the organization resolved to terminate all activities. The *Daily Worker* reported that the Council had been subjected to recent investigations by the Internal Revenue Service, the Justice Department (Foreign Agents Registration Division), and the New York State Joint Legislative Committee on Charitable and Philanthropic Organizations, as well as the SACB. Thus, a consideration in the dissolution of the Council was "the fact that 'continuing government harassment makes further effective work by the organization impossible.'"[6] Historian Hollis Lynch posited that the vote was taken in June 1955 to preclude appearing at another hearing before the SACB which was scheduled to begin in July. He concluded that "there is no evidence that the Council owed its origins or support to the American Communist Party" and that its demise represented "one more victim of McCarthyite repression."[7]

With the Council and *Freedom* newspaper disbanded, the internationalist appraisal of civil and human rights issues for which Robeson had advocated had fewer public proponents. The southern nonviolent movement against segregation, which was famously gearing up through the Montgomery bus boycott led by Martin Luther King in late 1955, concentrated its critique on the constitutionality of separate public accommodations for African Americans. This framework garnered some tangible victories such as the removal of the infamous physical signs of segregation that directed black bus riders to the rear of the vehicle or black moviegoers to the balcony entrance. However, King's more radical analysis of the connection between African American civil rights and freedom in the underdeveloped world came much later in his career. For example, in 1967, he linked the gross expenditures on the war in Vietnam with the economic subjugation of African Americans. King argued that there would be no progress toward economic prosperity for African Americans while government resources continued to fuel the war machine in Southeast Asia. King's denunciation of the Vietnam War was a logical successor to Robeson's position on Korea seventeen years earlier. Like Robeson, King suffered the ire of the press and the wrath of the federal government, especially President Johnson who had considered King an ally, when he dared to openly condemn U.S. foreign policy. By the late 1960s, U.S. cold war foreign policy toward the developing world was firmly entrenched. Yet, a generation earlier, progressive activists such as Robeson and the Council on African Affairs had questioned this strategy as it was just taking shape.

Despite the specter of controversy which trailed Robeson in the press, he continued to maintain a performance schedule as best he could through the 1950s. Newspapers across the country from this period are rife with reportage of banned Robeson appearances. For example, his 1952 concert tour sponsored by United Freedom Fund illustrated this pattern. *Freedom* newspaper listed sixteen stops on this tour and documentation of canceled venues or controversy was available for at least six of these cities.[8] Still, when he had trouble booking larger venues, many black churches kept their doors open to Robeson. In the early and middle 1940s, on any given night, Robeson was performing in stadiums or the most prestigious concert halls. Conversely, in the early and mid fifties, he was singing at Galilee Baptist Church in Newark and Calvary Baptist Church in Detroit. A flyer for a service at the Mt. Carmel Baptist Church summarized this spirit well: "Paul Robeson [will be the] main speaker. On this day let's all worship God and Honor the one who saved our Union. We must never forget Paul. He came to our rescue when the chips were down.... Don't miss this opportunity to thank God and show our sincere appreciation to Paul."[9] In a United Freedom Fund memorandum for a tour that was being planned for 1954, it was suggested that the "minimum schedule ... be fought for in each city." Notice the phrase "fought for." The organizers were aware and prepared for the challenges of booking a tour for Robeson. However, black churches were highlighted as potential venues, "In cities where outdoor concerts are not being planned, all efforts should be made to arrange the appearance at a leading Negro church."[10]

Several of Robeson's columns in *Freedom* recounted concerts in churches around the country. He was heartened by a meeting at Metropolitan Community Church in Chicago which made him "more than ever deeply proud and happy that I decided way back to give my talents and energy to the working masses." After a meeting with black ministers and union leaders, Robeson focused on the importance of solidarity between workers' unions and churches. On another occasion, he recalled his youth in the A.M.E. Zion Church and emphasized the necessity of unity among all denominations "because the influence of the church in the lives of our people is a powerful one."[11]

In May 1952, in a vital show of support, a conference in Brooklyn, New York, of three thousand delegates from the A.M.E. Zion Church voted to back Robeson in his passport suit against the State Department. When Bishop William Walls called for everyone who defended Robeson to stand, Edith Sampson, who worked for the State Department and later became an alternate U.N. delegate, was one of only two people present who remained seated.[12] In 1953 *Freedom* reported, "More than 6,000 people in Detroit welcomed Paul Robeson into their churches, their homes and their hearts during a week-long celebration for his birthday."[13] Several years later, in 1958, a Robeson appearance in Pittsburgh might have been cancelled had several leading churches not opened their doors for the concert.[14] That same year, Robeson's memoir, *Here I Stand*, underscored his upbringing by a minister in the A.M.E. Zion Church and the stability that "center of community life" lent to his formative years, particularly after the untimely death of his mother when he was only six years old.[15] The opening chapter of his autobiography was titled "A Home in That Rock." This label could also be applied to the decade of the 1950s. When Robeson was oppressed on various fronts; he found a reliable home in black churches, particularly the A.M.E. Zion Church.

During this time of controversy, Robeson's income plummeted. Performing mainly at union halls and churches was not nearly as profitable as bookings in major theaters and concert halls. Historian Philip Foner estimated that Robeson's annual income dwindled from "a high of over $100,000 in 1947 to about $6,000 in 1952."[16] P. L. Prattis, of the *Pittsburgh Courier*, commented on this trend in 1957: "I think such a sacrifice would be true of any Negro, Communist or not, who could disturb the authorities in his defense of Negro rights. . . . Bold defense of the Negro's rights is often a costly venture."[17] Robeson made this sacrifice voluntarily because he refused to compromise his principles or alter his political views. An interviewer for the *Afro-American* asked how he felt about giving up a lucrative career. Robeson responded, "I am willing to make a sacrifice for my people, because I cannot be happy otherwise. I feel that I have to speak out against injustice as I see it."[18] In his book *In Battle for Peace*, W. E. B. Du Bois contrasted Robeson's attitude with those who selected a more comfortable route: "For this appeal [for peace] he has been crucified and characteristically many rich and respectable Negroes have joined the slavery wolf-pack in return for cash and ease."[19]

In the early 1950s, when the doors of many concert halls and recording companies were closed to Robeson, his son, Paul, Jr., and Lloyd Brown created an independent recording company. The name of the company recalled Robeson's greatest success of the 1940s: Othello Recording Corporation. The company, which was run primarily by Robeson's son, released three records of Robeson's singing between 1953 and 1955. This new venture was an important source of income for Robeson during these lean years. The first album, *Robeson Sings*, was scheduled for release in January 1953, but could be preordered through *Freedom* in December, just in time for holiday shopping. A full page advertisement in *Freedom* featured a letter from Robeson along with an order form. The letter outlined his current struggle: "For the past several years a vicious effort has been made to destroy my career. . . . Although I have recorded for nearly every major recording company and sold millions of records both here and abroad, these companies refuse to produce any new recordings for me." Then he announced, "An independent record company has just been established that will make new recordings for me. . . . The big task is to make sure that the records will reach a mass audience in every part of the country."[20] The album, which included six songs, could be ordered for five dollars and sold quite well. Robeson biographer Martin Duberman noted that the album sold five thousand copies within four months.[21]

Robeson faced a similar obstacle in 1958 when no publishers in the United States were interested in his memoir, *Here I Stand*. This book was crucial to clarifying Robeson's endeavors and his political views. He noted in the prologue his purpose in writing: "I have sought to explain how I came to my viewpoint and to take the stand I have taken." Robeson further elucidated for whom the book was intended. He proclaimed that he cared "less than nothing" about what "the Big White Folks think of me and my ideas." On the other hand, he underscored, "But I do care—and deeply—about the America of the common people whom I have met across the land. . . ."[22] It was these folks, "all of that America of which I sang in the 'Ballad for Americans,'" that Robeson had in mind when creating this unique autobiography, which chronicled his life experiences in order to illuminate his political convictions. Othello Recording company expanded to include publishing and organized dissemination of the book in the United States. Now known as Othello Associates Incorporated, Robeson's company worked in tandem with other publishers who launched the book overseas. The FBI followed the developments of Robeson's book closely and even sent an agent to buy two copies. A report dated February 6, 1958, remarked that Robeson's book had been published on the third of February by Othello Associates and was currently only available at the Communist Jefferson Book Shop in Manhattan.[23]

Distribution of *Here I Stand* was based primarily on newspaper reviews and word of mouth, but it sold well. The book was enthusiastically endorsed by a number of newspapers including the *Daily Worker*, the *Baltimore Afro-American*, and the *Pittsburgh Courier*. Saunders Redding reviewed the book for the *Afro-American* and described it as "simple and sincere, it is primarily a statement of principles and convictions." Redding concluded, "But no American of whatever color can really quarrel with Robeson's principles and program."[24] The *Afro-American* did not stop there, however. The *Afro Magazine* serialized a large portion of *Here I Stand* in ten articles with photos between March and May 1958. This was very significant in that it made Robeson's own words available to a larger black audience who might not have had the money or opportunity to buy the book. Certainly, this series must have increased book sales as well. Additionally, the *Daily Worker* reviewed Robeson's memoir twice in its Sunday edition. The first review by Benjamin Davis, a friend of Robeson's, noted his recent renaissance and summarized other reviews of the book. A second review concluded, "No person reading it can fail to respond to its passion, a passion which, taken as their own by millions of people, will become an irresistible force."[25]

The enthusiasm for Robeson's book early in 1958 signaled an upsurge in his career toward the end of a troubling decade. The *Sunday Worker* reported in March 1958 that the word-of-mouth campaign for *Here I Stand* had led to two thousand book sales per week since it came out on February 14.[26] The book was sold at union meetings, concerts, and similar venues. Individuals even took it upon themselves to circulate Robeson's memoir, as one railroad worker sold seventy-five copies to co-workers. By April, the first ten thousand copies had sold and Othello Associates planned a new release of twenty-five thousand copies at a lowered price ($1.00 down from $1.50) for the paperback.[27] Finally, the *Pittsburgh Courier* noted in

May 1958 that *Here I Stand* had sold over one hundred thousand copies.[28] Though it did not possess the apparatus of an established publishing house, Othello Associates' distribution of Robeson's memoir was creatively pursued and fairly successful. Significantly, the title of this company indicated Robeson's continued association with the Moor of Venice. Throughout this decade of confinement in the United States, Robeson, with a network of supporters, resourcefully continued to perform and communicate his message of peace, civil rights for black Americans, and independence for the colonized world.

Robeson's Passport Case

One of the most debilitating strategies pursued against Robeson was the revocation of his passport. This illegal and capricious confinement in the United States crippled his performing career and his ability to make a living. During the 1950s, Robeson remained extremely popular overseas where his political views were not considered suspicious. He could have maintained a fruitful artistic career had he been able to travel. Yet, in July of 1950, Robeson, who had held a passport continuously since 1922, was asked by two agents of the State Department to relinquish his current passport. Robeson was about to leave the country for concert and speaking engagements across Britain and Europe. He refused to turn in his passport and was notified in August that it had been cancelled. All border control officials were notified that they should detain Robeson if he attempted to leave the country. That December, Robeson sued on the grounds that revoking a passport violated the First Amendment freedoms of speech, thought, assembly, petition, and association as well as the Fifth Amendment rights to own and secure property. In other words, depriving Robeson of his passport denied him not only the right to travel but the right to practice his profession. An article from the Associated Negro Press noted in January 1951 that the loss of a passport had already cost Robeson in excess of three thousand dollars in fees and royalties and "he will suffer the same amount of loss annually as the result of the cancellation of future . . . foreign appearances."[29]

Robeson was hardly alone in this regard. The State Department revoked or refused passports for many because of their political beliefs during the cold war period including W. E. B. Du Bois, Rockwell Kent, Howard Fast, Max Schachtman, and scientist Martin Kamen, as well as Otto Nathan, executor of Albert Einstein's estate.[30] On what grounds did the State Department use the arbitrary authority to prevent travel abroad? A 1952 press release declared, "For many years the Department has . . . refused passports to persons when it had in its files clear evidence that they had, on previous trips abroad, engaged in political activities in foreign countries." The document then specifically cited as an example the conviction of eleven leaders of the U.S. Communist Party who represented a "clear and present danger to the United States." Thus, if the State Department had reason to believe someone was "knowingly a member of a Communist organization or that his conduct abroad is likely to be contrary to the best interests of the United States," their right to travel was withheld.[31] Still, despite constant attempts to brand Robeson as a member of the Communist Party, such an affiliation was *not* cited as the primary reason he was confined to domestic travel. In February 1952, the State Department submitted its case to the appeals court and stated that Robeson's travel abroad would not be in the best interests of the United States due to his "frank admission that he has been for years extremely active politically on behalf of independence of the colonial people in Africa." Advocating for freedom for the underdeveloped world, it seemed, had been Robeson's most insidious endeavor. Furthermore, "the diplomatic embarrassment that could arise from the presence abroad of such a political meddler . . . is easily imaginable. . . ."[32] For Robeson, then, it was clear, as he explained, that his "concern for Negro rights is indeed at the heart of the [passport] case."[33]

In his book and his column in *Freedom*, Robeson addressed the historic importance of travel for African American activists. In *Here I Stand*, he compared his current struggle for the right to travel with the abolitionists, such as Frederick Douglass, who traveled abroad to gain support for the antislavery cause. Concerning his opposition to colonialism, Robeson posed an insightful question: "Can we oppose White Supremacy in South Carolina and not oppose that same vicious system in South Africa? . . . Those who oppose independence for the colonial peoples in Africa are the real un-Americans!" In answer to the State Department's claim that Robeson's travel would not be in the best interests of U.S. foreign policy, he asserted, "[T]he fact is that speaking the truth abroad has been of great value to the struggle for Negro rights in America. It has always been in our *best* interests." Furthermore, he contended, "The concept of *travel* has been inseparably linked in the minds of our people with the concept of freedom [his emphasis]."[34] Here, Robeson once again revealed his historical acumen. The link between travel and freedom was especially apparent during slavery when African Americans bravely sought freedom north of the Mason-Dixon Line or in Canada. Travel was also fundamental to the concept of freedom after the passage of the Thirteenth Amendment when black Americans could, for the first time, travel around the country to reunite with lost relatives. After Reconstruction, African Americans traveled to places like Kansas in an attempt to free themselves from the vigilantism of the South. Later, in the early twentieth century, African Americans traveled north to cities such as Pittsburgh and Chicago seeking economic freedom away from endless cycles of debt accrued through sharecropping.

Robeson also emphasized the historical importance of travel specifically for black artists, such as Ira Aldridge, in order to practice their profession. He maintained that "the right to travel has been a virtual necessity for the Negro artist. A century ago it was not possible for a Negro actor to appear on the American stage in any role—not even as a buffoon." Aldridge, famously, had relocated overseas in the nineteenth century where his artistry could flourish. In the twentieth century, scores of African American writers, dancers, and musicians visited or settled permanently in Europe where they were, for the most part, free from the injustice and hostility of the United States. Thus, Robeson reasoned, "[T]he right to travel is of special importance to the Negro artist. In view of this fact, is it not unjust to require that he remain silent about the conditions of his people in order for him to have this opportunity to practice his art and to earn his livelihood?"[35] Robeson viewed his passport case, then, as part of the continuing struggle of African Americans who were speaking out against injustice and, more specifically, black artists who relied on the international stage to practice their crafts.

A similar parallel was drawn in a pamphlet by Lloyd Brown titled "Lift Every Voice for Paul Robeson" published by Freedom Associates in 1951. Brown compared Robeson to Douglass: "But remember Frederick Douglass . . . he went to Europe to speak for his people's freedom. Robeson is the Douglass of today." Brown then quoted Robeson's attorneys who outlined the impetus behind his actions, "In all his public activities, [the] plaintiff's objectives have been . . . to vindicate and effectuate the rights guaranteed by the 13th, 14th and 15th Amendments and the rights set forth in the United Nations Universal Declaration of Human Rights."[36] It was important that Robeson's lawyers made the connection between the Reconstruction Amendments, which protected black freedom and civil rights, and the U.N. declaration. This link underscored Robeson's global perspective on civil rights and that he was not afraid to turn to the U.N. declaration to point out how the United States was failing to uphold the rights of black Americans. Robeson summarized his position in an editorial printed in the *Daily Worker*: "Instead of persecuting me for criticizing the conditions of Negroes in America, the U.S. ought to be down in Mississippi prosecuting those who have unleashed against our people a reign of terror and bloodshed."[37]

Robeson's insistence on relating the civil rights struggle of black Americans with the movement for independence in Africa was at the root of his conflict with the State Department. His passport case also spoke the larger problem of state formation in the developing world within a strictly communist vs. anticommunist rubric. The fact that an activist like Robeson was suppressed from speaking abroad about self-determination for Africa revealed the lengths to which the U.S. government was willing to go in order to preserve Western interests on the continent, whether or not those were in the best interests of the African people. Anticommunism as the driving force behind U.S. foreign policy confined voices like Robeson for political purposes. This stringent anticommunist agenda set up a nearly impossible framework in which emerging nations were forced to maneuver. When new states in Africa, starting with Ghanaian independence from Britain in 1957, sought to align their fledgling countries on the world stage, they had few options. The United States, along with most of Western Europe, had consistently taken the position against colonial independence within the forum of the United Nations during the early 1950s. On the other hand, the Soviet Union tended to vote in favor of independence for African colonies.

The publications of the Council on African Affairs made this point plain when it published how countries voted on colonial issues regularly in its newsletter. For example, *Spotlight on Africa* from January 8, 1953, revealed that the United States voted no or abstained from voting on all the questions regarding African self-determination and human rights violations in Africa by Europe. These questions included investigating the racial situation in South Africa, negotiations between France and Tunisia, suffrage for people in Togoland, criticizing British policies in Tanganyika, and one resolution "recommending that member states should 'uphold the principle of self determination of all peoples and nations' and should facilitate the exercise of this right in territories under their administration." This prompted the editor to query in frustration, "Is the U.N. supposed to be an organ for the protection of the colonial powers?" Unfortunately, the answer was often yes because the United States and Western Europe did not want to risk hegemony in Africa in favor of independence for African people with indigenous leadership that might not want to stay within their sphere of influence. In order for a developing country to receive aid from the West, it had to maintain alliances with the former colonizers and could not ally with the Soviet Union. On the other hand, an alliance with the Soviet Union meant solidifying the enmity of the United States and becoming vulnerable to CIA-backed coup attempts or other recriminations. Independence meant that new nations had to make extraordinarily difficult decisions based not on what was best for their people but on how to maneuver on a global stage based on a stringently two-pronged communist versus anticommunist cold war framework. As demonstrated by their U.N. votes, from the U.S. perspective, it was favorable to try to avoid independence altogether in order to protect Western interests. Thus, the strategy of stymieing the efforts of advocates such as Robeson who were outspoken supporters of self-rule in Africa was concomitant to the overall policy of maintaining Western supremacy at any cost.

The nonalignment movement was a response to this bifurcated approach to cold war alliances. Twenty-nine countries from Africa and Asia sent representatives to a meeting in Bandung, Indonesia, in 1955 to discuss peace, economic and cultural cooperation, human rights and self-determination for colonized people. The countries at the conference represented almost two-thirds of the world's population. Yet, President Eisenhower refused to send official greetings to Bandung.[38] Robeson, a strong proponent of peace and independence for colonized nations, was prevented from attending the conference due to passport restrictions. His message to the conference highlighted the need for diplomacy and discussion among nations: "If other nations of the world follow the example set by the Asian-African nations, there can be developed an alternative to the policy of force and an end to the threat of H-bomb war."[39] Moreover, it was upon the platform adopted at the Afro-Asian meeting that Robeson voiced his political stance in his 1958 book *Here I Stand*. He elucidated his position, saying that "when anyone asks me today what is the viewpoint I support in world affairs, I point to the Ten Principles of Bandung . . . ."[40] These tenets included: respect for human rights, respect for sovereignty of all nations, racial equality and equality among nations large and small, refraining from acts or threats of aggression, and settlement of international disputes by peaceful means. Despite being confined to the United States during the Bandung conference, Robeson energetically vocalized his support for the meeting. Still, he deeply regretted that he could not attend. Had he been able to travel to Indonesia in 1955, the image of Robeson's towering figure coming together with the diplomats and leaders from Africa and Asia would have conveyed a powerful message of solidarity between African Americans and the broader Afro-Asian world. This was precisely the reason the State Department did not want him there.

"From the outside, removed by the passage of time, we can hardly comprehend what it must have felt like to have been an American radical at the height of the Cold War," summarized Kent Worcester in his political biography of C. L. R. James.[41] Robeson and James had crossed paths in London in 1936 for their collaboration on James's play about Toussaint L'Ouverture. Though their analyses of Marxism deviated, James leaning toward Trotsky and Robeson toward the Communist Party, in the eyes of the American government, James and Robeson were both simply radicals. Thus, they were targeted by the government—Robeson by the State Department and James by the immigration authorities because of his precarious presence in the country as an alien. Some interesting parallels existed between James's and Robeson's cases which further illuminated responses to confinement during the high tide of cold war reactionism.

C. L. R. James had sailed to New York just two years after his play starring Robeson debuted on London's West End. Having honed his Trotskyist perspective while in England, James traveled to the United States, the heart of the capitalist enterprise. He had planned to leave in 1939 but was detained when war broke out in Europe and ended up staying over fourteen years. While in the United States he became "a central player in the country's peripheral far left" where he worked "cajoling and organizing a tiny, radicalized minority of American workers into adopting a militant, socialist perspective."[42] James's immigration trouble reached a critical point in 1952 when he was held in custody for passport violations. He then had to serve six months' detention at Ellis Island while his case for U.S. citizenship was considered. While the mention of Ellis Island conjured for many the sentimental image of wide-eyed huddled masses entering the United States through New York harbor for the first time, the isolation of the island also made it a convenient holding space for illegal immigrants awaiting deportation, political prisoners, and, in James's words, all manner of "mariners, renegades, and castaways." It was during his imprisonment on the island that James conceived one of his most eloquent studies of American culture through his reading of *Moby Dick* as a metaphor for the paradoxes in U.S. democracy. Being confined on the island shaped James's analysis of Melville, as the seclusion of the place and the castaways therein paralleled the journey of the *Pequod* and its crew. Both were steered by madmen, Ahab in the case of the *Pequod*, and "the anti-alien policy of the Department of

Justice" guided the "unprincipled regime of the island." Both James's island and Melville's ship encompassed "American officers and the nondescript people of the world."[43] James's ensuing monograph, *Mariners, Renegades and Castaways*, was intended to strengthen his case for U.S. citizenship. Just as Robeson clarified his political position and the details of his passport case in his memoir written during his confinement in the United States, the final chapter of James's book, titled "A Natural But Necessary Conclusion," described the specific circumstances of his case and his internment.

Robeson, a citizen, was constrained within the U.S. borders and prevented from pursuing his career abroad because of his political views. On the other hand, James, a foreign national, desired to live and work in the United States but was deported because of his politics. Robeson and James were both offered exit strategies for their legal predicaments by the federal government. Robeson was told his passport would be returned if he signed an affidavit affirming that he was not a member of the Communist Party. James was informed that he was not being detained against his will and was free to "leave and go to Trinidad . . . and drink my papaya juice" at any time.[44] Both men adamantly rejected these opportunities as violations of their rights. Robeson's passport revocation was based on his activism on behalf of the cause of African independence. In response, he sued the State Department on the grounds that denying his passport violated the right of free speech enshrined in the First Amendment. He also argued that restraining his career abroad violated the right to secure property protected by the Fifth Amendment. James's attorneys utilized the same constitutional amendments to bolster his case for citizenship. His case had been rejected due to the content of his writing, principally his ruminations in *The Rise and Fall of the Communist International*. The book was a critical assessment of the movement penned in 1937, the year prior to James's arrival in the United States. This led James to conclude "that the Department of Justice now assumes the right to say what a citizen or would-be citizen should study."[45] James's ultimately unsuccessful appeal fought the constitutionality of this decision, since the founding document "forbids the limitation of the free speech and free expression of opinion of any person in the United States." He elucidated the position carefully: "It specifically does not say citizen: it says person, meaning anybody. . . . [I]f an individual, citizen or alien, commits some action, breaks the law, then a Government is entitled to proceed against him, but not for what he says." This argument, however, did not hold up in the charged environment of cold war politics.

The limits of free speech during this acute period in history were illustrated well through James's and Robeson's confinement. James, a foreigner, was deemed unworthy of citizenship, even though he had a child who was a citizen, due to the substance of the books he had published. (Ironically, U.S. officials probably failed to recognize that James, as a Trotskyist, was critical of the Communist International.) Robeson, a citizen, was deprived of the right to travel from 1950 to 1958 because of his public comments not on communism but on self-determination in Africa. As James aptly pointed out, political leaders consistently assured the American public that the witch hunt against the Communist Party was not aimed at freedom of speech or intellectual expression but, rather, against an international conspiracy focused on establishing a totalitarian regime.[46] Robeson's and James's cases told a different story, however, one that revealed free speech being curtailed as a matter of political expediency. It was more convenient for the government to deport foreigners like James who were perceived as radicals but posed no threat to the country and had never been involved in attempting to secure a totalitarian regime in the United States. Similarly, it was pragmatic for the State Department to try to silence an outspoken advocate like Robeson rather than reconsider its political objectives in Africa. The outcomes of these cases diverged: James was forced to leave the country in 1953, and Robeson's confinement was ruled unconstitutional so he was permitted to travel outside the United States five years later. Interestingly, both men headed for England when they departed; James continued writing and agitating, and Robeson fulfilled a long-awaited theater engagement in Stratford-upon-Avon.

Performances on the Cold War Stage

Despite his domestic confinement and the controversy tailing his appearances in the United States, Robeson continued to perform in the venues that welcomed his singing and commentary on political issues. As in the previous decade, Robeson's recitals in the 1950s included some reflections on current politics, and his political appearances maintained a singular performative quality. Robeson's wife had observed in her 1930 biography that the simple act of walking down the street in Harlem became a public event as the blossoming performer was enthusiastically greeted by eager passersby. A similar trend took shape in the turbulent decade of the fifties, especially among the black working class. An article from 1951 remarked that when Robeson "stands on a street corner" it "immediately becomes the center of a throng." However, at this time, the phenomenon acquired a decidedly political undertone. Rather than greeting him and asking for an autograph, supporters declared, "Paul, I'm with you," or "Keep fighting 'em, Paul" and "I'm in your corner, Paul."[47] Robeson, ever the sturdy oak, was deeply rooted in the black community. These supporters were not simply gawking and acknowledging Robeson's celebrity but were consciously invoking his political stand. They offered a warm handshake or a word of encouragement during an extremely strenuous time. Robeson had always forthrightly identified with working people even though his fame and charisma could have enabled him to affiliate primarily with upper echelons of the wealthy and powerful. It was this important backing from segments of the black community and the working classes which provided the foundation from which Robeson, the cold warrior, could perform his politics.

Since its founding in 1946, Robeson had worked with the Civil Rights Congress (CRC), which was an organization headed by William Patterson, an attorney and leader in the Communist Party. The group had been inaugurated out of a merger between the International Labor Defense (ILD) and the remnants of the National Negro Congress (NNC), among other organizations, with a platform that included fighting for African American civil rights. Its battles, which were primarily in the courthouse, were memorable and historic. In the tradition of the ILD's defense of the Scottsboro boys in the 1930s, many CRC defendants were black men and women from the South who had been wrongly accused of rape or murder. They included Willie McGee, Rosa Lee Ingram, the Trenton six, and the Martinsville seven. The CRC also defended the eleven leaders of the Communist Party who were indicted under the Smith Act, as well as the Rosenbergs, who were executed for espionage in 1953. Paul Robeson was a close friend of Patterson's and a key speaker and performer at CRC fundraising events.

Robeson's involvement with the CRC culminated in the presentation of the human rights petition *We Charge Genocide* before the United Nations in 1951. The historic petition charged that the United States had committed genocide against the fifteen million African Americans living within the country's borders. The document tenaciously presented its case based closely on the definition of genocide adopted at the U.N. conference in 1948. Genocide, the petitioners pointed out, did not necessarily involve the complete destruction of a people but "any intent to destroy, *in whole or in part*, a national, racial, ethnic or religious group [their emphasis]." Thus, "the oppressed Negro citizens of the United States, segregated, discriminated against and long the target of violence, suffer from genocide as the result of consistent, conscious, unified policies of every branch of government."[48] Part of the evidence submitted included a scrupulous year-by-year recounting of lynchings and other individual acts of violence committed against African Americans that had deliberately gone unpunished. The petition was presented simultaneously on both sides of the Atlantic Ocean. To the Fifth Session of the General Assembly meeting in Paris, Patterson disseminated copies. When Patterson returned to the United States, his passport was promptly revoked.[49] Due to his restricted travel, Robeson led the delegation that submitted the document to the secretary general's office in New York. Against the backdrop of Patterson's words in the petition declaring that the CRC was the "implacable enemy" of any society "that denies democratic rights or one iota of human dignity to any human being," one can picture Robeson, tall, dignified, and full of purpose striding into the U.N. building to present a document that demanded the United States account for its history of racist policies before an international body.[50] *Freedom* newspaper announced the notable occasion with a drawing of Robeson by Charles White dominating its front page.[51] In the artist's rendering, a stern-looking Robeson stood elevated and poised with an almost larger-than-life accusatory hand pointing outward under the heading "The Charge IS Genocide." The picture communicated that Robeson's formidable presence brought credibility and authority to the accusations of the petition.

The United Nations chose not to respond to the Civil Rights Congress petition. However, the effort marked an important precedent in broadening the scope of the civil rights struggle of black Americans. Before his untimely death in 1965, Malcolm X was considering bringing similar charges against the United States before the world body. In 1970, *We Charge Genocide* was revisited and reprinted when a new campaign was launched by activists to again present a petition before the U.N. Within the global framework of cold war politics, the United States faced critiques of its racist policies not only from the Soviets but also from a subjugated minority group who endeavored to compel the United States to answer for its crimes in an international arena. In the view of Robeson, and all of the CRC petitioners, the United States should not have been exempt from recognizing and taking responsibility for the naked racism and fascist tendencies within its own borders.

Not surprisingly, the work of the CRC came under increasing government scrutiny after the presentation of the genocide petition. In 1955, the New York State Joint Legislative Committee on Charitable and

Philanthropic Agencies and Organizations subpoenaed Robeson because of his involvement with the CRC. The committee had charged the CRC with racketeering, which Patterson vehemently denied. In a foreshadowing of his performance before HUAC the following year, Robeson was not afraid to condemn the intentions of this state committee. He bravely countered that the committee was actually bent on destroying "organizations dedicated to the people's interests." He further denounced the committee's use of informers and seethed, "Don't play around. Don't ask me any questions on names." Robeson also emphasized that he was proud of his association with the CRC, which "has been working and fighting for the lives of Negro people."[52] It was hearings such as these that ultimately led to the dissolution of the CRC in 1956. The *Daily Worker* reported that "the intensification of defense activities against these attacks" had diverted its efforts in the "growing broad offensive against . . . the McCarran Act, Smith Act . . . [and] against the current Dixiecrat genocidal attacks on the Negro people. . . ."[53] Like the Council on African Affairs, the Civil Rights Congress was fatally impaired in its ability to carry out the stated goals of its platform because it was forced to constantly defend its very existence.

When major venues rejected Robeson appearances, creative alternatives revealed the tenacity of Robeson and his fan base. In early 1952, Robeson was turned away from the U.S.-Canadian border even though no passport was necessary to enter Canada at that time. He had been scheduled to speak at an event for the International Union of Mine, Mill, and Smelter Workers in Vancouver. Robeson addressed them via telephone from Seattle instead.[54] The FBI was following Robeson's movements at the border very closely and made certain that all ports in the area were alerted in order to prevent him from crossing the Canadian border.[55] When Robeson was turned back at the Washington/Canada border, a photo captured his reaction at the immigration office (figure 6.1). Perhaps the photo was Robeson's idea or that of an enterprising photographer who recognized the saliency of the moment as a symbol of cold war policies. The shot was clearly staged, with Robeson, dressed in smart, professional attire ready for his appearance, standing tall with a performer's posture outside the door to the office. His overcoat underscored his tremendous breadth and height, which seemed to engulf the doorway over which the small, seemingly insignificant sign marked that this was, in fact, the immigration office. Robeson's unassailable presence in this hallway made it hard to believe that any governing body could contain such a man. In the photo, Robeson's head was turned slightly, and he was glancing up at the "Immigration" sign with a sardonic grin on his face. His

6.1 Robeson is turned away at the Canadian border, 1952. Photographs and Prints Division, Schomburg Center for Research in Black Culture, The New York Public Library, Astor, Lenox and Tilden Foundations.

expression communicated so much: the irony of being turned away from entering a country where a passport was not necessary, the impudence of confining him against his constitutional right to travel and speak freely, the audacity of a government utilizing its resources to contain an artist merely for his outspoken political views and not because he had ever presented any threat to the nation. One can imagine Robeson, immediately after this photo was taken, perhaps pausing momentarily, breathing deeply and then striding briskly away, foreseeing a grave and protracted battle ahead of him. The photo represented a priceless symbol of the performer's indefatigable spirit in the face of cold war obstacles.

Exhibiting his resiliency, this event led to a highly successful concert series in Peace Arch Park at the border in Blaine, Washington, that took place annually from 1952 to 1955. Robeson and his backers reasoned that if he was barred from entering Canada, then he could sing in the park on the border so that Canadians and Americans could still demonstrate their support for him. Devotees came in droves to hear Robeson at these concerts sponsored by the International Union of Mine, Mill, and Smelter Workers. The *Vancouver Sun* reported that thirty thousand people crowded into Peace Arch Park in May 1952, forcing the border to close for more than an hour because of heavy traffic.[56] Thousands turned out in subsequent years as well, and, though there was occasionally some heckling from the U.S. side, these popular concerts remained peaceful.[57] Fortunately, some recordings were made of these important Robeson performances where he sang with longtime accompanist Lawrence Brown on piano and delivered stirring orations which commented on contemporary politics.

In his 1953 speech at Peace Arch Park, Robeson addressed three themes that he maintained throughout this period of confinement in the United States.[58] First, he assured the audience that he remained "the same Paul that you have known throughout all these years." This seemingly obvious point was significant within the context of the media reports that vilified him and his politics during the cold war. He wanted to make plain that his political outlook had not changed. He still fervently believed in peace, full citizenship for African Americans, and independence for colonized people around the world. It was the tenor of the country that had transitioned, not Robeson's political views. Second, he elucidated the circumstances of his passport case. Robeson lamented, "In America today, it's very difficult . . . to get a hall to sing in. Whenever I go to a city like St. Louis . . . the wrath of all the powers that be descends upon one single poor minister who wants to give me his church. . . ." He addressed his continued popularity abroad by noting the invitation to play Othello in England and declaring that the British Actors' Equity Association indicated that he would be welcome to perform there. The numerous requests for Robeson appearances overseas, however, did little to alter the implacable position of the State Department. Alluding to the State Department's case, Robeson was pointed but lighthearted. "Why do they take my passport away?" he queried the audience. "Because out of my own lips," he responded, "for many years I have been struggling for the independence of the colonial peoples of Africa and that is meddling in the foreign affairs of the U.S. government." Here he paused for dramatic effect as the audience chuckled at this ridiculous insinuation. Robeson continued jocularly, "Now that's just too bad 'cause I'm gonna have to continue to meddle," and the audience laughed and cheered. His fighting spirit was represented, but the consummate performer knew how to have fun with the crowd while still driving his point home.

Finally, his passion was at the forefront as the speech climaxed: Robeson focused on his roots in the black community and his commitment to continuing this struggle. His historical insight was revealed once again: "I speak as one whose fathers, whose mothers toiled in cotton . . . to help create the basic wealth upon which the great land of the United States was built." Robeson then declared with fervor, "And I say . . . that I have a right to speak out on their blood, on what they have contributed . . . I say right here that because of their struggle . . . a good piece of that American earth belongs to me [applause]." Observing that this was "the rock upon which I stand," Robeson ardently laid out his vision, "I go all around America . . . seeking a simple thing. It seems so simple that all people should live in full human dignity and in friendship." He then framed his continued dedication to achieving this goal with great feeling, saying, "I shall continue to fight as I see the truth . . . and I want everybody in the range of my voice to hear, official or otherwise, that there is no force on earth that will make me go backward one thousandth part of one little inch [spirited cheers and applause]." Harvey Murphy, head of the union, then led the crowd in a rousing spontaneous three cheers for Paul Robeson. His precisely controlled vocal inflections, especially at the close of the speech, showed that Robeson was a seasoned performer who understood how to effectively engage his audience. His recognition of the "official" presence in the crowd at Peace Arch Park demonstrated Robeson's knowledge that the authorities monitored him, but this did not inhibit his lively and strong-willed performance.

One of Robeson's most memorable and significant performances on the cold war stage was his testimony before the House Un-American Activities Committee on 12 June 1956. In 1938, HUAC had been established as a temporary committee in the House of Representatives under the leadership of Martin Dies from Texas. The committee became a tool for anti–New Dealers to raise suspicion of domestic communist activity within the expanded governmental social programs of the depression era. Dies's southern segregationist perspective and tight rein on the committee influenced the direction that their investigations took after becoming a standing committee in 1945. As the cold war opened, HUAC colluded with the FBI and other federal bureaus to help propagate the anticommunist hysteria that was also dramatically instigated by Joseph McCarthy and his histrionics in the Senate. The antiradical agenda at the heart of HUAC's program, illustrated well in their investigations of Alger Hiss and the Hollywood Ten, was also tinged by the racist views of the committee members. Involvement in left-wing civil rights activities opened the way for red-baiting specific black activists, such as Paul Robeson, to try to destroy their credibility within the African American community and the country. Representative Francis Walter succeeded Dies and John Wood, a Georgia Democrat, as chairman of HUAC and headed the proceedings when Robeson testified in 1956. Walter was not substantially different from his predecessors regarding racial issues. He was once queried about investigating the Ku Klux Klan and replied that they do not "constitute a threat to the liberties of Americans."[59] Similarly, in Robeson's prepared statement, he wondered, "Why does Walter not investigate the truly 'un-American' activities of [Mississippi senator James] Eastland and his gang, to whom the Constitution is a scrap of paper when invoked by the Negro people . . . ?" The indignant manner with which Walter treated Robeson during his testimony was, thus, not surprising. The following exchange exemplified Walter's attitude toward Robeson and all people of color: "Mr. Robeson: 'You are the author of all the bills that are going to keep all kinds of decent people out of the country.' The Chairman: 'No, only your kind.' Mr. Robeson: 'Colored people like myself. . . .' The Chairman: 'We are trying to make it easier to get rid of your kind, too.'"

Although the HUAC session was convened to investigate the unauthorized use of U.S. passports, the committee grilled Robeson on a variety of subjects, particularly his affiliation with the C.P. and known members of the party. In fact, the one time that Robeson directly engaged the passport case, Walter ducked the question: "Mr. Robeson: 'They have just invited me to come to London next week to sing to 140,000 miners up in Yorkshire. Do you think that you could let me go?' Mr. Chairman: 'We have nothing to do with that.'"[60] The analogy of Frederick Douglass was again invoked by Robeson during the hearing: "I am here because I am opposing the neo-Fascist cause which I see arising in these committees. You are like the Alien [and] Sedition Act, and Jefferson could be sitting here, and Frederick Douglass here. . . .'" Characteristically, Robeson was quick to point out the inherent racism in the committee: "I am not being tried for whether I am a Communist, I am being tried for fighting for the rights of my people who are still second-class citizens."[61]

Robeson invoked the Fifth Amendment when asked whether he was a member of the C.P., although he reiterated the fact that the Communist Party was a legal political party just like the Republican and Democratic parties. He further observed in his prepared statement that demanding to know someone's political membership was a violation of the constitutional rights of all Americans.[62] This was an important point that Robeson raised. At the root of this inquiry on Communist ties lay not the question of whether Robeson's political views favored the Soviet Union. The vital issue at stake was, rather, Robeson's constitutional right to free speech and to hold whatever political affiliation he desired even if that meant advocating for African independence. Thus, he invoked the Fifth Amendment rather than name names, perjure himself, or admit "guilt" for being a member of the C.P., when the party was, in fact, a legal political party.

Robeson asked Walter several times if he could read his prepared statement into the Congressional Record as other witnesses had done. However, Walter was fed up with Robeson's assertive posture as a witness and obstinately refused. Before Walter adjourned the hearing, Robeson blasted the very existence of the committee: "[Y]ou gentlemen belong with the Alien and Sedition Acts, and you are the nonpatriots, [sic] and you are the un-Americans and you ought to be ashamed of yourselves."[63] As Robeson had demonstrated in his meeting with Truman in 1946 and his testimony before a New York legislative committee in 1955, he was not afraid to speak truth to power even in the threatening period of the early cold war. The *Daily Worker* captured well the various dramatic intonations that undergirded Robeson's testimony: "Although the committee chairman and other members repeatedly tried to restrict him to the rigged question routine, Robeson's voice, sometimes angry, sometimes somber, sometimes chuckling, overwhelmed their heckling."[64] Robeson had undergone prostate surgery in the autumn of 1955 and had limited his appearances in early 1956. There had been some concern that he might not be fit enough to testify, but he had been in fine form before HUAC.

Robeson had maintained Othello's final monologue in his repertoire throughout the 1950s. It was a crowd pleaser and served as an important reminder of his triumph on Broadway as well as the fight to perform the role again overseas. For example, his 1952 concert tour, while fraught with controversy along the way, included a variety of folk songs and spirituals along with readings from poet Pablo Neruda and *Othello*. While on that tour, Robeson performed for tens of thousands of Americans and Canadians at Peace Arch Park in Blaine, Washington, where he told the crowd, "I am deeply moved to see that nothing can keep me from my friends in Canada." A recitation from *Othello* also closed that concert.[65] In 1955, Robeson made several notable appearances at colleges. He was pleased to be welcomed into these schools and observed in a *Freedom* article that the cold war was beginning to recede among the younger generation, saying, "It is good, these days, to get out to the college campuses and see the stirring of new life among the students. . . . The fresh breeze of free expression is beginning to filter into the stale atmosphere of the cold war classrooms."[66] Indicative of this pattern was Robeson's visit to the City College of New York that year. The engagement was so popular that hundreds of students had to be turned away a full half hour before the concert was scheduled to begin because the auditorium was already filled to capacity. At CCNY, his spirituals and peace songs were enthusiastically received and for "good measure" he recited from *Othello*.[67]

Though the school enrollment was only nine hundred, over a thousand students and visitors eagerly received Robeson's performance at Swarthmore College that year. While there, Robeson stressed to the students the importance of freedom and dignity for all people and that "mutual respect between peoples of different colors, cultures and ways of life is essential."[68] Robeson made a point of acknowledging that the Quaker heritage in his mother's family paralleled the college's Quaker origins. Between the concert, readings, and discussions of issues, Robeson spent six hours total with the students at Swarthmore. The student paper, the *Swarthmore Phoenix*, ran a lengthy and inspired review of Robeson's appearance.[69] The reporter, Tim Shopen, focused on the importance of welcoming the performer to the campus. His article reflected the move toward free expression that Robeson had noted in his *Freedom* column. Shopen observed, "That Mr. Robeson can be appreciated even though his audience disagrees with most of his political views is demonstrated by the warm and generous reception he received here. Indeed, the honor was all ours."

The unmistakable highlight of this engagement was Robeson's recitation from *Othello*. Shopen thoughtfully described it in detail: "The high point of the evening was the reading of the closing speech from 'Othello'. Mr. Robeson commented that, as he saw the part, Othello was to the end a man of great dignity, not one who had lost his pride but rather one of another culture in a strange land, who felt that he had been betrayed." The article concluded, "Robeson's reading was intelligently suited to this interpretation. His physical stature and voice coupled with his acting skill made for a tremendously powerful Othello." Shopen underscored the excited reception for Robeson's Othello, writing that "the consistently warm applause which followed each of his songs was exceeded by the near ovation called forth by the *Othello* reading." In this way, Robeson continued to emphasize Othello's dignity as he had on stage in the 1940s and, according to this review, was still able to move audiences with his affecting interpretation of

Shakespeare's Moor. In the 1950s, Robeson tended to perform a repertoire of pieces that symbolized the history of African American struggle, such as "No More Auction Block for Me," were particularly suited to current political circumstances, "Scandalize My Name," or were audience favorites, "Joe Hill" and "Ole Man River." *Othello* was vital both as an audience favorite and because it illustrated his continued affiliation with the play. Engaging the final monologue from *Othello* represented another creative strategy to defy his confinement. By reciting this speech, Robeson could simultaneously evoke his historic fame on Broadway, highlighting the ascendancy of his artistry, while also accentuating the current struggle to perform in Shakespeare's play abroad due to his passport case.

This spirit was also apparent at a press conference later in 1955. A judge had just upheld the State Department's right to force Robeson to sign an affidavit confirming his political association in order to travel abroad. Robeson held a press conference to accentuate that, despite this ruling, he would keep fighting and "continue to speak out for first class citizenship, full freedom, peace and civil liberties." Robeson also stressed that "he had always criticized the oppression of the Negro people at home and abroad and would continue to do so."[70] Significantly, Robeson concluded the press conference by reciting Othello's final speech. Whether it was on a theater stage, at a college, or in a meeting with the media, any venue where Robeson inhabited Othello's persona became a theatrical setting. As an activist, he utilized his range as an artist to communicate the urgency of the political situation. Robeson was an actor, but he was barred from practicing his craft overseas, where his career could have flourished, and neither could he perform in the United States on the prestigious stages he had once graced with his presence. In response to his confinement, any site where he was welcome to perform offered an opportunity to remind the audience of his artistic talent. By performing *Othello*, Robeson could convey to the audience how arbitrary and ludicrous his confinement appeared in contrast with his rich artistry. This was the portrayal which had, after all, garnered scores of accolades for him and steered a cast to a record number of performances on Broadway. It was also the role which had spurred his stand against theater segregation and solidified the marriage between his art and his political beliefs. All of these elements were symbolized in his recitations from *Othello* during the cold war. In no place was the passion or the profundity of Robeson's Othello more apparent than when he was invited back to Carnegie Hall in the spring of 1958.

Robeson's sold-out concert on May 9 proved to be such a success that another engagement was booked for later in the month. The *New York Times* reviewer characterized the unique versatility of Robeson's performance: "It would be forcing a point to call this event a recital. Mr. Robeson sang, lectured, [and] even danced a tiny bit. . . . As a lecturer, Mr. Robeson was superb—frequently witty, sonorous, completely uninhibited." He offered singular praise for Robeson's recitation from *Othello* as the focal point of the evening: "And the most musical vocalism of all came not on the singing but in the brief 'Othello' excerpt. Mr. Robeson's shading, his magnificent diction, his effective use of pauses and the sheer color of his speaking voice showed more art and vocal resource than anything heard during the musical portion of the program."[71] Undoubtedly, the speech was a piece Robeson knew well and could render with feeling and careful nuance. Here, the poise and enunciation of the actor, the vocalism of the singer, and the passion of the activist were beautifully conjoined. These components melded seamlessly, in part, because of his having maintained this speech in his varied program consistently through the 1950s.

While the *Times* focused solely on the concert at hand, Joseph North, reporting for the *Daily Worker*, connected Robeson's Carnegie Hall performance directly with his political advocacy: "New York critics . . . misunderstand the core of the man's magnetism when they sought to distinguish between Robeson, the artist, and Robeson, the crusader, the tribune of the people. For this singer . . . has wedded his indisputable genius as artist to that of the unconquerable crusader who champions all humanity that suffers indignity."[72] Fortunately, for those of us who could not attend, the momentous performance on May 9 was recorded.[73] The theme of dignity was reinforced in Robeson's ardent comments that prefaced the *Othello* recitation: "I'd like to do a short excerpt from Shakespeare's *Othello*. It is the last speech of Othello; he has killed Desdemona. From savage passion? No [with emphasis]. Othello came from a culture as great as that of ancient Venice. He came from an Africa of equal stature and he felt he was betrayed. His honor was betrayed and his human dignity was betrayed." Here, Robeson again confirmed the status of Othello's African heritage, which was reminiscent of his writing on Africa from the 1930s. He also highlighted the betrayal of a foreigner in a strange land, which had been a reliable theme in his interpretation of the role through the decades of his affiliation with the play. This speech resonated in an especially meaningful way at the second Carnegie Hall concert because a break in the passport case was on the horizon. Robeson announced at that show, "I'd like you to know that it looks like I'll be traveling all around soon."[74] After years of legal haggling and delay, Robeson would be playing Othello again on the British stage in less than a year. His passport was reissued in late June, and he was on his way to Britain and the Soviet Union to begin a concert tour in July 1958.

In conclusion, Robeson remained steadfast in the face of confinement in the 1950s. Perhaps the most trying time was in the middle of the decade when *Freedom* folded, the Council on African Affairs was dissolved, the Civil Rights Congress disbanded, and prostate surgery left Robeson convalescing during the autumn and winter of '55–'56. Events on the international stage cannot be forgotten either. Khrushchev's confirmation in 1956 of the atrocities committed under Stalin's regime coupled with the violent suppression of Hungary that year had a debilitating effect on Communist parties around the world. As troubling as it might be in retrospect, Robeson chose not to publicly denounce Stalin or the Soviet Union even after 1956. However, he had specific reasons for doing so. As a performer, he was nothing if not consistent. Audiences knew to expect spirituals, folk music, political analysis, and, if they were lucky, a little Shakespeare at a Robeson engagement. Crowds were familiar with his activist posture, his critique of U.S. foreign policy on Africa, his advocacy for all people to live in peace and human dignity, and his encouragement of friendship with the Soviets. To have publicly decried the Soviet Union might have undermined his message of friendship with the Soviet people. Moreover, the Soviets tended to share Robeson's critique of the racism and classism wrought under U.S. capitalism and European colonialism. Thus, Robeson aligned with the Soviets, in part, because they were the opponents of those who had subjugated him and his people: the U.S. government. It was the right wing of the federal government who Robeson believed represented the most dangerous threat to peace on the world stage. He, therefore, maintained his close relationship with the Soviet people, visiting Moscow for a jubilant concert in August 1958 soon after receiving his passport. At this concert, a reading from *Othello* was requested by an audience member as an encore.[75]

Though there were definitely strong pockets of support for Robeson in the black community, such as the A.M.E. Zion Church, Robeson's steadfast alliance with the Soviet Union, even after 1956, prevented unanimous support for him. While black Americans hated racism, most of them did not necessarily view Soviet Communism as a desirable alternative. African

Americans such as Richard Wright, who had supported the C.P., left the party because they discovered that the Soviet system represented another form of dominance. Moreover, the Communist Party in the United States had not always been reliable in the fight for black rights because support of Soviet policy was the top priority for the party. Might Robeson have felt betrayed by the Soviet Union, particularly after Khrushchev's revelations and the invasion of Hungary in 1956? Having never denounced Stalin, did Robeson inhabit Othello's line "one that loved not wisely but too well"? Robeson's actions in the late 1950s did not demonstrate a sense of betrayal, as he remained a frequent visitor to the Soviet Union once his passport was returned. He also spent time with Khrushchev in Crimea in August 1958. Moscow ebulliently received Robeson on one of his first stops when his passport was returned. Additionally, Robeson was in and out of hospitals and care facilities in the Soviet Union when his health wavered between 1959 and late 1963 when he finally returned to the United States. It might be tempting to correlate the trajectory of Robeson's life in the 1950s with the arc of Othello's tragedy. However, it would be a mistake to speculate whether Robeson was speaking for himself or his own personal sense of betrayal when quoting Othello's final monologue. Robeson was never one to allow anyone, not even Shakespeare, to put words in his mouth. As a performer, he identified with Othello to the extent that he identified with the struggles of all people of color and working people around the world.

A reporter for the *Pittsburgh Courier* posed the provocative question in 1958: "Has Paul Robeson re-enacted the role of the tragic Moor, Othello, in his decade of jousting with political enemies?" This reporter supposed that if Robeson's life reflected a formulaic tragedy, then he had, in fact, written his own monologue: "Mr. Robeson is now deep into the third act of his meaty real life role with his latest book, 'Here I Stand,' shining forth as his soliloquy."[76] Thus, Robeson had forthrightly articulated his political views in his memoir and this could serve as his own monologue. While *Othello* was a vital tool in his artistic arsenal, Robeson's own life was not a corporeal incarnation of Shakespeare's Moor. Robeson was not victimized by the Communist Party in the way that Othello had been duped by Iago's machinations. Robeson had not been an official member of the party though he was closely affiliated with party leaders and numerous campaigns of the CPUSA. Despite the unfortunate reality of Stalin's oppression of the Soviet people, the Soviet critique of U.S. racial politics was still valid. The United States could never fulfill its promise of making the world safe for democracy while citizenship rights of African Americans remained unprotected at home and African independence was thwarted. Thus, Robeson made a conscious decision, as a public figure, not to stand with the United States in their alignment against the Soviets. As a performer whose views were part of the public discourse, he instead remained consistent in his message of peace and his critical assessment of neofascist forces in the United States. Robeson had employed *Othello* as a vehicle to fight against segregation in the forties and as a vital symbol of his right to travel in the fifties. His Othello at Stratford in 1959 was a triumphant coda to the repressive political circumstances which had imbued that decade. The thunderous reception for Robeson at Memorial Theatre in April 1959 was as much for his portrayal of Shakespeare's Moor as it was for Robeson himself and the political turmoil he had surmounted to be able to perform in the formal theater for what would be the last time.

CHAPTER SEVEN

Robeson at Stratford

In May 1954, four years before deciding on travel restrictions, the U.S. Supreme Court ruled that racial segregation in public schools was unconstitutional in the landmark *Brown v. Board of Education* case. Following this decision, domestic black protest campaigns attracted the world's attention. The brutal murder of young Emmett Till in Mississippi in the summer of 1955 helped mobilize the postwar generation against racial violence and discrimination. The year-long boycott against segregated busses in Montgomery, Alabama, from late 1955 to 1956 roused the media and secured a Supreme Court decision against segregation in public transportation. A youthful preacher named Martin Luther King, Jr., headed the campaign in Montgomery and became the leader of the newly created Southern Christian Leadership Conference (SCLC) that would be at the forefront of nonviolent direct action on behalf of African American civil rights for the next decade. Meanwhile, in 1957, nine black students attempted to desegregate Central High School in Little Rock, Arkansas, which outraged segregationists across the south and inspired Governor Orval Faubus to surround the school with National Guard troops to prevent the students from entering. President Eisenhower then enforced the *Brown* ruling by sending federal troops to protect the right of the nine students to attend Central High.

The resolution of Paul Robeson's passport case and his departure abroad should be considered against the backdrop not only of anticommunist repression but also of the burgeoning movement for African and African American freedom. For example, the liberation of Ghana from Great Britain in 1957 signaled an upsurge in the movement for African independence for which Robeson had so ardently advocated. Several of Robeson's contemporaries relocated to Ghana, including his colleagues from the Council on African Affairs W. E. B. Du Bois and W. Alphaeus Hunton, who collaborated on the *Encyclopedia Africana* project at the invitation of President Kwame Nkrumah. For a fed-up and disgusted Du Bois, this move represented his final divorce from the repressive United States whose government he symbolically scorned by officially joining the U.S. Communist Party before parting for Ghana, never to set foot on United States soil again.

The southern nonviolent struggle for black civil rights in the United States was gaining momentum prior to Robeson's departure for England in the summer of 1958. However, this movement did not take shape the way Robeson had envisioned, as a coalition between white and black labor with the Communist Party at the vanguard. By the late 1950s, the CPUSA was largely in disarray due to the prosecution of its leaders, anticommunist repression, and disillusionment caused by Khrushchev's confirmation of Stalin's crimes in 1956. Rather, the civil rights movement of the 1950s and 1960s emphasized nonviolent direct action linked with Christian values as articulated by leaders like King and Bayard Rustin and organizations like SCLC, the Congress of Racial Equality (CORE), and the Student Nonviolent Coordinating Committee (SNCC). These groups concentrated on domestic reforms, such as desegregation of schools and public facilities as well as voting rights, while veering away from criticizing U.S. foreign policy toward Africa or making direct links between the cause for African American full citizenship and the need for liberation in the underdeveloped world. Cold war politics stifled such an internationalist critique of racial oppression as demonstrated by the folding of groups such as the Council on African Affairs and the Civil Rights Congress in the middle 1950s. King and leaders of SNCC did make plain these important global connections and were critical of capitalism but not until the mid-to-late 1960s after they had been radicalized by their early civil rights campaigns. Moreover, the new generation of freedom fighters that came of age in the 1950s was not necessarily closely acquainted with Robeson's legacy. This occurred, in part, because he left the country in 1958 and returned in ill health to retire in late 1963. The late fifties, then, witnessed a changing of the guard as smaller left-wing organizations such as the CAA, CRC, and *Freedom* disbanded while their message of solidarity between the working classes and the oppressed worldwide was overshadowed by the implementation of direct action nonviolence and the media attention it garnered.

Robeson's final triumph as Othello, then, was most enthusiastically celebrated in the U.K. where his popularity still flourished. The Stratford

Othello resonated on several important levels. First, it recalled Robeson's greatest success as Othello on Broadway when his artistry was at its height and his political views were more widely accepted. This was quite important given the way in which his career had been publicly marred through Peekskill, the passport case, the HUAC subpoena, and other manifestations of the anticommunist backlash in the United States. Second, the Stratford *Othello* provided a vital forum for British audiences to affirm their support for Robeson and celebrate his victory against the U.S. State Department in the passport case. Crowds came in droves to catch a glimpse of Robeson as Othello, and this underscored his continued status with audiences overseas despite his eight-year confinement in the United States. Whether or not they agreed with his political views, admirers abroad celebrated Robeson's courage and supported his right to free speech. Finally, if the revocation of Robeson's passport because of his advocating for African independence highlighted the obstacles for postwar state formation within a strict anticommunist rubric, then Robeson's victory in his passport case and release from domestic confinement reflected the early successes of the independence movements across Africa in the late 1950s and early 1960s. Robeson's internment in the United States ended at a moment when the likelihood of African self-determination seemed hopeful.

The censure of Joseph McCarthy in 1954 and the Supreme Court's recognition of the unconstitutionality of restricting travel for U.S. citizens in 1958 illustrated a slight thawing in domestic cold war ideologies that restricted civil rights. Still, the ascendancy of Robeson's final Othello would not have been possible in the United States in the late 1950s. If he was not vilified, his unapologetic affiliation with left-wing politics was still considered suspicious. In order to be truly symbolic of his passport victory and genuinely resuscitate his battered career, Robeson's artistry, now matured and weathered, had to come full circle by interpreting Shakespeare once again in England twenty-nine years after his debut in 1930.

Background on the Stratford Production

Stratford-upon-Avon, a bucolic village in the Cotswolds, would probably have remained quaint but undistinguished and relatively unknown save for the accidental fortune of having been the birthplace of England's most beloved playwright in 1564. It was in 1769 that renowned Shakespearean actor and producer David Garrick envisioned the first Shakespeare Jubilee.

Just over one hundred years later, in 1879, the Stratford Memorial Theatre, which would house the Royal Shakespeare Company, was erected on the bank of the Avon River. Thus began the annual Stratford Festival. London critics, at first, jeered that sustaining a repertory theatre dedicated to Shakespeare outside of the metropolis was "ridiculous."[1] Yet, the festival had blossomed by the turn of the twentieth century, with a birthday luncheon and procession celebrating the Bard becoming annual events by 1908. The 1959 season was significant in the annals of Stratford on several accounts: it was the one-hundredth season of the festival and it pointed toward a transition in leadership, as artistic director Glen Byam Shaw was soon to be replaced by the up-and-coming Peter Hall, who went on to direct the Royal Shakespeare Company from 1960 to 1968 to much acclaim. The play that opened this historic season billed Paul Robeson as the star and was, interestingly, the same one that Garrick had selected for his Shakespeare fete almost two centuries earlier.

Byam Shaw, along with actor/director Anthony Quayle, had achieved success at the Memorial Theatre through luring celebrities to play at Stratford. Though they had little more than "uncommonly hard work and modest salaries to offer," the Memorial Theatre had presented many luminaries, including John Gielgud, Richard Burton, Michael Redgrave, and Peggy Ashcroft (who had acted with Robeson in 1930).[2] For the one-hundredth season, in addition to Robeson's *Othello*, directed by Tony Richardson, an impressive list of stars were cast for the occasion: Laurence Olivier as Coriolanus, directed by Hall; Charles Laughton as King Lear, with Albert Finney and Ian Holm, directed by Byam Shaw; Dame Edith Evans in *All's Well That Ends Well*, directed by Tyrone Guthrie; and Michael Redgrave's daughter, Vanessa, in her Stratford debut in *A Midsummer Night's Dream*, directed by Hall. Albert Finney and Ian Holm also had roles in *Othello* playing Cassio and the Duke, while Vanessa Redgrave was the understudy to Desdemona that season.

However, Robeson's journey to becoming the headliner in *Othello* in 1959 had been fraught with obstacles. The passport case with the U.S. State Department was the chief cause of Robeson's belated appearance at Stratford. This fact was noted in several reviews of the production. One reviewer articulated the gravity of the opening, which represented much more than the theatre's anniversary: "It was also a climactic occasion in the life of a great artist. The unique opportunity to seize upon Robeson's presence in England again, at last, and the undoubted sympathy which his American passport and political troubles have engendered for him in Britain certainly was not lost on the Memorial Theatre directors."[3] Cedric Belfrage, writing for the *National Guardian*, noted the value of the opening for the Memorial Theatre's director: "And it was a night of supreme justification for Glen Byam Shaw . . . who long before Paul's passport was restored had stunningly rebuked the witch-hunters with the offer of a contract."[4] Byam Shaw's persistent invitation for Robeson to appear at Stratford had been important evidence in the passport case for his continued artistic status overseas.

Glen Byam Shaw's determined effort to have Robeson again perform Othello in England illustrated a broader trend of support for Robeson across the country. There had been a flurry of activity around the United Kingdom on behalf of Robeson's right to travel. For example, in 1955, a petition was launched in Scotland which collected over three thousand signatures including fourteen members of Parliament. Another delegation in London, led by the Amalgamated Union of Building Trades Workers, delivered a petition to the U.S. Embassy that had been signed by 3,165 people.[5] In May 1956, at a planning committee meeting, it was decided that the "scattered activities in support of Paul Robeson's effort to secure a passport" be "united on a national scale and extended." It was the "Let Robeson Sing" committee in Manchester that initiated this coordinated national endeavor. Cedric Belfrage was selected as chair of the national working committee.[6] In a 1956 phone interview, Robeson expressed his appreciation for the "very many" letters of support from Britons that he had received.[7] A high point in the U.K. struggle for Robeson's passport was in 1957 when he sang from New York via transatlantic cable to over a thousand fans gathered at St. Pancras Town Hall in London. The gathering was organized by the National Paul Robeson Committee and was addressed by several Ministers of Parliament who spoke on Robeson's behalf.[8]

In addition to his passport difficulties, Robeson's health was another obstacle that nearly prevented his performance at Stratford. He had fallen ill after renewing his passport and leaving the United States in the summer of 1958. The following January, he was booked into a Moscow hospital and diagnosed with bronchitis and exhaustion. By March, after a period of convalescence, Robeson had improved and decided to carry on with the plan to perform at Stratford. On the sixteenth of March, having arrived in England, Robeson announced, "I feel fit as a fiddle now."[9] In those intervening months, however, Robeson's *Othello* appearance had been in question, which concerned Glen Byam Shaw greatly since rehearsals were scheduled to begin in mid-February. At one point, Robeson's wife had canceled the Stratford engagement for the sake of his health.[10] When she notified Byam

Shaw, he tried to find a replacement "but then cabled Robeson begging him to reconsider ('I implore you Paul to help me or [the] Stratford season will be ruined')." Byam Shaw subsequently "promised to adjust rehearsal and performance schedules in such a way as to minimize all strain on him."[11] Robeson biographer Martin Duberman maintained that Byam Shaw's insistence helped minimize the trepidation Robeson felt about agreeing to perform under less than ideal circumstances.

Unfortunately, the 1959 *Othello* production was hampered from the beginning. Although it represented an important vindication of his right to travel, Robeson was not at his best artistically due to his recent illness and the demanding strain of constant appearances on his sixty-year-old body. Tony Richardson's unorthodox direction and poor casting further debilitated the production. Nevertheless, the Robeson charisma prevailed. Despite these liabilities, almost all of the critics extolled Robeson and, perhaps more important, the audiences buoyed his spirit with their bountiful applause. After fifteen curtain calls on opening night, Robeson felt confident that he had rallied, for he came off the stage knowing that "I was starting again, a new life as good as ever."[12]

❖ ❖ ❖

Robeson's arrival in London in July 1958 was a moment of fulfillment for him and his supporters. The *Sunday Worker* in New York reported that two hundred people greeted Robeson, and when he exited the plane "the traditional British '3 cheers'" were exclaimed.[13] Cedric Belfrage, the self-described "editor-in-exile" of the *National Guardian* newspaper, had moved to England to escape cold war repression. He observed that, during the 1950s, "my London flat became a kind of embassy for Americans trapped within their frontiers by the passport ban...." Belfrage remembered in his memoir that a "bouquet laden mob" had formed at the airport to welcome Paul and his wife. Moreover, the taxi hired to dispatch the Robesons to their apartment did so voluntarily, with the driver affirming that "I wouldn't take no fare from you, Mr. Robeson. The pleasure was mine." Belfrage further recalled that "[s]o many Londoners recognized the black peacemonger ... that even on his early morning walks there were hands to shake on every block."[14]

Robeson's performance at St. Paul's Cathedral in London in October 1958 was indicative of the tremendous outpouring of goodwill that he received in Britain. Eslanda Robeson, in a press release for the Associated Negro Press, noted that the only other time St. Paul's had been filled to capacity was for Victory in Japan Day in 1945.[15] Four thousand people crowded into the pews to hear Robeson sing at evensong, and, following the service, police had to "rescue" him from the throngs of admirers. Robeson commented to a reporter, "This is an historic moment in my life. I am terribly moved by this tremendous demonstration for me. I am close to tears about it."[16] This foreshadowed the prodigious reception Robeson received at the Memorial Theatre for the *Othello* opening.

In March 1959, Robeson arrived in Stratford for rehearsals. He was working with British director Tony Richardson, who was fairly young but was known for producing playwright John Osbourne's *Look Back in Anger* and *The Entertainer* for the stage in the mid-1950s. He subsequently directed these pieces for film as well. Richardson's film work was fundamental in the development of the British New Wave Cinema movement that emphasized class conflict and sought to give a voice to the poor. He was also associated with the "angry young men" of 1950s British stage realism. Richardson's critical success culminated when he won two Oscars for his film *Tom Jones* in 1963. He was not unfamiliar with *Othello*, however, for he had directed a version for BBC television in 1955 with African American actor Gordon Heath playing the title role.

The British actress and wife of John Osbourne, Mary Ure, was cast as Desdemona. She had previously worked with Richardson on *Look Back in Anger*. The villain, Iago, was played by Sam Wanamaker, which meant that Americans portrayed the two principals, irritating some London critics. However, Richardson had chosen another American deliberately, for he thought that would help Robeson's accent "blend more easily into the ensemble."[17] Wanamaker, though from Chicago originally, spent most of his professional life in England, having departed from the United States permanently in 1952 after HUAC blacklisted him for his work in the film *Mr. Denning Drives North*. Wanamaker was perhaps best remembered as the visionary behind the re-creation of the Globe Theatre in Southwark, London, that opened, after his death, in 1997.

In his memoir, Richardson explained the methodology behind the *Othello* production: "We had decided to take a traditional approach but very elaborate, with costumes inspired by Titian, and with the pace of an American musical." Most reviewers were critical of this technique, citing that the play was too fast paced and littered with superfluous gimmicks that added nothing to the plot and diverted attention from the actors. Richardson recalled in his autobiography that working with Robeson at this time in his career was a mixed blessing. He commented that "rehearsals were fascinating"; however, "the years and his persecutions had left their mark and he [Robeson] no longer had the energy and technique he once had." Richardson continued, "When it came to the great rages and explosions of jealousy, he could not totally rise to them." Yet, he admitted that he "had never seen an Othello who could." On the other hand, when Robeson "made his first entrance and when he told his entrancing story to the . . . Venetian senate, he was perfection." Richardson also confirmed what Robeson felt onstage opening night, that "the love and sympathy of the audience radiated toward him [and] sustained him." Richardson concluded, despite the production having been "mauled" by the critics, that he was "very, very proud and privileged to have been able to work with Paul."[18]

The promptbook specified that Richardson's production was divided into two acts, the first with five scenes and the second having seven scenes.[19] The curtain rose at 7:30 p.m., there was one eighteen-minute interval, and the curtain was slated to fall around 10:10 p.m., which meant that the entire performance lasted on average just over two and a half hours. The shorter running time indicated that cuts had been made to many of the speeches, especially Iago's, and this was particularly irksome to several reviewers. Some lines were also changed, or manipulated, which further dismayed critics.

For example, at the end of the final scene, Lodovico was originally slated to speak the closing lines of the play with Shakespeare's characteristic heroic couplet, "Myself will straight aboard, and to the state / This heavy act with heavy heart relate." However, the script was rearranged so that Cassio's lines, "This did I fear, but thought he had no weapon / For he was great of heart," closed the play instead. This was curious since Shakespeare's formula almost always assigned the character onstage who was the highest ranking official the last lines of his plays (in this case, Lodovico) and every act, particularly the final one, was concluded with a heroic couplet. This was a tradition with which the audience, especially the critics, would have been familiar, so they certainly must have noticed the change. Perhaps it was this alteration that prompted one reviewer to express that "the cutting throughout was shocking, and very confusing to anyone reasonably well acquainted with the play."[20] Robeson's emphasis when playing Othello had always been on his vocal ability and diction with Shakespeare's language, which put him at a disadvantage in a production that focused on extraneous flourishes like dogs and firecrackers rather than dialogue.

In this production, Robeson was scheduled to kiss Mary Ure six times throughout the play which, again, made the papers. However, in 1959, the headlines were more playful and matter-of-fact than indignant, with notices such as "Aging Robeson Wow[s] as Lover" and "Paul Robeson, Mary Ure in 'Othello': Kissed actress six times, takes 15 curtain calls."[21] Additionally, the program notes, written by veteran critic Ivor Brown, remarked casually in the plot summary, "Othello has raised a colour-bar [sic] problem by winning and marrying Desdemona, daughter of a Venetian Senator, Brabantio."[22] This was the only mention of race in the program, and the novelty of a dark-skinned Othello was, for the first time, not a major theme in the reviews. This marked a striking difference between the reviews from 1930 and those from 1959. Robeson was now known and esteemed across Britain. England had been a second home to him in the 1930s. His concert tours around Britain in the 1930s and 1940s were very enthusiastically received, as were film projects like *Proud Valley*, a 1938 movie about miners in Wales. A coalition backed by the labor movement in Britain had organized the "Let Robeson Sing" campaign to support his passport case. By 1959, then, Robeson had attained such a stature that it seemed natural for him to be performing Shakespeare in Shakespeare's birthplace.

Critics and Audiences Respond to the Stratford Opening

Othello opened Stratford's one-hundredth season on April 7, 1959, two days before Robeson's sixty-first birthday. The demand for tickets to see Robeson was intense, as it had been throughout the Broadway production. The scene at Shakespeare Memorial Theatre was described by W. A. Darlington: "Not only had the rush for tickets burned fiercer than ever, but an all-night queue of people determined to get in somehow and somewhere had formed outside the theatre, and had waited patiently all last Tuesday in a cruel, cold wind."[23] The *Wolverhampton Express and Star* commented that so many people were clamoring for seats that "a comfortable little black market in tickets had grown up for opening night."[24] The *Warwickshire Advertiser* ran an amiable piece about a couple trying to get last-minute tickets on opening night. They arrived at the theatre on a lark, hoping to get standby tickets but felt they would be satisfied merely experiencing the glamour of opening night. They were not disappointed. In the foyer, the couple saw television stars mingling with film actors, tourists from Holland and India, and they even rubbed shoulders with John Osbourne. Fortuitously, the couple got two tickets, which was a pleasant surprise since they had been told that the show was booked solid for the next four months.[25]

Darlington also characterized the dual reception of the production well. On one hand, "The curtain rose and fell a fantastic number of times, and still the audience continued to demand more. As a send-off to a gala season, nothing could have been more spectacular than this public reaction, or more spontaneous." Yet, he continued, "the critical reaction, understandably enough, is more restrained," except for the "almost unanimous praise of Mr. Robeson's solidly magnificent Othello." Here, Darlington touched on the chief themes emerging from the reviews: the unprecedented public enthusiasm exhibited opening night, the complimentary reviews of Robeson's performance, and the critiques of the production as a whole.

On opening night, the exultant crowd offered a nearly overwhelming ovation for the cast, especially Robeson, inducing one reviewer to caption his article "Robeson's Duel with the Curtain" since it was "bobbing up and down" so repetitively.[26] The London *Daily Worker* asserted that "our applause almost shook that solid brickwork on the banks of the Avon."[27] The journalist writing for the *Leamington Spa Courier*, who had attended most of the openings at Stratford for over twenty-five years, could not ever remember having witnessed "such a prolonged ovation."[28] Director Tony Richardson, however, might have suspected the reception on that first night would be spectacular, for backstage notes had been written for up to fifteen curtain calls.[29] Robeson disclosed in the wings to a *Daily Mirror* reporter, "I am overwhelmed by the reception I have been given tonight. It is the greatest moment of my life."[30]

Congratulatory telegrams also streamed into Robeson's dressing room from theater notables such as Michael Redgrave, John Gielgud, Peter Hall, and Sybil Thorndike Casson (who had played Emilia in the 1930 Savoy production), as well as old friends including Claudia Jones and the staff of the *National Guardian*.[31] London's *Daily Express* noted that although Robeson looked tired after the opening, he affirmed that "[e]verybody has been wonderful to me. Why I get stopped and have my hand shaken every yard in Stratford."[32] Furthermore, at a small reception after the opening, Glen Byam Shaw announced Robeson's approaching birthday and offered a toast, whereupon the cast contributed "a spirited rendering of 'happy birthday to you.'" Robeson, then, "looking a little shy responded with a short speech in which he again made it quite plain that he was truly happy to be at Stratford, 'This is one of the greatest nights of my life,' he said."[33]

Robeson was no doubt touched by the adulation which was showered on him at Stratford. The reports of opening night corroborated the way in which the affection of the crowds at Memorial Theatre helped bolster

Robeson and must have mollified his initial misgivings about performing given his recent poor health. In this way, the Stratford appearance functioned as a vital symbol of resurgence in Robeson's artistic career following the passport victory. Yet, his triumph at Stratford was also a public acknowledgment of Robeson's posture as a political performer during the cold war. One insightful critic writing about the Stratford opening, Mervyn Jones, asserted that the line between cheering for Robeson as Othello and Robeson's personal character was increasingly blurry: "Robeson could do it [play Othello] I feel, because of the man he is—brave, simple, loyal, supremely fitted to become, for a space, Othello. So we applauded him through I don't know how many curtain calls. We were not, I saw later, cheering a great piece of acting. We were welcoming Paul Robeson for what he is, and for that I will clap my hands sore any time."[34] Robeson's final Othello interpretation was an important emblem of Robeson as a performer in both the artistic and political realms, of one who had remained stalwart through years of cold war repression and emerged with his dignity and enthusiastic fan base safely intact.

The majority of critics lauded Robeson's portrayal of the Moor of Venice at Memorial Theatre. One theme in the reviews addressed Robeson's growth since the 1930 production. The *Stratford Herald* critic exclaimed, "How far has he progressed in these last 29 years."[35] Charles Graves, writing for the *Scotsman*, observed that "the years have given Paul Robeson's Othello a maturity it may not have had before. . . . Everything is now more controlled. . . ."[36] Another reviewer compared Robeson's two performances in Britain: "Others remember moments when he seemed to lack the confident authority that is essential to the character of a great general. He has that authority now and in consequence his Othello ranks among the best that I have ever seen. . . ."[37] Robeson's age also added depth to his characterization as noted by another critic: "Now in his 60's, his performance also had another added virtue . . . here was a man who, because he had 'declined into the vale of years,' was racked by suspicion of a young wife."[38] This was an aspect of the play that could not have been emphasized in Robeson's previous interpretations. There was only about a nine-year age difference between Robeson and his 1930 Desdemona, Peggy Ashcroft. Though Uta Hagen was about twenty years Robeson's junior on Broadway, Mary Ure had, by far, the greatest age differential: her twenty-six years juxtaposed against Robeson's sixty-one-year-old Othello (figure 7.1). A youthful, voluptuous Desdemona added depth to Othello's jealous reaction when he was confronted with suspicion of her infidelity. Thus, the Stratford *Othello*

7.1 Robeson as Othello at Stratford-upon-Avon in 1959 with Mary Ure as Desdemona. Angus McBean: Copyright Royal Shakespeare Company.

highlighted the theme of age, which was implicit in the text but had not been a focal point in his two earlier portrayals.

The superlatives for Robeson were not lacking in many of the reviews. J. C. Trewin felt strongly that Robeson was "great of heart," for he mentioned it twice in his review along with the observation that "Robeson is absorbed at once in the character; Othello has been recreated in his mind. . . ."[39] The reviewer for the *Birmingham Mail* admitted that there was much in the production that he did not enjoy, but "Mr. Robeson's performance finally left me defenceless [sic] and emotionally shattered."[40] A reporter from Coventry proclaimed, "If ever an actor has seemed born for a particular role that man is Paul Robeson and the role Othello." Moreover, "Robeson's Othello is the fruit of long study and past successes," which made the evening's triumph "mostly his."[41] Another critic began simply, "This is Paul Robeson's play."[42]

Cecil Wilson, who did not care for the production as a whole, believed, nevertheless, that "[o]nly Paul Robeson . . . seemed to inhabit the true spirit of the play."[43] In an editorial for the *Daily Worker* in London, Mike Myson declared that he could not "add to the praise already given—almost unanimous praise—to Paul Robeson." He then concluded with a quote from the play, which characterized the magic of seeing Robeson on stage: "It gives me wonder great as my content to see you here before me."[44] Another analysis of Robeson, pointed out by W. E. B. Du Bois's wife, Shirley Graham, spoke to the populist appeal of his Othello. She explained in the *Pittsburgh Courier* that she and her husband were accosted by a railway switchman on the train to Stratford from London who observed, "England will never find another Othello equal to Mr. Robeson." Graham noticed that while this man was hardly a theater critic he had certainly witnessed the onslaught of visitors who had journeyed to the Cotswolds not to pay homage to the Bard but to Robeson.[45]

Dignity was, as in the Broadway production, a prominent aspect of Robeson's interpretation that was cited in many reviews. Critics for the 1959 production did not merely mention Robeson's dignity in passing but some took care in articulating this idea. It is interesting to consider whether this reflected more on Robeson's dignified deportment or on how the reviewers might have grown in their ability to perceive Robeson's innate dignity onstage since the 1930 production. Either way, these reviews emphasized the centrality of dignity to Robeson's interpretation of Othello. For example, an inspired reporter asserted, "Mr. Robeson being the gigantic figure he is . . . somehow seems to shoulder the dignity of the whole Negro race."[46] A detailed review in the *Shakespeare Quarterly* pointed out, "Mr. Robeson's Othello had a dignity, an ease and an authority that was not present in the [1930] Savoy production."[47] Reviewer Neville Miller maintained, "Anyone who has ever seen Mr. Robeson in any context whatever knows that an aura of dignity, simplicity and an intensely human nobility is as much his as Othello's."[48]

Two themes were revealed here. First, these reviews were a far cry from the notices that Robeson received in 1930 when critics were torn over whether a black actor should even be playing Othello. Roughly 40 percent of the 1959 reviews examined for this study mentioned Robeson's dignity onstage. Locutions such as "majestic," "noble," "stately," and "sincere" also occurred repeatedly. The glaring racism of 1930 had diminished and the references to Robeson's dignity increased. Second, this pattern was indicative of the evolving racial dynamic that had emerged in Britain between

1930 and 1959, which was stimulated, in part, by the independence movements in British colonies such as India and Ghana. Yet, Robeson's personal stature and the impact of his political life should not be underestimated as an influence on the reviewers. Just as the critic Mervyn Jones emphasized that the first-night audience was applauding as much for Paul Robeson for who he was as for Robeson's Othello, the reiteration of this theme in the reviews suggested that Robeson's personal dignity shone clearly onstage as Othello. His performances on the cold war stage prior to Stratford had imbued Robeson's artistry with an unmistakable authority and maturity that complemented his inherently dignified comportment. Robeson's composure through cold war repression like the passport case and his HUAC testimony had enabled him to offer a more nuanced interpretation of Shakespeare that further blurred the line between Robeson's artistry onstage and his performances in the political arena. Thus, in 1959, the demarcation between Robeson's personal dignity and Othello's dignity onstage was almost imperceptible.

The theme of courage appeared in a couple of the Stratford reviews and was also directly linked to Robeson's political life. Unlike dignity, courage had not been an apparent theme in the notices for the 1930 or the Broadway productions. It was connected specifically to the 1950s context. For example, in its welcoming editorial in early March 1959, the London *Daily Worker* correlated Robeson's talent and return to the British stage with his courage through the cold war. Here, Mike Myson urged readers to join him in "welcoming back to our theatre this great representative of the progressive voice of America—a voice which refused to be drowned out by the shameful clamour [sic] of the McCarthyite years—readers will join with me in saluting him, for his courage, his unfailing loyalty to the cause of the common people of the world, and his great talent."[49] However, it was not especially surprising that the *Daily Worker*, the organ of the C.P., would make such an observation.

The mainstream *Daily Herald* also recognized Robeson's courage. In an interview with Robeson, the *Herald* highlighted the context of his recent ill health along with his political advocacy. Reporter Anthony Carthew pointed out that Robeson "would like to refer to Nyasaland in his Stratford curtain speech. He would like to say, 'You are very kind because I'm Paul Robeson. Would you be so kind to me in Nyasaland? It could be me, you know.'" Carthew then concluded, "This is Paul Robeson in 1959.... A man, I think, of great courage."[50] No evidence was found for this study that Robeson actually delivered a speech about Nyasaland on opening night, but he did make the connection in this interview which was published in a major newspaper. This article revealed two significant points. First, the iconic, political advocate of 1959 was not the same man as the young, blossoming actor of 1930. Second, this stemmed largely from his political advocacy. Robeson knew that the public in Britain adored him personally, yet he did not ignore the larger issue of self-determination for African people, like those in Nyasaland. Nyasaland was a British protectorate that was vying for independence in the late fifties and became the independent nation of Malawi in 1964. Pointing to germane current events in Africa was typical of Robeson in 1959 though this had not necessarily been true in 1930. In the Carthew interview, Robeson not only noted the case of Nyasaland, but he clearly signaled his solidarity with these Africans when he evocatively observed, "It could be me, you know." This was the continent where Robeson's ancestors had been born and from which they had been forcibly removed. Robeson was alerting Britons that it was not acceptable or logical for them to rally behind him, their beloved performer, and not simultaneously support African self-determination.

Additionally, critic Don Cook opined in a review, "Forget Paul Robeson's politics for a moment and consider the whole complex emotional background against which this eminent Negro faced the opening night . . . of 'Othello' last week."[51] William Patterson, a friend of Robeson's and a leader in the CPUSA, took offense to this remark, which he felt undermined the importance of Robeson's political life. Patterson responded to it in a letter to the editor of a Russian periodical. He protested, "How can we forget or submerge what has contributed so much to the making of a world renowned figure? Can Paul Robeson's devotion to the freedom struggles of his people, to the liberation struggles of all men, to respect for human dignity be forgotten? Can we forget his deathless devotion to the cause of peace? All this is indissolubly linked with that [Stratford] Othello."[52] Thus, Patterson plainly reinforced the connection between Robeson's dignity onstage at Stratford with his political advocacy. Robeson at the Memorial Theatre, then, represented not just a single portrayal of Othello but symbolized the international recognition of his artistry which had matured in large part because of the political posture he maintained throughout the cold war.

Still, a few critics were not as moved by Robeson's performance at Stratford. Several reviewers noticed that Robeson seemed fatigued following the opening. Robeson's Council on African Affairs colleague W. Alphaeus Hunton observed that "perspiration streamed down his face" and "he was obviously tired" after opening night.⁵³ Anthony Carthew also felt that his performance "showed strain" although he concluded that "Robeson triumphed."⁵⁴ Robeson's lassitude following the show could have stemmed from his recent hospitalization for exhaustion as well as the hectic schedule he was maintaining. The other chief complaints about Robeson included reference to a "stiff and monotonous" performance; that he was "humdrum and tentative in both voice and gesture"; and that his performance was "but an abstract arrangement of patterns and sounds."⁵⁵ Yet, even two of these reviewers conceded the quality of Robeson's voice, and one critic still felt that Robeson, at his best, could be stirring.

The drama critic for the *London Times* maintained that Robeson had again been "sadly handicapped by an over-clever production" as had been the case in 1930. He postulated that Robeson's considerably younger costars, Wanamaker and Ure, did not properly complement Robeson's matured interpretation: "The miscasting of both these actors robs Mr. Robeson of his best chance of making something memorable of the part."⁵⁶ Another critic agreed and lamented that, unfortunately, Robeson had no one of the caliber of Peggy Ashcroft or Sybil Thorndike to support him onstage at Stratford as he had had in 1930.⁵⁷ The issue of miscasting was corroborated in Sally Beauman's history of the Royal Shakespeare Company in which she posited that among "the heterogeneous collection of actors" that season, "nothing jelled." She continued, "This was most apparent in the production of *Othello*; Robeson was understrength vocally, but even so it was hard to understand how the combination of him, Sam Wanamaker as Iago, and Mary Ure as Desdemona—all actors from totally different traditions, and with totally different acting approaches—could possibly have worked."⁵⁸ Her commentary introduced one of the many criticisms levied against the Stratford production. While comparatively few reviews were critical of Robeson individually, the majority of reviews found fault with the overall production. The *Times* reviewer, in fact, proclaimed it to be "a freakish production and a grotesquely maimed text."

First, Mary Ure received consistently bad press, though her buxom appearance was pleasing to some critics. Sam Wanamaker did not fare much better, although some reviewers believed his machinations against Othello were convincing. One critic summed, "As Desdemona, Mary Ure probably came off more badly than anyone else with the possible exception of Sam Wanamaker as Iago."⁵⁹ Many critics felt that Ure did not complement Robeson's dignity ("Mary Ure has neither dignity nor poetry . . ."), nor did her "tiny voice" hold water next to his baritone.⁶⁰ Ure's Desdemona left a *Daily Worker* writer wondering how Othello could love "such an empty piece of femininity."[61] Moreover, Wanamaker's accent grated on a number of critics, one of whom commented, "Sam Wanamaker speaks Iago with the accents of Chicago." Indeed, "He acts the villain like a henchman in the Al Capone style."[62] Another reporter likened his Iago to a "street corner boy" who had been "bred in the slums."[63]

Wanamaker's performance was regarded as unorthodox as was a litany of other unnecessary elements in the production. For example, Ian Holm played the Duke of Venice as an asthmatic who hissed through his lines. Great Danes rushed across the stage in act I as Brabantio searched for his eloping daughter and son-in-law. Firecrackers and fog dramatically illustrated the storm off Cyprus. The calls of seagulls and loons as well as cannon fire and drums reverberated through other scenes.[64] The critic for the *Evening Dispatch* summarized, "The first [act] is a fine flurry of thunderous, breakneck speed with fireworks, four Great Danes, a set which looks like a gigantic palisade, a wheezing ... Duke, ... a wholesale storm, ... resounding fights and drinking songs." Yet, "[i]f you look carefully, you may catch the tragedy of 'Othello' getting under way."[65] Numerous critics were unimpressed by these contrivances. One review was aptly titled, "Othello Shocks the Purists."[66]

A chief concern of reviewers was that Shakespeare's language was lost beneath the spectacle. Desmond Pratt commented, "The deliberate emphasis on naturalistic treatment has meant that the dialogue is spoken at a great speed, giving it mainly the impression of prose."[67] Similarly, the *Western Daily Press* reviewer decried the production's "indifference to some of the poetry and its excessive striving for realism."[68] "At times there was so much business that one lost the words," asserted a reporter who, like many others, felt that the pace of the play made audibility problematic at times.[69] The staging was further hindered by poor lighting. The *Oxford Mail* synthesized the effect: "The production ... was a noisy, gaudy affair with its tempests, fireworks and grisly fight scenes. Smoke and clouds rolled across the stage, much of the time in semi-darkness, while the wind howled through Loudon Sainthill's scenery."[70]

A final liability ironically recalled the 1930 production quite closely. The placement of the bed in the final act was lambasted by critics because it was on a second floor and placed at an angle making it less visible and, thus, rendering the pathos of the murder scene less accessible. Tony Richardson, lamentably, made a similar error in the Stratford production. The reviewers in 1959 were, again, quick to point out this shortcoming that distanced the action of the play from the audience. J. C. Trewin expressed regret: "I am sorry that the director has staged the bed-chamber on an upper and remote level." He concluded that this play was "not altogether Shakespeare's."[71] Another critic bemoaned the fact that Richardson "contrives to give the play something of an anti-climax by providing Desdemona with a first floor bedroom at the back of the stage."[72] M. St. Clare Byrne, writing for *Shakespeare Quarterly*, sounded his frustration: "But the bedroom for the murder of Desdemona, set aloft on high arches and angled across two-thirds of the right side of the stage . . . far from being called for by the text made nonsense of parts of it, necessitated cuts, and was altogether an unhappy piece of designer's ingenuity. . . ."[73] This inopportune staging put Robeson again at a disadvantage, for his most tender and terrifying moments as Othello were potentially lost on the audience who was too far away to appreciate them.

The director, for his part, realized this unfortunate lapse, writing in his memoir, "But Loudon and I made one very bad mistake. We'd placed Desdemona's bedroom on the upper level of the stage; then, knowing that the scenes there need to bring the actors as close to the audience as possible, we had cantilevered it out. It gave anyone sitting near in the stalls a dangerous, vertiginous feeling."[74] However, Richardson recalled, that with only four weeks of rehearsals, there was no time to rectify the situation. All in all, the critics seemed disappointed that the producers appeared "determined to make the whole tragedy as un-Shakespearean as possible."[75] It was regrettable that both of Robeson's appearances as Othello in England suffered from tawdry productions that detracted from the impact of the play.

How did the black press in the United States react to the Stratford *Othello*? Robeson's 1959 *Othello* did not register in the black press with much fervor. The article carried by the *Chicago Defender* mentioned the production, but, reflecting cold war politics of the era, most of the piece recounted how Robeson had been "under the spell of Russian communism" since the 1930s.[76] A short notice from Claude Barnett's Associated Negro Press was picked up by the *Baltimore Afro-American* and the *Pittsburgh Courier*.[77] It mentioned the fifteen curtain calls for Robeson on opening night as well as the six kisses he exchanged with Mary Ure onstage. The brief article also noted that Robeson was the first African American to play Othello in the history of the Memorial Theatre. Although the *Afro-American* did run a photo of Robeson next to the short notice, *Othello* was somewhat overshadowed in the *Afro-American* by an extended article on Lorraine Hansberry's *A Raisin in the Sun*, which had recently premiered on Broadway and won a Drama Critics award, hinting at a changing of the guard to a younger generation of African Americans in the theater.

However, two of Robeson's colleagues from the Council on African Affairs were present at the Stratford opening. W. E. B. Du Bois, who felt like a "released prisoner" with his newly reissued passport, stopped in England with his wife to visit the Robesons. In an autobiography he noted of that trip, "I saw Paul Robeson and his splendid production of *Othello*."[78] W. Alphaeus Hunton wrote a lengthy press release that summarized the British reviews and the history of Robeson in *Othello*. In a letter to Robeson's wife, Eslanda, that accompanied the press release, Hunton remarked, "I'm everlastingly grateful to you for enabling me to be there for the opening."[79] Du Bois's wife, Shirley Graham, who had a background as an actress and playwright, was also enthusiastic about the Stratford *Othello*. The *Pittsburgh Courier* ran the laudatory piece that she wrote on the production in which she declared that she had seen all three of Robeson's interpretations of the Moorish general and believed this one to be "beyond all question" the best performance.[80]

Performances in 1959 and 1960

As he had during the Broadway production, Robeson characteristically made a variety of other appearances during the run of *Othello* in Stratford from April to November. For example, the play opened on April 7, and he attended the lunch that accompanied the celebrations for Shakespeare's birthday in Stratford just two weeks later. That same week, a capacity crowd gave Robeson a "tremendous welcome" when he made an appearance at an African Freedom Day concert in London, having "come straight from the Shakespeare Memorial Theatre at Stratford."[81] In June, Robeson spoke and sang at a peace rally in Trafalgar Square, London, where the protesters demanded that the British and U.S. governments take the lead in curbing the threat of nuclear war.[82] Later that summer, in August, Robeson traveled to Austria to visit the World Youth Festival in Vienna. Following a parade of children from more than eighty countries, the crowd gathered in the Hofburg Palace Park for a concert in which Robeson participated. Interestingly, the festival overlapped with Vice President Nixon's tour of Eastern Europe and Russia. Robeson seized the timely opportunity to publicly criticize U.S. foreign policy which, in his view, could not "talk of giving full freedom and democracy to Africa when 18,000,000 of us do not have full freedom in the U.S."[83] In the autumn, Robeson teamed up with Lawrence Brown for a series of ten radio programs on the BBC in which Robeson sang and talked about music.[84] Thus, while Robeson donned Othello's sword in service to the Venetians on the Stratford stage he also continued to advocate for peace and full citizenship for African Americans on the political stage.

Still, Eslanda Robeson was concerned throughout the *Othello* run that Robeson was overcommitting himself. The production took more of a toll on him than he was perhaps willing to admit at the time. Eslanda wrote to Claude Barnett of the show's closing, "Paul wound up his OTHELLO in a blaze of glory last Thursday at Stratford. He took 10 curtain calls, and the cast said that it was the best performance of the season. So that's finished, without having missed a single performance. Not bad."[85] In another letter to Barnett, she expressed her relief that they would rest for a period following *Othello*: "I am not undertaking anything until Paul finishes with OTHELLO . . . and then we will both take a good long much needed rest. After that we will plan. . . . But we are both very tired and are looking forward to that rest."[86]

However, Eslanda was more candid in a letter to Claudia Jones. She confided to Jones that Robeson had not complained much during the Stratford engagement, but afterwards he conceded that *Othello* had been a daily struggle. "Every performance, he said, he had the prompter, he was sure he would forget his lines. He did once, and it terrified him. But he always expected to. He suffered agonies with that Othello, from April to November, when it finished. Often he would stay in bed all day, with fear. It really is terrible, when you hear him tell it now." Though his wife worried that he was overextending himself, Robeson was in demand as a performer and often felt compelled to make appearances after his forced absence from foreign stages. This was especially true with *Othello* since it was the one-hundredth season and the Stratford invitation had figured prominently in his passport fight. Eslanda frankly characterized the situation: "And Paul with his conscientious self, again said . . . that he couldn't let them down. They had stuck their necks out for him, so he would have to struggle thru [sic] it somehow. He did, and no one will ever know at what cost, he said yesterday."[87]

Nevertheless, in the public sphere, Robeson's time in Britain from late 1958 through 1960, particularly the Stratford *Othello*, signaled resurgence in his artistic career. He gave recitals and made appearances in Europe and Russia during this period. In the spring of 1960, Robeson embarked on a concert tour of the U.K., which was enthusiastically received by the public and reviewers. Lawrence Brown, the familiar face alongside Robeson since 1925, again accompanied him. The *Liverpool Post* described the crowd's eager devotion, noting that the evening proceeded like "a succession of encores interrupted by a programme [sic]. . . ."[88] Robeson naturally wove his political analysis into the program of spirituals and other musical offerings. One reviewer observed, "But he is generous with encores, shamelessly enthusiastic in the cause of music . . . and equally passionate in the cause of freedom."[89] Some critics preferred Robeson's singing to his politics; one remarked, "He never lets us forget that his father was a slave, but he does make us feel that the road to complete emancipation and race equality can be travelled with less weariness and bitterness because of the gift of song."[90]

After a special appearance at a concert sponsored by Claudia Jones and the *West Indian Gazette*, Robeson departed for his first visit to Australia and New Zealand in the fall of 1960. Lawrence Brown toured with Robeson on this trip, which was fervently received. Australians and New Zealanders were obviously thrilled to see the iconic Robeson in person. One reporter in New Zealand believed that when Robeson stepped on the stage and began to sing, "A legend had come true."[91] Robeson, of course, could not be deterred from including political commentary during his appearances. At a press conference in Auckland, "Mr. Robeson's manager tried to dissuade him from talking about political questions. Mr. Robeson rebuked him. 'I don't need to be protected, he said.'"[92] At Midland Junction, Robeson sang for an outdoor lunchtime concert, and two thousand people crowded around to hear him while children climbed trees to get a better view of the luminary.[93] Perhaps the most memorable concert he gave was a spontaneous show at the brand-new Sydney Opera House, which was still being erected at the time. A notice in the *Daily Telegraph* commented, "Seagulls and workmen today will be the first to hear a performance from Sydney's . . . Opera House." A public relations officer was quoted: "I don't know what he plans to sing, but I assume they will be songs the workmen know."[94]

During this period, Robeson continued to mingle Shakespeare's poetry with his singing. Indeed, as he had throughout the 1950s, Robeson recited from *Othello* on his tour of Australia and New Zealand. This component always seemed to have a great impact on the audience. For example, in Auckland, a reviewer proclaimed, "[P]erhaps most interesting of all, was a speech from Shakespeare's 'Othello.'"[95] Russell Bond, reporting on a show in Wellington, was also moved. He wrote emphatically that the concert "alone would have been enough to show how compelling and commanding he must be on the dramatic stage had he not reinforced it strongly later on with a short speech from 'Othello'. . . ."[96] When they heard him intoning Shakespeare's poetry, new audiences could share some of the excitement of Robeson's recent triumph in Stratford. Othello's final monologue, then, was an important highlight of this, what would be his last, major concert tour.

In conclusion, playing Othello in England for a second time fittingly brought Robeson's career full circle. It was in England that he had debuted as the Moorish general on the West End, and it was where he became increasingly politically engaged in the 1930s. Importantly, the British public, as well as specific individuals such as Glen Byam Shaw, had steadily supported Robeson during his domestic confinement in the 1950s. As a result, the Stratford *Othello* became a crucial symbol of Robeson's brief renaissance following his eight-year internment in the United States. The production itself was not without its weaknesses: miscasting, poor set design, and an extravagant use of spectacle, as well as Robeson's own compromised health. These issues notwithstanding, the ebullient public response bolstered Robeson. A reporter inquired if he could stand the strain of a season running from April to November, and Robeson replied, "I think so, because I get a warmth from British audiences which I don't get in America. It seems the British can still like an artist even if they disagree with his politics."[97] This affection was especially meaningful to Robeson, not only because of his recent poor health but because of his lengthy absence from the U.K. due to the passport struggle. He mentioned this in an interview with the *Daily Worker* in London: "The reception that I have had here has passed all bounds. It is something that could not happen to some visiting artist who just dropped in after ten years."[98] The extended ovations for the production on opening night were undoubtedly as much, if not more, for Robeson, the performer and political advocate, as for his interpretation of Othello. Shirley Graham pointed out in her review that Shakespeare's play was new to many of the theatergoers who patiently waited for hours with the faint hope of snatching a standing ticket to the show. "In fact, some make no secret of the fact that they would prefer hearing Paul sing," she ventured. "But they are willing 'to take' Shakespeare's lines so long as it's Paul Robeson giving them."[99] Imagine Shakespeare purists gasping at the notion of audience members making a pilgrimage to the heart of Shakespeare country on Shakespeare's birthday merely "to take" the poetry of his iambic pentameter! Such was the singular magnetism of Robeson's appearance in the Bard's hometown. It was Paul Robeson's personal courage and dignity, reflected onstage as Othello, which stood out to reviewers and, doubtlessly, to the public who so ardently embraced Robeson's performance at Memorial Theatre. Robeson, the cold warrior, stood his ground through the fifties, and the audiences loved him "for the dangers I had pass'd." On the whole, it was his three interpretations of Shakespeare's noble character that elucidated the trajectory of his unique politically infused artistic career. Robeson's enduring relationship with the great playwright of Stratford-upon-Avon embodied W. E. B. Du Bois's enlightening reflection in *The Souls of Black Folk*: "I sit with Shakespeare and he winces not."[100]

Conclusion

1963 was an iconic year in the southern nonviolent civil rights movement. The previous year, Martin Luther King, Jr., and the Southern Christian Leadership Conference's strategy of direct action nonviolence had received little press attention and achieved few tangible goals in the fight against segregation in Albany, Georgia. However, moving on to Alabama in the spring of 1963, SCLC's campaign to challenge segregation confronted Birmingham's notorious police chief Eugene "Bull" Connor. His tactics secured national and international headlines. Connor infamously ordered the assault of the nonviolent activists, including young people and children, with police dogs and fire hoses which filled nightly news broadcasts and prompted an outcry from around the United States. In a display of cold war politics, newspapers in the Soviet Union jumped at the opportunity to lambast the failures of U.S. domestic policy, especially in the wake of the recent botched invasion and missile crisis in Cuba. Following the violence in Birmingham and the subsequent international criticism, President Kennedy was finally moved to take his strongest stand yet on racial discrimination by promising to bring a comprehensive civil rights bill before Congress.

Organizers built on the momentum generated that spring to bring to fruition A. Philip Randolph's decades-long vision of a mass march on Washington, D.C., in August. Some of the most enduring images from the civil rights years occurred when an interracial assembly of about 250,000 crowded around the reflecting pool on the mall. Generational paradigms were also apparent that day. For example, the college-aged were represented by folk music revivalists Bob Dylan and Joan Baez singing anthems of the era and the movement such as "Blowin' in the Wind" and "We Shall Overcome." John Lewis, of the Student Nonviolent Coordinating Committee, was requested to tone down the rhetoric of his speech because it was deemed by veteran organizers such as Bayard Rustin as overly critical of the

Kennedy administration. In the eyes of SNCC activists, JFK and attorney general RFK had done little to protect their constituents who were being brutalized in the South. However, Lewis altered the speech out of respect for the elder generation of activists, especially Randolph. Still, many SNCC members remained disapproving of the president as well as the march itself, which some later characterized as a "castrated giant," for failing to address any critiques of Kennedy or engaging in civil disobedience.[1] King, only in his early thirties at the time, delivered the most celebrated speech of the day which cemented his prominence as a national symbol of the contemporary civil rights movement. Rather than criticizing the Kennedy brothers, King focused on a hopeful message of future reconciliation and racial equality. Thus, a changing of the guard was evident that historic afternoon as representatives of a younger generation took center stage on the steps of the Lincoln Memorial. Paul Robeson had delivered an antilynching address at that very monument in 1946, but he and another distinguished cold warrior were conspicuously absent that warm summer day in 1963.

Thousands of miles across the Atlantic and far from the spotlight, two deans of the twentieth-century struggle for civil rights followed news of the mass march. The venerable, ninety-five-year-old W. E. B. Du Bois, who had expatriated to Ghana at the invitation of Kwame Nkrumah, had heard about the planned protest through the Ghanaian media but died quietly in his sleep as the march commenced.[2] On another continent, Paul Robeson and his wife, Eslanda, monitored the coverage of that memorable August day from Europe. In a piece she penned in October, Mrs. Robeson recorded the connection that both Robesons felt with the protest in Washington. She noted, "We could almost feel ourselves there, in person, in Washington. We certainly felt ourselves an intimate part of this history."[3] Significantly, she linked the campaign in Washington to Robeson's legacy of activism.

In 1958 when his passport was returned, Robeson had headed to perform for friendlier audiences overseas. Yet his exit occurred just as direct action nonviolence, as implemented by groups like SCLC and later SNCC, was burgeoning. In December 1963, the sixty-five-year-old returned with weakened health to retire in the country which had kept him confined within its borders for speaking out in favor of African independence. As if to underscore his absence during pivotal years of civil rights action, a reporter at the airport unthinkingly queried whether Robeson would be joining the civil rights movement. Though he smiled silently at most questions directed toward him upon his arrival, to this inquiry Robeson cogently retorted, "Yes, I've been part of it all my life."[4] The disconnect between this reporter's question and Robeson's life as an activist stemmed in part from what the *New York Times* labeled his five-year "self exile."[5] Additionally, a new generation of civil rights activists who came of age in the postwar years was now at the forefront of the struggle. While the mainstream press tended to characterize Robeson's return as something like that of a prodigal son who had been swayed by Communism and was detached from the contemporary struggle, the progressive journal *Freedomways*, in an editorial which welcomed him home, made explicit the relationship between Robeson and the current fight. The editors thoughtfully noticed that "the winds of Freedom are once again blowing across the south; sparked by a new generation of Negro youth who proudly inherit the traditions of courage and dedication of which Paul Robeson is such a towering symbol and legend in his own time."[6]

In September 1964, after the signing of the Civil Rights Act that summer, Robeson published an article in the *Afro-American* that commented on his return as well as present issues. He correlated observations from his 1958 memoir with the current movement for civil rights by recollecting that he had called for mass involvement in the final chapter, "The Power of Negro Action." By 1964, he was pleased that the idea was now "manifesting itself throughout the land," as "[t]he 'long hot summer' of struggle for equal rights has replaced the 'cold war' abroad as the concern of our people." Finally, Robeson affirmed the role of artists in the current movement. "It is especially heartening," he declared, "for me to see the active and often heroic part that leading colored artists . . . are playing today in the Freedom struggle." As opposed to the forties and fifties, Robeson ruminated, "Today it is the colored artist who does not speak out who is considered to be out-of-line. . . ." In recognition of contemporary civil rights leadership, his closing acknowledged King's famed speech at the March on Washington. Robeson, the seasoned activist, was a bit more reserved than the younger King, yet still optimistic. He suggested, "But if we cannot as yet sing: 'Thank God Almighty, we're free at last,' we surely can all sing together: 'Thank God Almighty, we're moving!'"[7]

A generational shift was also evident at an event for Robeson in April 1965 hosted by the journal *Freedomways*. Over two thousand acolytes, celebrities, and activists, including Ossie Davis, Ruby Dee, Billy Taylor, Pete Seeger, John O. Killens, and Lloyd Brown, gathered at the Americana Hotel in New York for a cocktail party followed by a four-hour tribute to the performer.[8] The *Liberator*, a journal of the younger generation of black artists and advocates, dedicated a page to discussing the Robeson event. In its notice, the *Liberator* observed that the "fearless and uncompromising leadership which Robeson exerted before his departure" was "a type of leadership which we sorely lack today."[9] This article also pointed out that the only speech of the evening which highlighted the contemporary struggle was delivered by SNCC's John Lewis, who had recently participated in the Selma to Montgomery march. Robeson biographer Martin Duberman noted that when asked to prepare a keynote address, Lewis sought help from another SNCC member because Robeson's history was unfamiliar to him.[10] Nevertheless, the speech made critical linkages between Robeson's activism and the SNCC generation.[11]

He opened by acknowledging that for two generations "Paul Robeson represented the entire Negro people of this country." It was significant that Lewis, as well as the *Liberator* article, accepted Robeson as a leader in the African American community. This role had been denied by those who denounced Robeson after his remarks in Paris in 1949 but was now being documented by the subsequent generation. Lewis continued, "Tonight, as we salute Paul Robeson, we salute more than a man, we salute a cause." In addition, "We salute the dreams . . . of an oppressed people whether they be in Selma, Alabama . . . or in Vietnam." In this way, Lewis recognized the internationalism of Robeson's civil rights activism. Robeson had critiqued U.S. involvement in Korea in the early 1950s while the imperialist war of Lewis's generation was in another country in Southeast Asia: Vietnam.

Noting that SNCC, like Robeson, had been accused of being radicals of "Communist influence," Lewis wondered what was so dangerous about Robeson and later SNCC. In reply, he perceived that both maintained "faith in the numberless poor and uneducated" while believing that "they must be free" to "decide their own political destiny." He then thoughtfully suggested that the audience pay homage to Robeson's activism by supporting SNCC and the Mississippi Freedom Democratic Party's challenge to unseat the legislators who were elected in absence of the African American vote. Most memorable was Lewis's assertion that "we of S.N.C.C. are Paul Robeson's spiritual children." Indeed, Lewis had been a child at the time of Robeson's triumph on Broadway in the middle 1940s when his artistry and political advocacy were successfully conjoined. Robeson came forward to make a few comments following Lewis's speech. There must have been a moment when the legendary, now senior, artist and the youthful practitioner of nonviolent direct action met, and perhaps shook hands, marking a discernable transition between generations of civil rights proponents.

What was instructive about Robeson's career as a performer was not solely the substance of his politics, though that was vital and should be intrinsic to any examination of his artistry. Rather, it was the unique melding of his politics with his artistic talent that illuminated the role of the artist during times of crisis. When stymied by discrimination from pursuing a career in law, this budding scholar did not subvert his political acuity in favor of a livelihood in the arts but, over the years, he employed creative methods to unite his singing and stagecraft with his antifascism. Through the *Othello* production on Broadway, his stand against segregation was boldly manifested onstage as well as outside of the theater. As the political climate intensified, in the postwar years, Robeson did not divest himself from his commitment to being a politically minded artist. Instead, he sacrificed the financial remuneration of a purely artistic career in order to remain true to his political principles. His stalwart posture in the face of cold war repression was unmistakable in his persistent struggle to play Othello in England again.

As Shakespeare's character ruminated in act I, "Were it my cue to fight, I should have known it / Without a prompter...." Robeson, like Othello, knew when it was his cue to fight. The performer took his cue in the battles against fascism, discrimination, and colonialism in favor of freedom, dignity, and self-determination. Robeson brought to these fronts an arsenal of talent: an unforgettable resonant baritone shaped by the artist, a noble physique with the dignified comportment of the actor, and a sharp mind along with the courage to speak truth to power in trying political circumstances. As James Baldwin poetically observed at the *Freedomways* event, "[I]n the days when it seemed that there was no possibility of applying the rigors of conscience, Paul Robeson spoke in a great voice...."[12] Whether he was discussing African independence, peace with former allies, or the Bard of Stratford, and whether he was performing on a theater stage, at a press conference, or during a demonstration, when Paul Robeson voiced "a word or two before you go," many heads turned to listen.

NOTES

Introduction

1. Fredi Washington, "Entertainment World Fights Jimcro," *People's Voice*, 27 May 1944.
2. "An Interview with Paul Robeson," *Afro-American*, 1 March 1958.
3. Benjamin Davis, "A Great Man Writes a Great Book," *Sunday Worker*, 6 April 1958.
4. Ossie Davis, interview by St. Clair Bourne for the film *Paul Robeson: Here I Stand* (Menair Media International, Inc., 1999), transcript provided by St. Clair Bourne.
5. Anna Grimshaw, ed., *The C.L.R. James Reader* (Oxford: Blackwell, 1992), 237.
6. "And Yet He Can't Travel," *The Worker*, 12 January 1958.
7. Susan Curtis, *The First Black Actors on the Great White Way* (Columbia: University of Missouri Press, 1998), 21.
8. Philip Foner, ed., *Paul Robeson Speaks* (New York: Citadel Books, 2002), 118–19.

Chapter One

1. Virginia Mason Vaughan, *Othello: A Contextual History* (Cambridge: Cambridge University Press, 1994), 3–4.
2. Lois Potter, *Othello*, Shakespeare in Performance Series, ed. J. R. Mulryne and J. C. Bulman (Manchester: Manchester University Press, 2002), 6–8.
3. Carl Woodring, *Table Talk Volume II, The Collected Works of Samuel Taylor Coleridge*, ed. Kathleen Coburn, vol. 14 (Princeton, NJ: Princeton University Press, 1990), 31.
4. John Quincy Adams, "Misconceptions of Shakespeare upon the Stage," in *Notes, Criticism and Correspondence Upon Shakespeare's Plays and Actors*, ed. James Henry Hackett (New York: Carleton, 1863), 224.
5. William Winter, *Shakespeare on the Stage* (New York: Moffat, Yard and Company, 1911), 252.
6. Ania Loomba, *Shakespeare, Race and Colonialism* (Oxford: Oxford University Press, 2002), 111.

7. Celia R. Daileader, "Casting Black Actors: Beyond Othellophilia," in *Shakespeare and Race*, ed. Catherine M. S. Alexander and Stanley Wells (Cambridge: Cambridge University Press, 2000), 177.

8. Ian Smith, "Barbarian Errors: Performing Race in Early Modern England," *Shakespeare Quarterly* 49 (Summer 1998): 173.

9. Vaughan, 14 and 58; Loomba, 71.

10. Bernard Harris, "Portrait of a Moor," in *Shakespeare and Race*, ed. Alexander and Wells, 23.

11. Vaughan, 56; Smith, 175.

12. Loomba, 101.

13. Marvin Rosenberg, *The Masks of Othello* (Berkeley: University of California Press, 1971), 200.

14. Paul H.D. Kaplan, "The Earliest Images of Othello," *Shakespeare Quarterly* 39 (Summer 1988): 171–86.

15. John E. Bruce, *Was Othello a Negro?* (New York: privately printed, 1920), 10.

16. "Robeson Talks in London for Audience Here," *New York Herald Tribune*, 9 June 1930.

17. Mythili Kaul, *Othello: New Essays by Black Writers* (Washington DC: Howard University Press, 1997), 18.

18. Rudolph Elie, Jr., "Robeson Gives 'Othello' Great Power, Starring in Revival with White Troupe," *Variety*, 12 August 1942.

19. "Paul Robeson as Othello: Large Audience Acclaims His American Debut in Role," *The Christian*, 11 August 1942.

20. Rosenberg, 1.

21. Charles Shattuck, *Shakespeare on the American Stage from the Hallums to Edwin Booth* (Washington DC: Folger Shakespeare Library, 1976), 3–5, 16.

22. Potter, 27; Winter, 246–48.

23. Potter, 36–37; Shattuck, 66.

24. Potter, 37; Rosenberg, 70. For more on the riot, see chapter seven in Vaughan.

25. Shattuck, 45–46.

26. Potter, 30–31.

27. Charles B. Lower, "Shakespeare as Black on Southern Stages, Then and Now," in *Shakespeare in the South*, ed. Philip C. Kolin (Jackson: University Press of Mississippi, 1983), 199–228.

28. Potter, 29–30.

29. Vaughan, 163.

30. Potter, 45.

31. Vaughan, 168.

32. Lawrence Levine, *The Unpredictable Past: Explorations in American Cultural History* (Oxford: Oxford University Press, 1993), 142.

33. Elaine Brousseau, "'Now Literature, Philosophy, and Thought are Shakespearized': American Culture and Nineteenth Century Shakespearean Performance 1835–1875," (Ph.D. diss., University of Massachusetts, Amherst, 2003),74.

34. Ibid., 84–88.

35. Ibid., 91.

36. Levine, 171.

37. Ibid., 140.

38. Ibid., 153.

39. Rena Fraden, *Blueprints for Black Federal Theatre 1935–1939* (Cambridge: Cambridge University Press, 1994), 2.

40. Errol Hill, *Shakespeare in Sable* (Amherst: University of Massachusetts Press, 1984), 77.

41. Errol Hill, "The African Theatre to Uncle Tom's Cabin," in *A History of African American Theatre*, ed. Errol Hill and James Hatch (Cambridge: Cambridge University Press, 2003), 27.

42. Ibid., 82.

43. Ibid., 257.

44. *Crisis* 3 (March 1912): 198–99.

45. Sister M. Francesca Thompson, "The Lafayette Players 1917–1932," in *The Theatre of Black Americans: A Collection of Critical Essays*, ed. Errol Hill (New York: Applause Theatre Book Publishers, 1987), 211.

46. Ibid., 220.

47. "Shakespeare All Over the City," *New York Times*, 25 April 1916.

48. "Negroes Play Othello First Time Here," *Boston Herald*, 9 May 1916.

49. "Tree Hears Negro in Part of OTHELLO," *New York Times*, 3 April 1916.

50. *The Standard* (London), 14 April 1833.

51. *The Times* (London), 11 April 1833.

52. Hill, *Shakespeare in Sable*, 17.

53. James Hatch and Errol Hill, "Educational Theatre," in *A History of African American Theatre*, ed. Hill and Hatch, 257.

54. Roger D. Abrahams, "Traditions of Eloquence in Afro-American Communities," *Journal of Interamerican Studies and World Affairs* 12 (October 1970): 516.

55. C. Eric Lincoln and Lawrence H. Mamiya, *The Black Church in the African American Experience* (Durham: Duke University Press, 1990), 277.

56. Paul Robeson, *Here I Stand* (Boston: Beacon Press, 1988), 25.

57. Lamont H. Yeakey, "A Student Without Peer: The Undergraduate Years of Paul Robeson," *The Journal of Negro Education* 42 (Autumn 1973): 502.

58. Marcus H. Boulware, *The Oratory of Negro Leaders 1900–1968* (Westport, CT: Negro Universities Press, 1969): 68.

Chapter Two

1. Robeson, *Here I Stand*, 19.

2. Reprinted in *Freedom* 3 (April 1953): 3.

3. "Paul Robeson's Shakespearean Debut: Talk with the Negro Othello," *The Era*, 21 May 1930.

4. J. Murray Smith, "Paul Robeson on: Was Othello a Negro," Paul Robeson Collection, Manuscript Division, Moorland-Spingarn Research Center, Howard University, Washington DC.

5. "Robeson Talks in London for Audience Here," *New York Herald Tribune*, 9 June 1930.

6. "How Paul Robeson Mastered Pronunciation," *The Bulletin*, 21 May 1930.
7. Irma Kraft, "Paul Robeson Tells the Story of His Othello," *New York Herald Tribune*, 15 June 1930.
8. G. W. Bishop, "Robeson Acclaimed in Othello Role," *New York Times*, 20 May 1930.
9. *The Bulletin*, 21 May 1930.
10. *The Era*, 21 May 1930.
11. "Was Othello a Negro?" Paul Robeson Collection, Manuscript Division, Moorland-Spingarn Research Center, Howard University, Washington DC.
12. Smith, "Paul Robeson on: Was Othello a Negro?"
13. "'My Ordeal as Othello': How Paul Robeson Mastered Pronunciation," *Evening Standard*, 20 May 1930.
14. *The Era*, 21 May 1930.
15. James Agate, "The Dramatic World: Mr. Robeson's Othello," *Sunday Times* (London), 25 May 1930.
16. "Mr. Robeson on 'Othello,'" *The Observer*, 18 May 1930.
17. "Paul Robeson's Othello," *Morning Post*, 21 May 1930.
18. George Warrington, "At the Theatre," *Country Life*, 31 May 1930.
19. "The Negro Othello," *Daily Mail* (London), 21 May 1930.
20. "The Negro Othello," *Daily Mail* (London), 25 May 1930.
21. "Was Othello a Negro?"; "Paul Robeson Tells How It Feels for a Negro to Play Othello Role," *New York World*, 9 June 1930.
22. "Robeson Talks in London for Audience Here."
23. *The Era*, 21 May 1930.
24. "Interview with William Lundell," Paul Robeson Collection, Manuscript Division, Moorland-Spingarn Research Center, Howard University, Washington DC.
25. "Mr. Robeson's Kisses in 'Othello,'" *Daily Mail* (London), 21 May 1930.
26. "Robeson May Alter Othello Role Here," *New York Times*, 22 May 1930.
27. "Robeson Talks in London for Audience Here."
28. *Daily Sketch*, 21 May 1930.
29. Michael Billington, *Peggy Ashcroft* (London: John Murray Publishers, Ltd., 1988), 41.
30. "Othello's Way with a White Wife," *The Star* (London), 21 May 1930.
31. C. L. R. James, *Letters from London* (Port of Spain: Prospect Press, 2003), 83.
32. D. F. Kanaka, "Colour Bar," *Daily Herald* (London), 10 April 1934.
33. "Black Othello: No Letter of Protest About Paul Robeson Performance," *Daily Sketch* (London), 22 May 1930.
34. Billington, 41.
35. Hannen Swaffer, "Hannen Swaffer Looks at the Theatre," *Daily Express* (London), 21 May 1930.
36. *The Era*, 21 May 1930.
37. "Paul Robeson's Othello," *Morning Post*, 21 May 1930.
38. "Interview with William Lundell."
39. "'Othello' Surprise: Mr. Maurice Browne Suddenly Resigns His Part," *Sunday Dispatch*, 8 June 1930.
40. "Interview with Maurice Browne," *Sunday Dispatch*, 29 June 1930.

NOTES

41. "Robeson to Play Othello," *New York Times*, 4 September 1929.
42. Eslanda Robeson, *Paul Robeson, Negro* (New York: Harper and Brothers, 1930), 165.
43. "Negro Othellos," *The Observer* (London), 4 May 1930.
44. Sheila Tully Boyle and Andrew Bunie, *Paul Robeson: The Years of Promise and Achievement* (Amherst: University of Massachusetts Press, 2001), 222.
45. Eslanda Robeson Collection, Manuscript Division, Moorland-Spingarn Research Center, Howard University, Washington DC.
46. "Paul Robeson's Triumph," *Sunday Express*, 25 May 1930.
47. Ellen van Volkenburg, "The Script of Othello as Produced at the Savoy Theatre London, May 19th 1930," microfilm edition, Promptbook Collection, Folger Shakespeare Library, Washington DC.
48. W. Keith, "A Negro Athlete, Scholar, Singer and Tragedian," *The Star* (London), 20 May 1930.
49. "A Negro Artist," *The Times* (London), 20 May 1930.
50. John St. Ervine, "Paul Robeson: Negro," *The Observer* (London), 25 May 1930.
51. R. S. Pippett, "Book of the Day: Paul Robeson—by His Wife," *Daily Herald* (London), 19 May 1930.
52. Paul Robeson, Jr., *The Undiscovered Paul Robeson: An Artist's Journey 1898–1939* (New York: John Wiley and Sons, Inc., 2001), 170.
53. Eslanda Robeson, *Paul Robeson, Negro*, 70.
54. Ibid., 163.
55. Ibid., 73.
56. Ibid., 167.
57. Ibid., 151.
58. Ibid., 156.
59. Paul Robeson, Jr., 171.
60. Eslanda Robeson, *Paul Robeson, Negro*, 171.
61. Paul Robeson, Jr., 173.
62. "American Actor Gets Big Ovation," *Chicago Defender*, 24 May 1930.
63. "London Press on Robeson," *Afro-American*, 7 June 1930.
64. *Pittsburgh Courier*, 12 July 1930.
65. Ivan H. Browning, "Ivan Browning Tells of Struggles of Paul Robeson in 'Othello,'" *Pittsburgh Courier*, 14 June 1930.
66. "A Black Outlook at the Savoy," *The Bystander*, 28 May 1930.
67. "Behind the Footlights: Coloured Player as Othello," *Corydon Times*, 5 July 1930.
68. "'Othello' at the Savoy," *The Era*, 21 May 1930.
69. "Paul Robeson as Othello: A Fine Performance," *Irish Times*, 21 May 1930.
70. "The Theatres," *Hampstead Express*, 31 May 1930.
71. "Paul Robeson's English," *Everyman* 3 (1930): 546; "Paul Robeson's New Accent: How It Will Help Him in Othello," *Daily Herald* (London), 7 May 1930.
72. "Paul Robeson: A Great Othello," *Newcastle Chronicle*, 22 May 1930.
73. Thomas Moult, "A Shakespeare Invasion," *City News*, 8 June 1930.
74. "'Othello': Mr. Robeson's Interpretation," *Yorkshire Post*, 20 May 1930.
75. "Mr. Paul Robeson's Othello," *Sporting Life*, 23 May 1930.
76. Elizabeth Montizambert, "The London Theatre," *Montreal Gazette*, 7 June 1930.

NOTES

77. "Negro Othello," *Sporting Times*, 26 May 1930.
78. "Mr. Paul Robeson: Negro Actor's Great Success as Othello," *Sheffield Telegraph*, 20 May 1930.
79. "London Theatres: Paul Robeson in 'Othello,'" *Scotsman*, 21 May 1930.
80. "The Humanities," *Church Times*, 23 May 1930.
81. "London Theatres: The Savoy 'Othello' Revived," *The Stage*, 22 May 1930.
82. "Mr. Robeson's Othello," *Western Morning News*, 22 May 1930.
83. Richard Dyer, *Heavenly Bodies: Film Stars and Society* (New York: Routledge, 2004), 75.
84. "Paul Robeson as Othello," *Christian Science Monitor*, 21 June 1930.
85. C. B. Purdom, "Paul Robeson as 'Othello,'" *Everyman*, 29 May 1930.
86. "A Terrifying Othello," *Sunday News*, 26 May 1930.
87. "Splendid Robeson," *The Sunday Chronicle*, 25 May 1930.
88. "Paul Robeson as Othello," *Eastern Daily Press*, 21 May 1930.
89. Purdom, "Paul Robeson as Othello."
90. Hannen Swaffer, "Hannen Swaffer Looks at the Theatre," *Daily Express*, 21 May 1930.
91. "'Othello' at the Savoy Theatre," *Birmingham Post*, 21 May 1930.
92. "Negro Actor as Othello: Great Triumph for Paul Robeson," *Daily Telegraph*, 20 May 1930.
93. "Memorable Othello of Paul Robeson," *The Evening News*, 20 May 1930.
94. "Othello and Desdemona," *Sphere*, 31 May 1930.
95. "Paul Robeson's Triumph," *Sunday Express*, 25 May 1930.
96. "Mr. Robeson's Othello," *Daily Chronicle*, 20 May 1930.
97. "'Othello,'" *The Sunday Graphic*, 25 May 1930.
98. Elizabeth Sprigge, *Sybil Thorndike Casson* (London: Victor Gollancz Ltd., 1971), 194.
99. "'Othello,'" *Illustrated Sporting and Dramatic News*, 31 May 1930.
100. Edward J. MacDonald, "Robeson's Othello," *G. K.'s Weekly*, 31 May 1930.
101. "Robeson in 'Othello,'" *Englishman*, 9 June 1930.
102. Ivor Brown, "The Play: One of Our Conquerors," *The Weekend Review*, 24 May 1930.
103. "Changes for the Bad," *The Referee*, 25 May 1930.
104. "'Othello,'" *Curtain*, 1 June 1930.
105. Ivor Brown, "This Week's Theatres: 'Othello,'" *The Observer*, 25 May 1930.
106. E. A. Baughan, "Robeson as Othello," *Daily News*, 20 May 1930.
107. "Terrifying Passion: Paul Robeson Makes Othello a Slow-Witted Creature," *Daily Sketch*, 20 May 1930.
108. A. E. Wilson, "Paul Robeson as Othello: Magnificent Performance but More Careful than Inspired," *The Star*, 20 May 1930.
109. James Agate, "The Dramatic World: Mr. Robeson's Othello," *Sunday Times* (London), 25 May 1930.
110. *Empire News*, 25 May 1930.
111. *Liverpool Post*, 16 May 1930.
112. "A Black Outlook at the Savoy," *The Bystander*, 28 May 1930.
113. Sprigge, 193.

114. "Theatre: A Negro Othello," *Lady*, 29 May 1930.
115. Alan Parsons, "Mr. Paul Robeson's Othello," *The Daily Mail*, 20 May 1930.
116. "In the Limelight: Too Much Reserve in 'Othello' Command Performances," *Sunday Pictorial*, 28 May 1930.
117. James Agate, "The Dramatic World: Mr. Robeson's Othello."
118. Herbert Farjeon, "The London Stage: Mr. Paul Robeson's Othello," *The Graphic*, 31 May 1930.
119. George Warrington, "At the Theatre," *Country Life*, 31 May 1930.
120. "The Theatres: Ol' Man Othello," *Truth*, 28 May 1930.
121. M. Willson Disher, "Greenroom Gossip: Robeson's Othello," *The Scotsman*, 31 May 1930.
122. Eslanda Robeson Collection, Manuscript Division, Moorland-Spingarn Research Center, Howard University, Washington DC.
123. Billington, 37.
124. Sheridan Morley, *Sybil Thorndike: A Life in the Theatre* (London: Wiedenfeld and Nicolson, 1977), 98.

Chapter Three

1. Interview reprinted in Foner, 123–27.
2. "Paul Robeson's Velvet Voice in Sheffield," *The Daily Independent*, 20 January 1934.
3. *Time*, 28 August 1933.
4. Article reprinted as: Paul Robeson, "What I Want From Life," in *Paul Robeson Tributes and Selected Writings*, ed. Roberta Yancy Dent (New York City: Paul Robeson Archives, Inc., 1976), 55–59.
5. Article reprinted as: Paul Robeson, "Primitives," in Dent, 59–64.
6. Paul Robeson, "The Culture of the Negro," *The Spectator* (London), 15 June 1934.
7. Paul Robeson, "Negroes—Don't Ape the Whites," *Daily Herald* (London), 5 January 1935.
8. Ibid.
9. Article reprinted as: Paul Robeson, "Thoughts on the Colour Bar," in Foner, 82–84.
10. Ibid., 84.
11. Sterling Stuckey, "'I Want to Be African': Paul Robeson and the Ends of Nationalist Theory and Practice 1914–1945," *Massachusetts Review* 17 (Spring 1976): 81–138.
12. Dyer, 69.
13. C. L. R. James, "Paul Robeson: Black Star," in *C. L. R. James: Spheres of Existence* (Westport, CT: Lawrence Hill & Co., 1980), 260–61.
14. Alain Locke, ed., *The New Negro* (New York: Touchstone Books, 1997), 4.
15. Ibid., 19.
16. Ibid., 23.
17. W. E. B. Du Bois, *The Souls of Black Folk* in *Three Negro Classics*, ed. John Hope Franklin (New York: Avon Books, 1965), 387.

18. W. E. B. Du Bois, *The Gift of Black Folk*, ed. Herbert Aptheker (Millwood, NY: Kraus-Thomson Organization Limited, 1975), 320.

19. Stuckey, 82.

20. Claude McKay, *A Long Way from Home* (New York: Harcourt, Brace and World, 1970), xi.

21. Ibid., 349.

22. Wayne Cooper, *Claude McKay: Rebel Sojourner in the Harlem Renaissance* (New York: Schocken Books, 1987), 254.

23. Robeson, "Negroes—Don't Ape the Whites."

24. Dent, 59.

25. Robeson, "Negroes—Don't Ape the Whites."

26. Locke, 4.

27. *Paul Robeson Live at Carnegie Hall: The Historic May 9, 1959 Concert* (Santa Monica: Vanguard Records, 1987).

28. Paul Robeson, "Here's My Story," *Freedom* 3 (June 1953): 11.

29. Foner, 71–72.

30. Grimshaw, 222.

31. Ibid., 234.

32. James, "Paul Robeson: Black Star," 257.

33. Grimshaw, 230.

34. James, "Paul Robeson: Black Star," 256.

35. Robert A. Hill, "In England 1932–38," in *C. L. R. James: His Life and Work*, ed. Paul Buhle (New York: Allison and Busby, 1986), 73.

36. James, "Paul Robeson: Black Star," 261–62.

37. Michelle Stephens, *Black Empire: The Masculine Global Imaginary of Caribbean Intellectuals in the United States 1914–1962* (Durham, NC: Duke University Press, 2005), 221.

38. James, "Paul Robeson: Black Star," 256.

39. Grimshaw, 236.

40. "Two Great Negroes," *The People* (London), 22 March 1936.

41. Grimshaw, 6.

42. Anna Grimshaw, "Notes on the Life and Work of C. L. R. James," in *C. L. R. James: His Life and Work*, 13.

43. Grimshaw, *Reader*, 230.

44. Kent Worcester, *C. L. R. James: A Political Biography* (Albany: State University of New York Press, 1996), 36.

45. Stephens, 218.

46. Ibid., 220.

47. "Two Great Negroes."

48. M. Willson Disher, "Mr. Paul Robeson's Thrilling Part," *Daily Mail* (London), 17 March 1936.

49. "Toussaint L'Ouverture at the Stage Society," *The New Statesman and Nation*, 21 March 1936.

50. No title, Paul Robeson Collection, Manuscript Division, Moorland-Spingarn Research Center, Howard University, Washington DC.

51. "The Theatre," *The Keys* 2 (April–June 1936): 68.

52. "Robeson Calls for Aid to Negroes Defending Democracy in Spain," *Negro Worker* 7 (June 1937): 1–2.
53. Foner, 120.
54. "News Items," *The Keys* 5 (January–March 1938): 71.
55. Robeson, *Here I Stand*, 51–52.
56. Dent, 74–75; Foner, 118–19.
57. Robeson, *Here I Stand*, 53.

Chapter Four

1. Constantin Stanislavsy, *Creating a Role*, trans. Elizabeth Reynolds Hapgood (Methuen, NY: Theatre Arts Books, 1988), 35.
2. Nathaniel Buchwald, "Paul Robeson in Othello," *Morning Freiheit*, 23 October 1943.
3. Margaret Webster, *Don't Put Your Daughter on the Stage* (New York: Alfred A. Knopf, 1972), 88.
4. Quoted in H. L. Brock, "The Taming of the Bard," *New York Times*, 30 January 1944.
5. Milly S. Barranger, *Margaret Webster: A Life in the Theater* (Ann Arbor: University of Michigan Press, 2004), 135.
6. Margaret Webster, *Shakespeare Without Tears* (New York: Premier Books, 1957), 162.
7. Ibid., 176.
8. Margaret Webster, "Pertinent Words on his Moorship's Ancient," *New York Times*, 17 October 1943.
9. Webster, *Shakespeare Without Tears*, 178–80.
10. Foner, 145.
11. Ibid., 145–46.
12. Grimshaw, *Reader*, 246 and 231.
13. Foner, 163–64.
14. Webster, *Don't Put Your Daughter on the Stage*, 107.
15. Margaret Webster, "Robeson and Othello," *Our Time* 3 (June 1944): 5.
16. Webster, *Don't Put Your Daughter on the Stage*, 106.
17. Martin Duberman, *Paul Robeson: A Biography* (New York: Ballantine Books, 1989), 263.
18. Webster, "Robeson and Othello."
19. Webster, *Don't Put Your Daughter on the Stage*, 107.
20. Barranger, 133.
21. Margaret Webster, Promptbook for *Othello*, New York Public Library for the Performing Arts, Billy Rose Theatre Collection, New York.
22. Margaret Webster and John Haggot, typescript for *Othello*, New York Public Library for the Performing Arts, Billy Rose Theatre Collection, New York.
23. Margaret Webster, "Shakespeare and the Modern Theatre," Margaret Webster Papers, Manuscript Division, Library of Congress, Washington DC.
24. "Othello Costume Inventory," Margaret Webster Papers.

25. Margaret Webster, "Shakespeare and the Modern Theatre," 22–23.
26. Robert van Gelder, "Robeson Remembers," *New York Times*, 16 January 1944.
27. Margaret Webster, letter dated 9 July 1942, Margaret Webster Papers.
28. Margaret Webster, letter dated 30 July 1942, Margaret Webster Papers.
29. Uta Hagen, interview by St. Clair Bourne for the film *Paul Robeson: Here I Stand* (Menair Media International, Inc., 1999), transcript provided by St. Clair Bourne.
30. Margaret Webster, letter dated 14 August 1942, Margaret Webster Papers.
31. "Robeson as Othello," *New York Times*, 16 August 1942.
32. Joyce Dana, "Paul Robeson Magnificent in 'Othello' at Cambridge," *Boston Evening American*, 11 August 1942.
33. Margaret Williamson, "'Othello' in August," *Christian Science Monitor*, 28 August 1942.
34. "Robeson Stars as Othello at Cambridge," *Boston Daily Globe*, 11 August 1942.
35. "Paul Robeson Makes First U.S. Appearance as Othello at Cambridge Theater," *Boston Traveler*, 11 August 1942.
36. "'Othello' at Brattle Hall," *Harvard Crimson*, 12 August 1942.
37. Elinor Hughes, "Paul Robeson's 'Othello,'" *Boston Herald*, 11 August 1942.
38. "Paul Robeson as Othello: Large Audience Acclaims His American Debut in Role," *The Christian*, 11 August 1942.
39. Rudolph Elie, Jr., "Robeson Gives 'Othello' Great Power, Starring in Revival with White Troupe," *Variety*, 12 August 1942.
40. "A Negro Othello," *Pittsburgh Courier*, 5 September 1942.
41. *New York Times*, 16 August 1942.
42. *Boston Daily Globe*, 11 August 1942.
43. *The Christian*, 11 August 1942.
44. Owen Dodson, "Hampton Critic Reviews 'Othello'; Calls Play Race Angle Non-Existent," *People's Voice*, 5 September 1942.
45. Elliot Norton, "Robeson 'Othello' Was Something to See," *Boston Sunday Post*, 16 August 1942.
46. Quoted in Duberman, 265.
47. Ralph Warner, "Paul Robeson Creates an Immortal Othello up in Cambridge," *Sunday Worker*, 16 August 1942.
48. Webster, *Don't Put Your Daughter on the Stage*, 112–3.
49. Margaret Webster, letter dated 14 August 1942, Margaret Webster Papers.
50. Margaret Webster, letter dated 16 August 1942, Margaret Webster Papers.
51. "Robeson Concert Dates Delay Broadway Othello," *People's Voice*, 29 August 1942.
52. Susan Specter, "Margaret Webster's 'Othello': The Principal Players Versus the Director," *Theater History Studies* 6 (1986): 101; Janet Barton Carroll, "A Promptbook Study of Margaret Webster's Production of Othello" (Ph.D. diss., Louisiana State University, 1977), 30–31.
53. Margaret Webster, letter dated 12 August 1943, Margaret Webster Papers.
54. "Ferrers Quit 'Othello,'" *New York Times*, 17 August 1943.
55. Margaret Webster, letter dated 25 August 1943, Margaret Webster Papers.
56. Sam Zolotow, "Changes in 'Othello,'" *New York Times*, 27 August 1943.
57. Margaret Webster, letter dated 29 August 1943, Margaret Webster Papers.
58. Hagen, interview by St. Clair Bourne.

59. Ibid.
60. Webster, *Don't Put Your Daughter on the Stage*, 117.
61. "William Shakespeare and the Theatre Guild," Paul Robeson Collection, Manuscript Division, Moorland-Spingarn Research Center, Howard University, Washington DC.
62. Ely Silverman, "Margaret Webster's Theory and Practice of Shakespearean Production in the United States 1937–1953" (Ph.D. diss., New York University, 1969).
63. Llewellyn Ransom, "Question of the Week," *People's Voice*, 6 May 1944.
64. Margaret Webster, letter dated 20 October 1943, Margaret Webster Papers.
65. John Chapman, "A Black Man as Othello," *Sunday News* (New York), 24 October 1943.
66. Louis Kronenberger, "Going to the Theater," *PM*, 30 October 1943.
67. *New York Post*, 20 October 1943.
68. "The Moor Holds the Record," *New York Herald Tribune*, 5 March 1944.
69. Rosamond Gilder, "Broadway in Review," *Theatre Arts* (December 1943): 700.
70. Robert Garland, "Theatre Guild Production Directed by Margaret Webster Opens Here," *New York Journal American*, 20 October 1943.
71. Ward Morehouse, "'Othello' as Done by Guild and Miss Webster Provides Exciting Evening," *New York Sun*, 20 October 1943.
72. Howard Barnes, "The Theaters," microfilm edition of Claude A. Barnett Papers, Part 3, Series D, Reel 5, Frame 471.
73. Wilella Waldorf, "'Othello' and the Dramatic Renaissance of the Theatre Guild," *New York Post*, 23 October 1943.
74. *New York Post*, 20 October 1943.
75. Lewis Nichols, "Robeson as Othello," *New York Times*, 24 October 1943.
76. Lewis Nichols, "The Play in Review," *New York Times*, 20 October 1943.
77. *Variety*, 27 October 1943.
78. Burton Rascoe, "Guild's 'Othello' a Triumph," *New York World Telegram*, 20 October 1943.
79. E. C. Sherburne, "Paul Robeson as Othello," microfilm edition of Claude A. Barnett Papers, Part 3, Series D, Reel 5, Frame 741.
80. Richard P. Cooke, "Robeson's Othello," *Wall Street Journal*, 23 October 1943.
81. Edwin Schallert, "New Othello Sensational at Biltmore," *Los Angeles Times*, 23 January 1945.
82. Carl Diton, "Broadway Likes Paul Robeson in 'Othello,'" *Chicago Defender*, 30 October 1943.
83. Ruth Rolen, "Lotta Hugs and No Kisses in Paul Robeson's Portrayal of Othello," *Chicago Defender*, 16 October 1943.
84. "Star's Portrayal of the Moor Rated Best of Them All," *Pittsburgh Courier*, 30 October 1943.
85. W. E. B. Du Bois, "As the Crow Flies," Paul Robeson Collection, Manuscript Division, Moorland-Spingarn Research Center, Howard University, Washington DC.
86. J. A. Rogers, "Rogers Says: In Shakespeare's Day Negroes Were Called Moors," *Pittsburgh Courier*, 13 November 1943.
87. Dan Burley, "Paul Robeson as Othello Strikes Big Blow at Intolerance," *New York Amsterdam News* (Brooklyn/Queens edition), 30 October 1943.

88. Reprinted in *Freedom* 5 (April 1955).
89. Mike Gold, "A Genius and the People Merge at Shubert in 'Othello,'" Paul Robeson Collection, Manuscript Division, Moorland-Spingarn Research Center, Howard University, Washington DC.
90. Samuel Sillen, "The Discussion of Othello," *Daily Worker*, 9 November 1943.
91. Samuel Putnam, "Paul Robeson's Great Othello," *Sunday Worker*, 24 October 1943.
92. Bernard R. Boxill, "Self-Respect," in *Blacks and Social Justice* (1984; rvsd. Lantham, MD: Rowman and Littlefield, 1992), 195.
93. Frederick Douglass, "The Claims of the Negro Ethnologically Considered," in *Negro Social and Political Thought 1850–1920*, ed. Howard Brotz (New York: Basic Books, Inc., 1966), 229.
94. W. E. B. Du Bois, "Criteria for Negro Art," in *African American Literary Theory*, ed. Winston Napier (New York: New York University Press, 2000), 23.
95. Ossie Davis, interview by St. Clair Bourne for the film *Paul Robeson: Here I Stand* (Menair Media International, Inc., 1999), transcript provided by St. Clair Bourne.
96. Otis Guernsey, Jr., "The Playbill: Paul Robeson Is an Othello Ready Made," *New York Herald Tribune*, 17 October 1943.
97. Boxill, 195.
98. Joyce Dana, "Paul Robeson Magnificent in 'Othello' at Cambridge," *Boston Evening American*, 11 August 1942.
99. "The Moor Holds the Record," *New York Herald Tribune*, 5 March 1944.
100. Dyer, 136.
101. Doris Allen, "Singer Finds Moor Role in Othello Exhausting," *Rochester Times-Union*, 3 October 1944.
102. P. L. Prattis, "Why Has Robeson Been Called One of the World's Greatest Intellects?" Paul Robeson Collection, Manuscript Division, Moorland-Spingarn Research Center, Howard University, Washington DC.
103. Ashton Stevens, "Stevens Finds 'Othello' Spectacular—But," *Chicago Herald-American*, 11 April 1945; Ashton Stevens, "The Quicker, the Better," *Chicago Herald-American*, 15 April 1945.
104. Robert Pollak, "'Othello' Is All They Said About It in NY," *Chicago Times*, 11 April 1945.
105. John Cottrell, *Laurence Olivier* (Englewood Cliffs, NJ: Prentice-Hall, Inc., 1975), 337.
106. Allen, "Singer Finds Moor Role in Othello Exhausting"; "Robeson Foresees Social Advancement after War," *Vancouver News-Herald*, 11 January 1945; Foner 161.
107. Paul and Eslanda Robeson FBI File, report dated 6 July 1945.
108. Margaret Marshall, "Drama," *The Nation*, 30 October 1943, 507–508.
109. Miles Jefferson, "The Negro on Broadway—1944," *Phylon* 6 (1945): 42–52.
110. Langston Hughes, "Simple Sees 'Othello,'" *Chicago Defender*, 3 June 1944.
111. C. L. R. James, "'Othello' and 'The Merchant of Venice,'" in *C. L. R. James: Spheres of Existence* (Westport, CT: Lawrence Hill & Co., 1980), 141–50.
112. Anna Grimshaw, ed., *Special Delivery: The Letters of C. L. R. James to Constance Webb 1939–1948* (London: Blackwell Publishers, 1996), 90.
113. Ibid.

114. Margaret Webster, letters dated 17, 19, 23, 26 February 1944, Margaret Webster Papers.
115. Uta Hagen, interview by St. Clair Bourne.
116. Margaret Webster, letter dated 10 October 1943, Margaret Webster Papers.
117. Margaret Webster, "Robeson and Othello."
118. Uta Hagen, interview by St. Clair Bourne.
119. Louis Lytton, no title, Margaret Webster Papers.
120. Eslanda Robeson, *Paul Robeson, Negro*, 89.
121. John K. Hutchens, "Paul Robeson," *Theatre Arts* (October 1944): 579–85.
122. Webster, *Daughter*, 108–109.
123. Hutchens, 581.
124. Robeson, *Here I Stand*, 15.
125. Barranger, 135.
126. Stanislavsky, 8.
127. Ibid., 9.
128. Jerome Beatty, "America's No. One Negro," in microfilm edition of Claude A. Barnett Papers, Part 3, Series D, Reel 5, Frames 636–40.
129. Robert van Gelder, "Robeson Remembers," *New York Times*, 16 January 1944.
130. Stanislavsky, 49.
131. Constantin Stanislavsky, *Building a Character* (New York: Routledge, 1949), 73.
132. Stark Young, "Othello," *The New Republic*, 1 November 1943, 622.
133. "No 'Othello' Jimcro for Paul Robeson," *People's Voice*, 8 July 1944.
134. Marvel Cooke, "Headlines and Footlights," *People's Voice*, 15 July 1944.
135. Uta Hagen, interview by St. Clair Bourne.
136. Paul Robeson, "Here's My Story," *Freedom* 1 (September 1951).
137. "Robeson to Play Shakespearean Role at Rally for Ben Davis, Jr.," Paul Robeson Collection, Manuscript Division, Moorland-Spingarn Research Center, Howard University, Washington DC.
138. Alexander Baron, "Actors Are Citizens," *New Theatre* 5 (April 1949): 2–3.
139. Foner, 151.
140. Mela Underwood, "Joe and Uta," *Collier's*, 20 May 1944, 21.
141. Fredi Washington, "Fredi Says," *People's Voice*, 25 August 1945; "End of Race Hate Held Vital to UN," *New York Times*, 13 April 1946.
142. "Robeson Tells Artists Socialism Is Here," *People's Voice*, 12 January 1946.
143. Barranger, 155.
144. Margaret Webster, "Plea for a Rebirth of the Theatre," *New York Times*, 25 November 1945.
145. Richard Hays, "Paul Robeson Acclaimed in Drama at Met," *Seattle Times*, 26 December 1944.
146. Hutchens, 585.
147. V. Rogov, "Othello in the American Theatre," *Literatura I Iskustvo*, 2 September 1944. Translation in Margaret Webster Papers, Manuscript Division, Library of Congress, Washington DC.
148. Paul Robeson, "Preface for *Ira Aldridge* for Shevchencko Anniversary," Paul Robeson Collection, Manuscript Division, Moorland-Spingarn Research Center, Howard University, Washington DC.

Chapter Five

1. Zora Neale Hurston, "Characteristics of Negro Expression," in *African American Literary Theory*, ed. Winston Napier (New York: New York University Press, 2000), 31.
2. *New Africa* 2 (November 1943): 2.
3. Paul Robeson, "American Negroes in the War: Address Delivered by Paul Robeson at the New York Herald Tribune Forum on Current Problems November 16, 1943," distributed by the Anti-Discrimination Committee of the Indiana State CIO.
4. Langston Hughes, "The Negro Artist and the Racial Mountain," in *African American Literary Theory*, ed. Winston Napier (New York: New York University Press, 2000), 30.
5. W. E. B. Du Bois, "Criteria of Negro Art," in *African American Literary Theory*, ed. Winston Napier, 23.
6. Michael Denning, *The Cultural Front* (New York: Verso, 1996), 115.
7. Joe Bostic, "Encores I'd Enjoy Immensely," *People's Voice*, 31 March 1945.
8. *New York Times*, 18 August 1940.
9. "Concert and Opera Asides," *New York Times*, 17 January 1943.
10. Denning, 132.
11. *People's Voice*, 22 May 1943.
12. "Wallace Assures Russia Priority," *New York Times*, 9 November 1942; Paul and Eslanda Robeson F.B.I. File, report dated 8 December 1942; "'I am anti-fascist'—Robeson," *People's Voice*, 14 November 1942.
13. Foner, 123.
14. "Manhattan Vignettes," *Wall Street Journal*, 25 September 1942.
15. *New York Times*, 6 September 1942.
16. Nell Dodson, "Corny Direction Aids 'Tom' in Protest Film," *People's Voice*, 3 October 1942.
17. Wendell Green, "No More Hollywood—Robeson," in microfilm edition of Claude A. Barnett Papers, Part 3, Series D, Reel 5, Frame 549.
18. "Robeson Hits Hollywood," *New York Times*, 23 September 1942.
19. Nell Dodson, "Corny Direction Aids 'Tom' in Protest Film."
20. "Question of the Week," *People's Voice*, 14 February 1942.
21. "Double Victory Rally Backs Ben Davis Jr.," *New York Amsterdam News*, 30 October 1943.
22. W. E. B. Du Bois, "Closing Ranks Again," *New York Amsterdam News*, 14 February 1942; W. E. B. Du Bois, "The Negro and the War," *New York Amsterdam News*, 9 May 1942.
23. Amiri Baraka, "Paul Robeson" (paper delivered at the International Conference on Paul Robeson: His History and Development as an Intellectual, Lafayette College, Easton, PA, 2005), 25.
24. Foner, 151.
25. "Cox Retracts Admissions' on Betting, Gets New Hearing Before Landis Today," *New York Times*, 4 December 1943.
26. "A Tribute to Paul Robeson," souvenir program dated 23 January 1945, Paul Robeson Collection, Manuscript Division, Moorland-Spingarn Research Center, Howard University, Washington DC.
27. Souvenir program dated 24 February 1945, Paul Robeson Collection, Manuscript Division, Moorland-Spingarn Research Center, Howard University, Washington DC.

28. *Chicago Defender*, 21 April 1945.

29. "Robeson to Solo on Overseas Tour," *People's Voice*, 23 June 1945; "Robeson Breaks USO Color Rule," *People's Voice*, 4 August 1945.

30. Robert Dillner, "Robeson Troupe Scores Smash at Ingolstadt," *Ninth Division News* (Ingolstadt, Germany), 25 August 1945.

31. Frank Godden, "GI's in Paris Inspired as Robeson Sings, Talks," in microfilm edition of Claude A. Barnett Papers, Part 3, Series D, Reel 5, Frame 551.

32. "Paul Robeson Tenth to Win Lincoln Award," *People's Voice*, 20 February 1943.

33. "Paul Robeson Gets Hamilton Degree," *New York Times*, 22 January 1940.

34. "You Truly Are the People's Artist," reprinted in *Freedom* 5 (April 1955).

35. *Pittsburgh Courier*, 17 October 1944; *People's Voice*, 12 May and 20 October 1945; "Field Lauds Negro Achievement in Presenting Spingarn Award to Robeson," in microfilm edition of Claude A. Barnett Papers, Part 3, Series D, Reel 5, Frame 550.

36. Duberman, 301.

37. Robert Alan, "Paul Robeson: The Lost Shepard," *Crisis* 58 (November 1951): 569–73; Roy Wilkins, "Robeson Speaks for Robeson," *Crisis* 56 (May 1949): 137; Walter White, "The Strange Case of Paul Robeson," *Ebony* (February 1951).

38. Joe Powers and Mark Rogovin, "Paul Robeson Rediscovered: An Annotated Listing of His Chicago History from 1921–1958" (Chicago: Columbia College Chicago Paul Robeson 110th Birthday Committee, 2000), 15.

39. Russell McLaughlin, "Big Audience Attends Paul Robeson's Recital," *Detroit News*, 1 February 1943.

40. *People's Voice*, 5 January and 12 January 1946.

41. *Daily Worker*, 5 June 1946.

42. "Oppression of Negroes in South Africa," *New York Post*, 4 June 1946.

43. *PM*, 15 May 1946; *New York Herald Tribune*, 5 June 1946; *New York Times*, 3 June 1946; *New York Post*, 4 June 1946.

44. Paul Robeson, "Address by Paul Robeson Madison Square Garden Rally, June 6th," Paul Robeson Collection, Schomburg Center for Research in Black Culture, New York Public Library, New York.

45. "Williams Alleges 'Terrorism' in South," *New York Times*, 19 September 1946.

46. *New York Times*, 23–24 September 1946; Foner, 174–76, 528.

47. *Chicago Defender*, 28 September 1946; Foner, 529.

48. "Robeson to Leave Stage," *New York Times*, 27 January 1947.

49. Jack Goodman, "Robeson Quits Formal Concert Field," *New York Times*, 16 March 1947.

50. Paul Robeson, "Speech of Paul Robeson at Rally of Council on African Affairs, Friday, April 25th, 1947," Paul Robeson Collection, Schomburg Center for Research in Black Culture, New York Public Library, New York.

51. *Honolulu Observer*, 12 March 1948.

52. "Paul Robeson Thrills Panamanians," *People's Voice*, 28 June 1948.

53. W. E. B. Du Bois, "Du Bois Asks: What Is Wrong With the United States?" *National Guardian*, 9 May 1955.

54. News release from the Council on African Affairs dated 11 May 1949, Matt N. and Evelyn Graves Crawford Papers, Manuscript, Archives, and Rare Book Library, Emory University, Atlanta, Georgia.

55. *New York Times*, 21 April 1949.

56. Speech made by Paul Robeson at the Congress of the World Partisans of Peace translated from French by W. W. Smith, Paul Robeson Collection, Manuscript Division, Moorland-Spingarn Research Center, Howard University, Washington DC.
57. "Robeson Assails Stettinius," *New York Times*, 21 April 1949.
58. Duberman, 341–42.
59. David L. Lewis, *W. E. B. Du Bois: The Fight for Equality and the American Century 1919–1963* (New York: Henry Holt and Company, 2000), 544–45.
60. "Robeson as Speaker for Negroes Denied," *New York Times*, 25 April 1949.
61. Wilkins, "Robeson Speaks for Robeson," 137.
62. "Negroes and Whites Hit Robeson's 'Negro Won't Fight Russia' Talk," in microfilm edition of Claude A. Barnett Papers, Part 3, Series D, Reel 5, Frames 559–60.
63. Walter White, "A Reaction to Robeson," *New York Tribune*, 1 May 1949.
64. *New York Times*, 9 and 19 July 1949.
65. *Daily Worker*, 11 and 19 July 1949.
66. Reprinted in *Daily Worker*, 14 July 1949.
67. Jackie Robinson with Alfred Duckett, *I Never Had It Made* (New York: G. P. Putnam and Sons, 1972), 96.
68. Paul Robeson, "For Freedom and Peace" (New York: Council on African Affairs, 1949), 13–14.
69. Louise Thompson Patterson, "Paul Robeson," Louise Thompson Patterson Papers, Manuscript, Archives, and Rare Book Library, Emory University, Atlanta, Georgia. Other firsthand accounts consulted: "Eyewitness to Peekskill, USA" (White Plains, NY: Westchester, NY, Westchester Committee for a Fair Inquiry into the Peekskill Violence, October 1949); Howard Fast, *Peekskill, USA: A Personal Experience* (New York: Civil Rights Congress, 1951).
70. Howard Fast, "Howard Fast's Eyewitness Account of Fascist Mob's Attack," *Daily Worker*, 30 August 1949.
71. Joseph North, "Lynch Mob Runs Amok at Robeson Concert," *Daily Worker*, 28 August 1949.
72. "Turning Point to Robeson," *New York Times*, 31 August 1949; "Robeson to Sing in Peekskill This Sunday," *Daily Worker*, 2 September 1949.
73. "25,000 Hear Robeson at Peekskill," *Daily Worker*, 5 September 1949.
74. Thompson Patterson, 4; "Cops Help Peekskill Mob Attack on Homegoing Busses and Cars," *Daily Worker*, 6 September 1949.
75. Paul Robeson, "My Answer," reprinted in "Eyewitness to Peekskill."
76. Thompson Patterson, 5–7.
77. "6000 Jam Church, Crowd Street to Hear Robeson Speak, Sing in Chicago," in microfilm edition of Claude A. Barnett Papers, Part 3, Series D, Reel 5, Frame 577.
78. Thompson Patterson, 8.

Chapter Six

1. Paul Robeson, "Here's My Story," *Freedom* 2 (April 1952): 5.
2. John Pittman, "Mr. Freedom, Himself," *The Worker Magazine*, 15 April 1951.

3. Paul Robeson, "Statement by Paul Robeson, March 3, 1954," Paul Robeson Collection, Schomburg Center for Research in Black Culture, New York Public Library, New York.

4. W. A. Hunton, "The Council on African Affairs Answers Attorney General Brownell," Matt N. and Evelyn Graves Crawford Papers, Manuscript, Archives, and Rare Book Library, Emory University, Atlanta, Georgia.

5. *Spotlight on Africa* 12 (January 1953): 1; *Spotlight on Africa* 12 (December 1953): 1; *Spotlight on Africa* 14 (January 1955): 10.

6. "African Affairs Council Dissolves," *Daily Worker*, 20 June 1955.

7. Hollis Lynch, "Black American Radicals and the Liberation of Africa: The Council on African Affairs 1937–1955," (Ithaca, NY: Africana Studies and Research Center, 1978), 52.

8. "Paul Robeson Birthday Concert Tour," *Freedom* 2 (May 1952): 6. For example: *New York Times*, 26 April 1952; *The Voice* (San Francisco), 23 May 1952; *San Francisco Examiner*, 22 May 1952; *Denver Post*, 4 May 1952; *Milwaukee Sentinel*, 30 May 1952; *Cleveland Plain Dealer*, 7 May 1952.

9. Flyer in Paul Robeson Collection, Schomburg Center for Research in Black Culture, New York Public Library, New York.

10. "The Paul Robeson 1954 Tour," Paul Robeson Collection, Schomburg Center for Research in Black Culture, New York Public Library, New York.

11. *Freedom* 1 (March 1951): 1; *Freedom* 1 (September 1951): 1; *Freedom* 2 (May 1952): 1.

12. *Freedom* 2 (June 1952): 1.

13. *Freedom* 3 (May 1953).

14. *Pittsburgh Courier*, 19 April 1958.

15. Paul Robeson, *Here I Stand*, chapter one.

16. Foner, 40.

17. *Pittsburgh Courier*, 9 March 1957.

18. "What Makes Him Tick?: Paul Robeson," *Afro-American*, 8 March 1958.

19. W. E. B. Du Bois, *In Battle for Peace* (New York: Masses and Mainstream, 1952), 179.

20. *Freedom* 2 (December 1952): 8.

21. Duberman, 409.

22. Robeson, *Here I Stand*, 3–4.

23. Paul and Eslanda Robeson FBI File, reports dated 6 February and 20 June 1958.

24. Saunders Redding, "Book Review," *Afro-American*, 15 March 1958.

25. Benjamin Davis, "A Great Man Writes a Great Book," *Sunday Worker*, 6 April 1958; Philip Bonosky, "The Education of Paul Robeson," *Sunday Worker*, 4 May 1958.

26. *Sunday Worker*, 16 March 1958.

27. *Sunday Worker*, 6 and 20 April 1958.

28. *Pittsburgh Courier*, 3 May 1958.

29. "Robeson Files Suit Against Secretary of State Acheson for Return of Passport," in microfilm edition of Claude A. Barnett Papers, Part 3, Series D, Reel 5, Frame 583.

30. Luther Huston, "Passport Cases Irk Government," *New York Times*, 1 January 1956.

31. State Department press release dated 24 May 1952, in microfilm edition of Claude A. Barnett Papers, Part 3, Series D, Reel 5, Frames 601–603.

32. "Fact Sheet on the Paul Robeson Passport Case," Paul Robeson Collection, Manuscript Division, Moorland-Spingarn Research Center, Howard University, Washington DC.

33. Robeson, *Here I Stand*, 63.

34. Ibid., 64–69.

35. Ibid., 71.

36. Lloyd Brown, "Lift Every Voice for Paul Robeson" (New York: Freedom Associates, 1951), 12–13.

37. Paul Robeson, "The Real Issues Behind the Denial of Robeson's Passport," *Daily Worker*, 17 October 1955.

38. *Daily Worker*, 19 April 1955.

39. *Spotlight on Africa* 14 (April 1955): 18.

40. Robeson, *Here I Stand*, 46.

41. Worcester, 144.

42. Ibid., 55.

43. C. L. R. James, *Mariners, Renegades and Castaways: The Story of Herman Melville and the World We Live In* (Hanover, NH: University Press of New England, 2001), 145.

44. Ibid., 138.

45. Ibid., 157.

46. Ibid., 158.

47. John Pittman, "Mr. Freedom, Himself," *The Worker Magazine*, 15 April 1951.

48. William Patterson, ed., *We Charge Genocide: The Crimes of Government Against the Negro People* (New York: International Publishers, 1971), xiv.

49. Brenda Gayle Plummer, *Rising Wind: Black Americans and U.S. Foreign Affairs 1935–1960* (Chapel Hill: University of North Carolina Press, 1996), 202–203.

50. Patterson, xvi.

51. *Freedom* 2 (February 1952).

52. "Patterson, Robeson Hit Effort to Cripple Defense Organizations," *Daily Worker*, 28 February 1955.

53. "Dissolution Voted by Civil Rights Congress," *Daily Worker*, 9 January 1956.

54. *Freedom* 2 (March 1952): 1.

55. Paul and Eslanda Robeson FBI File, report dated 22 January 1952.

56. "Robeson Show Jams Border Traffic," *Vancouver Sun*, 19 May 1952.

57. "Robeson Heckled at Peace Arch Concert," *Vancouver Sun*, 17 August 1953.

58. *Paul Robeson: The Peace Arch Concerts* (Naperville, IL: Folk Era Records, 1998).

59. Charlotte Pomerantz, ed., *A Quarter Century of Unamericana* (New York: Marzani and Munsell, Inc., 1963), 74.

60. Foner, 432.

61. Ibid., 427, 421.

62. Ibid., 416, 436.

63. Ibid., 433.

64. "Un-Americans Cite Robeson as He Blasts Racism," *Daily Worker*, 13 June 1956.

65. "40,000 Hear Robeson Sing," *People's World*, 20 May 1952.

66. *Freedom* 5 (May–June 1955): 1.

67. *Daily Worker*, 10 January 1955.

68. *Daily Worker*, 13 May 1955.

69. Tim Shopen, "Paul Robeson Sings, Talks, Acts; Sees Peace Basis in Culture," *Swarthmore Phoenix*, 3 May 1955.

70. *Daily Worker*, 18 August 1955.

71. Harold Schonberg, "Paul Robeson Sings, Lectures in First City Recital in 11 Years," *New York Times*, 10 May 1958.

72. Joseph North, "Robeson Triumphs Here," *Sunday Worker*, 18 May 1958.

73. *Paul Robeson Live at Carnegie Hall: The Historic May 9, 1958 Concert* (Santa Monica: Vanguard Records, 1987).

74. *Pittsburgh Courier*, 31 May 1958.

75. Kate Baldwin, *Beyond the Color Line and the Iron Curtain: Reading Encounters Between Black and Red 1922–1963* (Durham: Duke University Press, 2002), 308.

76. Harold Keith, "Paul Robeson States His Case," *Pittsburgh Courier*, 22 February 1958.

Chapter Seven

1. "100th Season Quells Once and For All the Cry 'Ridiculous,'" *Stratford-upon-Avon Herald*, 3 April 1959.

2. Stephen Watts, "Stratford Fete," *New York Times*, 29 March 1959.

3. Don Cook, "Robeson's Othello at the Home Park," Paul Robeson Collection, Manuscript Division, Moorland-Spingarn Research Center, Howard University, Washington DC.

4. Cedric Belfrage, "The Spectator: Robeson at Stratford," *National Guardian*, 20 April 1959.

5. *Daily Worker* (NY), 21 November 1955 and 22 February 1956.

6. *Daily Worker* (NY), 6 June 1956.

7. *Daily Worker* (NY), 16 February 1956.

8. *Reynolds News* (London), 26 May 1957; *Daily Worker* (London), 29 May 1957.

9. "A Welcome for Paul," *Birmingham Evening Dispatch*, 16 March 1959.

10. Eslanda Robeson, undated letter to Claudia Jones, Claudia Jones Memorial Collection, Schomburg Center for Research in Black Culture, New York Public Library, New York.

11. Quoted in Duberman, 475.

12. "Robeson Aims at Middlebrow," *Auckland Star* (New Zealand), 17 October 1960.

13. John Williamson, "London Gives Hero's Welcome to Paul Robeson," *The Worker* (Sunday), 20 July 1958.

14. Cedric Belfrage and James Aronson, *Something to Guard: The Stormy Life of the National Guardian* (New York: Columbia University Press, 1978), 234 and 240.

15. Eslanda Robeson, "Paul Robeson Sings at St. Paul's Cathedral," in microfilm edition of Claude A. Barnett Papers, Part 3, Series D, Reel 5, Frames 491–92.

16. "Fans Mob Robeson Outside St. Paul's," *Daily Mail*, 13 October 1958.

17. Tony Richardson, *The Long Distance Runner: An Autobiography* (New York: William Morrow Co., 1993), 129.

18. Ibid., 129–30.

19. "Promptbook from *Othello*, 1959, Shakespeare Memorial Theatre," Shakespeare Centre Library, Stratford-upon-Avon, U.K.

20. M. St. Clare Byrne, "The Shakespeare Season at the Old Vic, 1958–59 and Stratford-upon-Avon, 1959," *Shakespeare Quarterly* 10 (Autumn 1959): 553.

21. Clippings in microfilm edition of Claude A. Barnett Papers, Part 3, Series D, Reel 5, Frame 691.

22. Program from *Othello*, Shakespeare Memorial Theatre, 1959, Shakespeare Centre Library, Stratford-upon-Avon, U.K.

23. W. A. Darlington, "Robeson's Performance in 'Othello' is Hailed by Stratford Playgoers," *New York Times*, 12 April 1959.

24. "Sensitive 'Othello' by Paul Robeson at Stratford Centenary," *Wolverhampton Express and Star*, 8 April 1959.

25. "A First 'First Night' on the Spur of the Moment," *Warwickshire Advertiser*, 10 April 1959.

26. *Birmingham Mail*, 8 April 1959.

27. "Robeson as the Moor Dominates the Show," *Daily Worker* (London), 9 April 1959.

28. "Hundredth Festival," *Leamington Spa Courier*, 10 April 1959.

29. "'Othello' Curtain Calls," Shakespeare Centre Library, Stratford-upon-Avon, U.K.

30. *Daily Mirror*, 8 April 1959.

31. Telegrams in Paul Robeson Collection, Manuscript Division, Moorland-Spingarn Research Center, Howard University, Washington DC.

32. "The Century at Stratford," *Daily Express*, 8 April 1959.

33. "'Happy Birthday' for Robeson on Greatest Night of Career," *Stratford-upon-Avon Herald*, 10 April 1959.

34. Mervyn Jones, "Robeson the Great," Paul Robeson Collection, Manuscript Division, Moorland-Spingarn Research Center, Howard University, Washington DC.

35. Edmund Gardner, "A Mighty Spectacle but Not a Truly Great Production," *Stratford-upon-Avon Herald*, 10 April 1959.

36. Charles Graves, "Paul Robeson's Othello Mature and Noble," *Scotsman*, 9 April 1959.

37. W. A. Darlington, "Two U.S. Actors Star on British Stage," *New York Times*, 8 April 1959.

38. Felix Barker, "Robeson Kills an Illusion," *Daily Herald*, 8 April 1959.

39. J. C. Trewin, "'Othello' at Stratford," *Birmingham Post*, 8 April 1959.

40. "The Othello of a Lifetime," *Birmingham Mail*, 8 April 1959.

41. "This 'Othello' a Personal Triumph for Paul Robeson," *Coventry Evening Telegraph*, 8 April 1959.

42. "Paul Robeson's Majestic Moor," *Evesham Journal*, 10 April 1959.

43. Cecil Wilson, "A Hell for Leather Othello," Paul Robeson Collection, Manuscript Division, Moorland-Spingarn Research Center, Howard University, Washington DC.

44. Mike Myson, "'Wonder Great as My Content,'" *Daily Worker* (London), 13 April 1959.

45. Shirley Graham, "Praise Heaped on Robeson for London 'Othello' Role," *Pittsburgh Courier*, 20 June 1959.

46. "Othello by Candlelight," *The Statesman*, 18 April 1959.

47. Byrne, 552.

48. Neville Miller, "A Miracle of Mechanics," *South Wales Argus*, 9 April 1959.

49. Mike Myson, "Robeson's So Welcome Return to 'Othello,'" *Daily Worker* (London), 6 April 1959.

50. Anthony Carthew, "Robeson Has Sell-Out for 'Othello,'" *Daily Herald*, 4 April 1959.

51. Don Cook, "Robeson's Othello at the Home Park," Paul Robeson Collection, Manuscript Division, Moorland-Spingarn Research Center, Howard University, Washington DC.

52. Quoted in Baldwin, 303.

53. W. Alphaeus Hunton, "Press Release on Stratford Othello," Paul Robeson Collection, Manuscript Division, Moorland-Spingarn Research Center, Howard University, Washington DC.

54. Anthony Carthew, "Robeson Best 'Othello' I've Seen," Paul Robeson Collection, Manuscript Division, Moorland-Spingarn Research Center, Howard University, Washington DC.

55. Philip Hope-Wallace, "Paul Robeson's Othello at Stratford," *Manchester Guardian*, 9 April 1959; "Paul Robeson's Moving Othello at Stratford, *The Stage and Television Today*, 9 April 1959; Michael Mac Llammoir, "Shakespeare, Ibsen and Ibsen," *Observer* (London), 12 April 1959.

56. "Miscasting Handicaps Robeson's Othello," *London Times*, 8 April 1959.

57. Charles Graves, "Paul Robeson's Othello Mature and Noble," *Scotsman*, 9 April 1959.

58. Sally Beauman, *The Royal Shakespeare Company: A History of Ten Decades* (Oxford: Oxford University Press, 1982), 232.

59. "Paul Robeson Gives Superb Performance of Othello," *Glasgow Herald*, 9 April 1959.

60. "Robeson's 'Othello' Stands Alone Triumphantly Alone," *Leamington Spa Courier*, 10 April 1959; "'Othello' at Stratford," *Berrows Worcester Journal*, 10 April 1959.

61. Mike Myson, "Moor of Great Magic," *Daily Worker* (London), 8 April 1959.

62. John Thompson, "Othello Finds an Al Capone Villain," Paul Robeson Collection, Manuscript Division, Moorland-Spingarn Research Center, Howard University, Washington DC.

63. "Paul Robeson Is a Moving Othello," *Warwickshire Advertiser*, 10 April 1959.

64. "'Othello': Music Cues Rehearsal," Shakespeare Centre Library, Stratford-upon-Avon, U.K.

65. Norman Holbrook, "Robeson Rescue That Nearly Came Off," *Evening Dispatch*, 8 April 1959.

66. Christine Cartwright, "Othello Shocks the Purists," *The Mercury*, 12 April 1959.

67. Desmond Pratt, "Centenary 'Othello' Triumph for Director," *Yorkshire Post*, 9 April 1959.

68. Peter Rodford, "Robeson at Stratford," *Western Daily Press* (Bristol), 9 April 1959.

69. "This 'Othello' a Personal Triumph for Paul Robeson," *Coventry Evening Telegraph*, 8 April 1959.

70. Michael Hand, "Robeson's Othello," *Oxford Mail*, 8 April 1959.

71. J. C. Trewin, "'Othello' at Stratford," *Birmingham Post*, 8 April 1959.

216 NOTES

72. "Sensitive 'Othello' by Paul Robeson at Stratford Centenary," *Wolverhampton Express and Star*, 8 April 1959.

73. Byrne, 552.

74. Richardson, 130.

75. Cecil Wilson, "A Hell for Leather Othello."

76. "Robeson Returns in Othello," *Chicago Defender*, 8 April 1959.

77. "Paul Robeson Wows England as 'Othello,'" *Pittsburgh Courier*, 18 April 1959; "Robeson Acclaimed," *Afro-American*, 18 April 1959.

78. W. E. B. Du Bois, *The Autobiography of W. E. B. Du Bois* (New York: International Publishers, 1968), 11, 409.

79. W. Alpaeus Hunton, "Press Release on Stratford Othello."

80. Shirley Graham, "Praise Heaped on Robeson for London 'Othello' Role," *Pittsburgh Courier*, 20 June 1959.

81. "Robeson Gets Great Welcome," *Daily Worker* (London), 20 April 1959.

82. "Rally Assails H-Bomb," *New York Times*, 29 June 1959.

83. *New York Times*, 2, 4, 10 August 1959.

84. Eslanda Robeson, letter to Claude Barnett dated 13 October 1959 in microfilm edition of Claude A. Barnett Papers, Part 3, Series D, Reel 5, Frame 497.

85. Eslanda Robeson, letter to Claude Barnett dated 2 December 1959 in microfilm edition of Claude A. Barnett Papers, Part 3, Series D, Reel 5, Frame 500.

86. Eslanda Robeson, letter to Claude Barnett dated 24 October 1959 in microfilm edition of Claude A. Barnett Papers, Part 3, Series D, Reel 5, Frame 498.

87. Eslanda Robeson, undated letter to Claudia Jones, Claudia Jones Memorial Collection.

88. "The Paul Robeson Charm Remains," *Liverpool Daily Post*, 11 May 1960.

89. Ernest Bradbury, "Paul Robeson's Recital Varied and Memorable," *Yorkshire Post*, 29 April 1959.

90. "Robeson Returns to Thrill Again," *The Journal* (Newcastle, U.K.), 15 March 1960.

91. Owen Jensen, "He Transcends the Rules: Paul Robeson is a Truly Great Artist," *Evening Post* (Wellington, NZ), 21 October 1960.

92. "Robeson's Political Creedo: Marx Still Suits Him," *New Zealand Herald* (Auckland), 18 October 1960.

93. "Ol' Man River," *The West Australian*, 3 December 1960.

94. "Opera House to 'Open' for Paul," *Daily Telegraph* (Sydney), 9 November 1960.

95. "Ol' Man River Triumphed," *New Zealand Herald* (Auckland), 19 October 1960.

96. Russell Bond, "Captivated by Paul Robeson," *The Dominion* (Wellington, NZ), 21 October 1960.

97. Anthony Carthew, "Robeson Has Sell-Out for Othello," *Daily Herald* (London), 4 April 1959.

98. Bob Leeson, "'I'll Be There' Pledge by Robeson," *Daily Worker* (London), 14 January 1960.

99. Shirley Graham, "Praise Heaped on Robeson for London 'Othello' Role," *Pittsburgh Courier*, 20 June 1959.

100. W. E. B. Du Bois, *The Souls of Black Folk*, 284.

Conclusion

1. Michael Thelwell, "The August 28th March on Washington: The Castrated Giant," in *Duties, Pleasures, and Conflicts: Essays in Struggle* (Amherst: University of Massachusetts Press, 1987).

2. Lewis, 570.

3. Eslanda Robeson, "The March on Washington from a Distance," in microfilm edition of Claude A. Barnett Papers, Part 3, Series D, Reel 5, Frames 508–14.

4. Peter Kihss, "Robeson Ends Self Exile," *New York Times*, 23 December 1963; Earl G. Talbott, "Robeson Ends U.S. Exile," *Detroit News*, 23 December 1963.

5. *New York Times*, 23 December 1963.

6. "Welcome Home, Paul Robeson," *Freedomways* 4 (Winter 1964): 7.

7. Paul Robeson, "'Thank God Almighty, We're Moving,'" *Afro-American*, 5 September 1964.

8. *Daily Worker* (London), 26 April 1965; *Amsterdam News*, 1 May 1965; *Afro-American*, 8 May 1965.

9. "Mr. Paul Robeson: Welcome Home," *Liberator* 5 (June 1965): 4.

10. Duberman 528.

11. Speech reprinted in: The Editors of *Freedomways*, *Paul Robeson: The Great Forerunner* (New York: International Publishers, 1998), 292–95.

12. Doug Archer, "2000 Hail Paul Robeson at Freedomways Tribute," *The Worker* (Sunday), 2 May 1965.

SOURCES

Primary Sources

MANUSCRIPT COLLECTIONS

Claude A. Barnett Papers (Associated Negro Press), microfilm edition (Frederick, MD: University Publications of America, 1984)
Lawrence Brown Papers, microfilm edition, Schomburg Center for Research in Black Culture, New York Public Library, New York, NY
Matt N. and Evelyn Graves Crawford Papers, Manuscript, Archives and Rare Book Library, Emory University, Atlanta, GA
Shirley Graham Du Bois Papers, Schlesinger Library, Radcliffe Institute, Harvard University, Cambridge, MA
Claudia Jones Memorial Collection, Manuscripts, Archives and Rare Book Division, Schomburg Center for Research in Black Culture, New York Public Library, New York, NY
Helen Armstead Johnson Miscellaneous Theater Collection, Manuscripts, Archives and Rare Book Division, Schomburg Center for Research in Black Culture, New York Public Library, New York, NY
Louise Thompson Patterson Papers, Manuscript, Archives and Rare Book Library, Emory University, Atlanta, GA
Promptbook Collection, microfilm edition, Folger Shakespeare Library, Washington DC
Paul and Eslanda Robeson Collections, Manuscript Division, Moorland-Spingarn Research Center, Howard University, Washington DC
Paul and Eslanda Robeson FBI File, electronic edition, Federal Bureau of Investigation Online Reading Room
Paul Robeson Collection, microfilm edition, Schomburg Center for Research in Black Culture, New York Public Library, New York, NY
Royal Shakespeare Company Archive, Shakespeare Birthplace Trust, Shakespeare Centre Library and Archive, Stratford-upon-Avon, U.K.
Margaret Webster Papers, Manuscript Division, Library of Congress, Washington DC

SOURCES

NEWSPAPERS AND PERIODICALS

Afro-American (Baltimore), 1930–65
Amsterdam News (New York), 1925–30, 1940–59
Courier (Pittsburgh), 1925–59
Crisis (New York), 1900–12, 1930–32, 1949–55
Daily Herald (London), 1925–36, 1958–60
Daily Mail (London), 1925–30, 1936, 1958–60
Daily Worker (New York), 1940–60
Defender (Chicago), 1930–59
Freedom, 1951–55
Freedomways, 1961–70
The Keys (London), 1935–38
New Africa, 1943–50
People's Voice (New York), 1942–48
Spotlight on Africa, 1952–55
Sunday Worker (New York), 1940–60
The Times (London), 1925–30, 1936, 1958–60
The Times (New York), 1919–76
Wall Street Journal, 1925–30, 1942–59

BOOKS, ARTICLES, PAMPHLETS

"Eyewitness: Peekskill USA." White Plains, NY: The Westchester Committee for a Fair Inquiry into the Peekskill Violence, 1949.
"Freedom's Fight Is Now." New York: Civil Rights Congress, 1946.
"Let Freedom Ring: National Conference 1947." Chicago: Civil Rights Congress, 1947.
"Lynching Northern Style." New York: Civil Rights Congress Committee to Free the Trenton Six, 1948.
"The Negro Question: Outline and Study Guide for Five Session Course." New York: New York State Communist Party, 1949.
"Petition to Oust Bilbo." New York: Civil Rights Congress, 1946.
"Petition to the President of the United States." New York: Civil Rights Congress, 1946.
"A Report on the Conference for Free Expression in the American Arts." New York: National Negro Congress, 1947.
"Wallace, Robeson Banned: Stem the Attack on Free Speech and Art." New York: Civil Rights Congress, 1947.
Adams, John Quincy. "Misconceptions of Shakespeare upon the Stage." In *Notes, Criticism and Correspondence Upon Shakespeare's Plays and Actors*, edited by James Henry Hackett. New York: Carleton, 1863.
Belcher, Fannin S., Jr. "The Negro Theater: A Glance Backward." *Phylon* 2 (Second Quarter 1950): 121–26.
Brown, Lloyd. "Lift Every Voice for Paul Robeson." New York: Freedom Associates, 1951.
Bruce, John E. *Was Othello a Negro?* New York City: privately printed, 1920.

Cox, Oliver. "The New Crisis in Negro Leadership Among Leaders." *Journal of Negro Education* 19 (1950): 459–65.

Douglas, Carlyle. "Paul Robeson: Farewell to a Fighter." *Ebony*, April 1976, 33–42.

Du Bois, W. E. B. *The Autobiography of W. E. B. Du Bois*. New York: International Publishers, 1968.

———. "A Chronicle of Race Relations." *Phylon* 3 (Fourth Quarter 1942): 417–34.

———. *Dusk of Dawn: An Essay toward an Autobiography of a Race Concept*. New York: Schocken Books, 1968.

———. *The Gift of Black Folk*. Edited by Herbert Aptheker. Milwood, NY: Kraus-Thomson Organization Limited, 1975.

———. *In Battle for Peace*. New York: Masses and Mainstream, 1952.

———. "The Real Reason Behind Robeson's Persecution." *National Guardian*, 7 April 1958.

———. *The Souls of Black Folk*. In *Three Negro Classics*, edited by John Hope Franklin. New York: Avon Books, 1965.

Gilder, Rosamond. "Broadway in Review." *Theatre Arts* (December 1943): 699–703.

Grant, George C. "The Negro in Dramatic Art." *The Journal of Negro History* 17, no. 1 (1932): 19–29.

Hunton, W. Alphaeus. *Decision in Africa*. New York: International Publishers, 1957.

Hutchens, John K. "Paul Robeson." *Theatre Arts* 28 (October 1944): 579–85.

Isaacs, Edith. "The Negro in the American Theatre: A Record of Achievement." *Theatre Arts* 26 (August 1942): 513.

Jefferson, Miles. "The Negro on Broadway—1944." *Phylon* 6 (First Quarter 1945): 42–52.

Locke, Alain, ed. *The New Negro*. New York: Touchstone, 1997.

Lovell, John. "Shakespeare's American Play." *Theatre Arts* 28 (June 1944).

Marshall, Margaret. "Drama." *The Nation*, 30 October 1943, 507–8.

Robeson, Eslanda. *African Journey*. New York: The John Day Co., 1945.

———. *Paul Robeson, Negro*. London: Victor Gollancz, 1930.

Robeson, Paul. "The Culture of the Negro." *The Spectator*, 15 June 1934.

———. *Forge Negro Labor Unity for Peace and Jobs*. New York: Harlem Trade Union Council, 1950.

———. *Here I Stand*. 2d ed. Boston: Beacon Press, 1988.

———. *The Negro People and the Soviet Union*. New York: New Century Publishers, 1950.

Sillen, Samuel. "No Borders for Art." *Masses and Mainstream* (June 1954): 4–5.

St. Clare Byrne, M. "The Shakespeare Season at the Old Vic, 1958–59 and Stratford-Upon-Avon, 1959." *Shakespeare Quarterly* 10 (Autumn 1959): 545–67.

Webster, Margaret. *Don't Put Your Daughter on the Stage*. New York: Alfred A. Knopf, 1972.

———. "Promptbook from Othello." Billy Rose Theater Collection, New York Public Library for the Performing Arts, New York, NY.

———. "Robeson and Othello." *Our Time* 3 (June 1944): 5.

———. *Shakespeare Today*. London: J. M. Dent and Sons Ltd., 1957.

———. *Shakespeare Without Tears*. New York: McGraw-Hill, 1942.

———. "Typescript from Othello at Sam Shubert Theater." Billy Rose Theater Collection, New York Public Library for the Performing Arts, New York, NY.

Winter, William. *Shakespeare on the Stage.* New York: Moffat, Yard and Company, 1911.
Yergan, Max. "A Petition to the United Nations on Behalf of 13 Million Oppressed Negro Citizens of the United States." New York: National Negro Congress, 1946.
Young, Stark. "Othello." *The New Republic* 109 (November 1943): 621–22.

Secondary Sources

BOOKS AND ARTICLES

Abrahams, Roger D. "Traditions of Eloquence in Afro-American Communities." *Journal of Interamerican Studies and World Affairs* 12 (October 1970): 505–27.
Alexander, Catherine M. S., and Stanley Wells, eds. *Shakespeare and Race.* Cambridge: Cambridge University Press, 2000.
Anthony, David Henry, III. *Max Yergan: Race Man, Internationalist, Cold Warrior.* New York: New York University Press, 2006.
Aptheker, Herbert, ed. *The Correspondence of W. E. B. Du Bois.* Vol. 3. Amherst, MA: University of Massachusetts Press, 1978.
Baldwin, James. *The Devil Finds Work.* New York: Dial Press, 1976.
Baldwin, Kate. *Beyond the Color Line and the Iron Curtain: Reading Encounters Between Black and Red 1922–1963.* Durham: Duke University Press, 2002.
Barranger, Milly S. *Margaret Webster: A Life in the Theater.* Ann Arbor: University of Michigan Press, 2004.
Beauman, Sally. *The Royal Shakespeare Company: A History of Ten Decades.* Oxford: Oxford University Press, 1982.
Belfrage, Cedric, and James Aronson. *Something to Guard: The Stormy Life of the National Guardian 1948–1967.* New York: Columbia University Press, 1978.
Billington, Michael. *Peggy Ashcroft.* London: John Murray Publishers Ltd., 1988.
Boulware, Marcus H. *The Oratory of Negro Leaders 1900–1968.* Westport, CT: Negro Universities Press, 1969.
Boxill, Bernard R. "Self-Respect." In *Blacks and Social Justice.* Lanham, MD: Rowman and Littlefield, 1992.
Boyle, Sheila Tully, and Andrew Bunie. *Paul Robeson: The Years of Promise and Achievement.* Amherst, MA: University of Massachusetts Press, 2001.
Breathett, George. "William Edward Burghardt Du Bois: An Address to the Black Academic Community." *Journal of Negro History* 60 (1975): 45–52.
Brotz, Howard. *Negro Social and Political Thought 1850–1920.* New York: Basic Books, 1966.
Brown, Lloyd. *The Young Paul Robeson: On My Journey Now.* Boulder, CO: Westview Press, 1997.
Buhle, Paul, ed. *C. L. R. James: His Life and Work.* New York: Allison and Busby, 1986.
Carby, Hazel. *Race Men.* Cambridge: Harvard University Press, 1998.
Carr, Robert. *The House Un-American Activities Committee.* New York: Octagon Books, 1979.
Cooper, Wayne. *Claude McKay: Rebel Sojourner in the Harlem Renaissance.* New York: Schocken Books, 1987.

Cottrell, John. *Laurence Olivier*. Englewood Cliffs, NJ: Prentice-Hall, Inc., 1975.
Curtis, Susan. *The First Black Actors on the Great White Way*. Columbia: University of Missouri Press, 1998.
Denning, Michael. *The Cultural Front: The Laboring of American Culture in the Twentieth Century*. New York: Verso, 1996.
Dent, Roberta Yancy, ed. *Paul Robeson Tributes and Selected Writings*. New York City: Paul Robeson, Archives, Inc., 1976.
Dorinson, Joseph, and William Pencak, eds. *Paul Robeson: Essays on His Life and Legacy*. Jefferson, NC: MacFarland and Co., 2002.
Draper, Theodore. *The Roots of American Communism*. Chicago: Ivan R. Dee, Inc., 1957.
———. *American Communism and Soviet Russia*. New York: Viking Press, 1960.
Duberman, Martin. *Paul Robeson: A Biography*. New York: Ballantine Books, 1989.
———. "Writing Robeson." In *Left Out: The Politics of Exclusion/Essays/1964–1999*. New York: Basic Books, 1999.
Dyer, Richard. *Heavenly Bodies: Film Stars and Society*. 2d ed. New York: Routledge, 2004.
The Editors of *Freedomways*. *Paul Robeson: The Great Forerunner*. New York: International Publishers, 1998.
Epps, Archie. "Olivier's Othello." *Harvard Journal of Negro Affairs* 1, no. 3 (1967): 1–11.
Foner, Philip S., ed. *Paul Robeson Speaks*. New York: Citadel Books, 2002.
Fraden, Rena. *Blueprints for a Black Federal Theater 1935–1939*. Cambridge: Cambridge University Press, 1994.
Grimshaw, Anna, ed. *The C. L. R. James Reader*. London: Blackwell Publishers, 1992.
———, ed. *Special Delivery: The Letters of C. L. R. James to Constance Webb 1939–1948*. London: Blackwell Publishers, 1996.
Habib, Imtiaz. *Shakespeare and Race*. New York: University Press of America, Inc., 2000.
Hill, Errol. *Shakespeare in Sable*. Amherst: University of Massachusetts Press, 1984.
———, ed. *The Theater of Black Americans: A Collection of Critical Essays*. New York: Applause, 1987.
Hill, Errol G., and James V. Hatch. *A History of African American Theatre*. Cambridge: Cambridge University Press, 2003.
Honneth, Axel. "Integrity and Disrespect: Principles of a Conception of Morality Based On a Theory of Recognition." In *The Fragmented World of the Social: Essays in Social and Political Philosophy*, edited by Charles W. Wright. Albany: State University of New York Press, 1995.
Horne, Gerald. *Black and Red: Du Bois and the African American Response to the Cold War*. Albany: State University of New York Press, 1986.
———. *Communist Front? The Civil Rights Congress 1946–1956*. London: Associated University Presses, 1988.
Hunton, Dorothy. *Alphaeus Hunton: The Unsung Valiant*. Privately printed, 1986.
Isserman, Maurice. *Which Side Were You On?: The American Communist Party During the Second World War*. Middletown, CT: Wesleyan University Press, 1982.
James, C. L. R. *Letters from London*. Port of Spain: Prospect Press, 2003.
———. *Mariners, Renegades and Castaways: The Story of Herman Melville and the World We Live In*. Reencounters with Colonialism: New Perspectives on the Americas. Hanover, NH: University Press of New England, 2001.

———. "'Othello" and "The Merchant of Venice."' In *Spheres of Existence: The Selected Writings of C. L. R. James*. London: Allison and Busby, 1980.

———. "Paul Robeson: Black Star." In *Spheres of Existence: The Selected Writings of C. L. R. James*. London: Allison and Busby, 1980.

Kaplan, Paul H. D. "The Earliest Images of Othello." *Shakespeare Quarterly* 39 (Summer 1988), 171–86.

Kaul, Mythili, ed. *Othello: New Essays by Black Writers*. Washington DC: Howard University Press, 1997.

Klehr, Harvey, and John Earl Haynes. *The American Communist Movement: Storming Heaven Itself*. New York: Twayne Publishers, 1992.

Kolin, Philip C., ed. *Shakespeare in the South*. Jackson: University Press of Mississippi, 1983.

Leab, Daniel J. "'All Colored' but Not Much Different: Films Made for Negro Ghetto Audiences 1913–1928." *Phylon* 36 (Third Quarter 1975): 321–39.

Levine, Lawrence. *The Unpredictable Past: Explorations in American Cultural History*. New York: Oxford University Press, 1993.

Lewis, David L. *W. E. B. Du Bois: The Fight for Equality and the American Century 1919–1963*. New York: Henry Holt and Company, 2000.

Loomba, Ania. *Shakespeare, Race and Colonialism*. Oxford: Oxford University Press, 2002.

Lynch, Hollis. *Black American Radicals and the Liberation of Africa: The Council on African Affairs 1937–1955*. Ithaca, NY: Africana Studies Center, 1978.

McCullough, Norman Verrle. *The Negro in English Literature*. Devon: Arthur H. Stockwell Ltd., 1962.

McKay, Claude. *A Long Way From Home*. New York: Harcourt, Brace and World, 1970.

Meriwether, James. *Proudly We Can Be Africans: Black Americans and Africa 1935–1961*. Chapel Hill: University of North Carolina Press, 2002.

Morley, Sheridan. *Sybil Thorndike: A Life in the Theater*. London: Wiedenfeld and Nicolson, 1977.

Naison, Mark. *Communists in Harlem During the Depression*. Chicago: University of Illinois Press, 1983.

Napier, Winston, ed. *African American Literary Theory*. New York: New York University Press, 2000.

Navasky, Victor. *Naming Names*. New York: Viking Press, 1980.

Nunez, Elizabeth. "Could Shakespeare Have Known." *Journal of Negro Education* 45 (Spring 1976): 192–96.

O'Connor, Garry. *The Secret Woman: A Life of Peggy Ashcroft*. London: Wiedenfeld and Nicolson, 1997.

O'Reilly, Kenneth. *Black Americans: The F.B.I. Files*. New York: Carroll and Graf Publishers, Inc., 1994.

———. *Hoover and the Un-Americans*. Philadelphia: Temple University Press, 1983.

———. *Racial Matters*. New York: Free Press, 1989.

Ottanelli, Fraser. *The Communist Party of the United States from the Depression to World War II*. New Brunswick: Rutgers University Press, 1991.

Patterson, William. *The Man Who Cried Genocide*. New York: International Publishers, 1971.

———. *We Charge Genocide*. 2d ed. New York: International Publishers, 1970.
Plummer, Brenda Gayle. *Rising Wind: Black Americans and U.S. Foreign Affairs 1935–1960*. Chapel Hill: University of North Carolina Press, 1996.
Pomerantz, Charlotte, ed. *A Quarter Century of Un-Americana*. New York: Marzani And Munsell, Inc., 1963.
Potter, Lois. *Othello*. In *Shakespeare in Performance*, edited by J. R. Mulryne and J. C. Bulman. Manchester University Press, 2002.
Richardson, Tony. *The Long Distance Runner: An Autobiography*. New York: William And Morrow Co., Inc., 1993.
Robeson, Paul, Jr. "Paul Robeson Jr. Refutes Misrepresentation." *Jewish Currents* (April 1983): 22–30.
———. *The Undiscovered Paul Robeson*. New York: John Wiley and Sons, Inc., 2001.
Robeson, Susan. *The Whole World in His Hands: A Pictorial Biography of Paul Robeson*. Secaucus, NJ: Citadel Press, 1981.
Robinson, Jackie, with Alfred Duckett. *I Never Had It Made*. New York: G. P. Putnam and Sons, 1972.
Rosenberg, Daniel. "Paul Robeson in the Era of Reaganism." *New World Review* 50 (July–August 1982): 20–30.
Rosenberg, Marvin. *The Masks of Othello*. Berkeley: University of California Press, 1961.
Seton, Marie. *Paul Robeson*. London: Dennis Dobson, 1958.
Shattuck, Charles. *Shakespeare on the American Stage from the Hallums to Edwin Booth*. Washington DC: Folger Shakespeare Library, 1976.
Smith, Ian. "Barbarian Errors: Performing Race in Early Modern England." *Shakespeare Quarterly* 49 (Summer 1998), 168–86.
Smith, Judith. *Visions of Belonging: Family Stories, Popular Culture, and Postwar Democracy 1940–1960*. New York: Columbia University Press, 2004.
Solomon, Mark. *The Cry Was Unity: Communists and African Americans, 1917–1936*. Jackson: University Press of Mississippi, 1998.
Spector, Susan. "Margaret Webster's 'Othello': The Principal Players Versus the Director." *Theatre History Studies* 6 (1986): 93–108.
Sprigge, Elizabeth. *Sybil Thorndike Casson*. London: Victor Gollancz Ltd., 1971.
Stanislavsky, Constantin. *Building a Character*, 21st ed. Translated by Elizabeth Reynolds Hapgood. New York: Routledge Theatre Arts Books, 1987.
———. *Creating a Role*. 12th ed. Translated by Elizabeth Reynolds Hapgood. New York: Routledge Theatre Arts Books, 1988.
Stephens, Michelle Ann. *Black Empire: The Masculine Global Imaginary of Caribbean Intellectuals in the United States 1914–1962*. Durham: Duke University Press, 2005.
Stewart, Jeffrey C., ed. *Paul Robeson: Artist and Citizen*. New Brunswick: Rutgers University Press, 1998.
Stuckey, Sterling. "'I Want to Be African': Paul Robeson and the Ends of Nationalist Theory and Practice 1914–1945." *Massachusetts Review* 17 (Spring 1976): 81–138.
Thelwell, Michael. *Duties, Pleasures, and Conflicts: Essays in Struggle*. Amherst: University of Massachusetts Press, 1987.
Trewin, J.C. *Shakespeare on the English Stage 1900–1964*. London: Barrie and Rockliff, 1964.

Vaughan, Virginia Mason. *Othello: A Contextual History*. Cambridge: Cambridge University Press, 1994.
Von Eschen, Penny. *Race against Empire: Black Americans and Anti-Colonialism 1937–1957*. Ithaca: Cornell University Press, 1997.
Whalum, Wendell Phillips. "James Weldon Johnson's Theories and Performance Practices of Afro-American Folksong." *Phylon* 32 (Fourth Quarter 1971): 383–95.
Woodring, Carl, ed. *Table Talk Vol. II*. In *The Collected Works of Samuel Taylor Coleridge*, edited by Kathleen Coburn. Princeton: Princeton University Press, 1990.
Worcester, Kent. *C. L. R. James: A Political Biography*. Albany: State University of New York Press, 1996.
Worthen, William B. "Stanislavsky and the Ethos of Acting." *Theatre Journal* 35 (March 1983): 32–40.
Yeakey, Lamont H. "A Student Without Peer: The Undergraduate College Years of Paul Robeson." *The Journal of Negro Education* 42 (Autumn 1973): 489–503.
Zacharia, Don. "My Legacy." *Kenyon Review* (Winter 1985): 97–110.

RECORDINGS

Paul Robeson Live at Carnegie Hall: The Historic May 9, 1959 Concert. Vanguard Records, 1987.
Paul Robeson: The Peace Arch Concerts. Folk Era Records, 1998.
Shakespeare, William. *Othello*. Cast recording. New York: Columbia Records, 1951.

DISSERTATIONS AND OTHER UNPUBLISHED ITEMS

Baraka, Amiri. "Paul Robeson and the Theater." Paper presented at the International Conference on Paul Robeson, Lafayette College, 2005. Copy purchased from author.
Bourne, St. Clair. Transcripts of interviews with Uta Hagen and Ossie Davis for film *Paul Robeson: Here I Stand*. Menair Media, 1999. Transcripts provided by director.
Brousseau, Elaine. "'Now Literature, Philosophy, and Thought, Are Shakespearized': American Culture and Nineteenth-Century Shakespearean Performance 1835–1875." Dissertation, University of Massachusetts, 2003.
Carroll, Janet Barton. "A Promptbook Study of Margaret Webster's Production of Othello." Dissertation, Louisiana State University, 1977.
Lamphere, Lawrence. "Paul Robeson, Freedom Newspaper and the Black Press." Dissertation, Boston College, 2003.
McCartney, John. "The Influence of Marxism-Leninism on Paul Robeson's Intellectual Development." Paper presented at the Conference on Paul Robeson, Lafayette College, 2005.
Perucci, Anthony Thomas. "Tonal Treason: Paul Robeson and the Politics of the Cold War." Dissertation, New York University, 2004.
Powers, Joe, and Mark Rogovin. "Paul Robeson Rediscovered: An Annotated Listing of His Chicago History 1921–1958." Chicago: Columbia College Paul Robeson 100th Birthday Committee, 1998.
Scholsser, Anatol. "Paul Robeson: His Career in the Theater, in Motion Pictures and on the Concert Stage." Dissertation, New York University, 1970.

Silverman, Ely. "Margaret Webster's Theory and Practice of Shakespearean Production in the United States 1937–1953." Dissertation, New York University, 1969.

Streater, John Baxter. "The National Negro Congress 1936–1947." Dissertation, University of Cincinnati, 1981.

Welch, Rebeccah. "Black Art and Activism in Postwar New York 1950–1965." Dissertation, New York University, 2002.

INDEX

Aaron the Moor (*Titus Andronicus*), 12, 15, 22
Abraham Lincoln Brigade, 52, 68
Africa: Bandung conference and, 149–50; CAA and, 52, 123–24, 130, 137, 140–41, 148; civil rights and, 168–69; colonies in, 8, 10, 61, 66, 140, 148, 169; culture of, 10, 23, 33, 52, 113; Elizabethan England and, 12–15, 29; *Freedom* on, 138–39; C. L. R. James on, 60, 62–64; Robeson on, 33, 53–59, 61, 64, 101, 126, 136, 139, 146, 148–49, 151–52, 157, 160, 163–64, 166–67, 181, 185, 191; and slavery, 23, 92; WWII and, 112, 116, 123. *See also* Colonialism; Self determination; South Africa
Africanus, Leo, 14, 29
Aldridge, Amanda, 23, 34
Aldridge, Ira, viii, 7, 15, 20, 22, 23, 34, 38, 98, 106, 107, 119, 147
All God's Chillun Got Wings, 5
American Federation of Labor (AFL), 26
A.M.E. Zion Church, 5, 24, 58, 142, 164
Anticommunism: colonialism and, 136, 148–49, 152, 167, 169; Peekskill and, 132; Robeson's passport case and, 118; after WWII, 8, 127, 128, 136–37, 158, 169. *See also* Communism; Communist Party in U.S.
Antifascism: Robeson's position on, 8, 52, 61, 64–67, 71, 105–6, 108, 109, 121, 127, 135, 194; Soviet Union and, 128; U.S. policy and, 125. *See also* Fascism

Arab vs. Ethiopian debate, concerning Othello's character, 29, 42, 47, 87
Ashcroft, Peggy, 31–32, 34–35, 38–39, 42, 49, 78, 170, 177, 182

"Ballad for Americans," 111–12, 128
Bandung conference, 137, 140, 149
Bethune, Mary McLeod, 119, 124, 130
Broadway, 4, 7, 10, 16, 20, 40, 49, 51, 121, 126, 137, 160, 162, 184, 193; *Othello* revival on, 10, 19, 20, 33, 35, 38, 52, 60, 64, 69–107, 108–10, 115, 117, 135, 169, 175, 177, 179, 180, 185, 194
Brown, Lawrence, 37, 120, 157, 186–87
Brown, Lloyd, 138, 143, 147, 192
Browne, Maurice, 28, 32–37, 39, 43, 46, 48–49, 77

Canada, 104, 147; concerts at Peace Arch Park, 157, 160; Robeson turned away at border, 155
Carnegie Hall, 26, 59, 162–63
Civil Rights Congress (CRC), 51, 123, 132, 137, 153; dissolution of, 155, 164, 168; petition to United Nations, 154
Cold war: anticommunism and, 132, 149, 184; Bandung conference and, 149; colonies in Africa and, 128, 139, 168; HUAC and, 158; Paris Peace Conference and, 128, 130; passport revocations during, 145, 172; peace with Soviets during, 25, 123, 135; repression of civil liberties in U.S.

during, 5, 8, 132, 135, 150–51, 160, 169; Robeson's repertoire during, 10, 132, 137, 152–66, 189; Stratford *Othello* revival and, 7, 177, 180, 181, 194; U.S. foreign policy during, 141, 190

Colonialism: Britain and, 12, 59, 62, 99, 180; and cultural theory, 13; W. E. B. Du Bois on, 130; C. L. R. James on, 62–63, 99; Robeson on, 60–61, 64, 67, 75, 128, 135, 145–46, 157, 194; Soviet Union and, 164; struggle against, 63–64, 123–24, 139, 148–49; U.S. policy and, 8, 124, 136, 140, 148

Communism: and African Americans, 51, 164; in China, 129; HUAC and, 158–59; and Korea, 136; Truman Doctrine and, 136. *See also* Anticommunism; Communist Party in U.S.

Communist Party in U.S. (CPUSA): and African Americans, 165; cold war and, 152; Du Bois joins, 168; and "front" organizations, 140, 146; indictment of leaders, 136, 146, 153; leaders in, 51, 116, 132, 153; Lincoln Brigade and, 68; organizing in 1930s, 26; Robeson and, 62, 83, 126, 128, 142, 150–51, 159, 160, 164–65, 168, 184, 192–93; WWII and, 115. *See also* Anticommunism; Communism

Congress of the World Partisans of Peace (Paris Peace Conference), 128–30

Council on African Affairs (CAA), 19, 109, 112, 123, 137, 139; and cold war, 140–41; on colonial issues, 148; coverage of Paris Peace Conference, 129, 131; dissolution of, 155, 164, 168; famine relief, 130; founding of, 52; response to Peekskill, 132, 133; sponsor of *Othello* performance, 118

Daily Worker, 7, 66, 92, 123, 131, 132, 140, 144, 148, 155, 160, 163, 176, 179, 180, 183, 188

Davis, Benjamin, 5, 105, 116, 124, 144

Davis, Ossie, 6, 93–94, 192

Desdemona (*Othello*), 12, 15–18, 28, 29, 58, 73, 89, 163, 175, 177; Peggy Ashcroft as, 31, 34; Uta Hagen as, 72, 76–78, 84, 90, 99; Mary Ure as, 170, 173, 177, 182, 184

Dignity: during cold war repression, 10, 137, 154, 164, 177, 194; and fight against racial oppression, 5–6, 10, 59, 64, 71, 93–94, 110–11, 117, 133–34, 158, 161, 163, 181; and Robeson's character, 36, 38, 80, 188; and Robeson's Othello interpretation, 4, 18, 29, 38–39, 41, 83, 92, 94–95, 98, 103, 119, 163, 179–80, 182; and theater audience, 7, 106; and Toussaint role, 64

Double Victory campaign ("Double V"), 64, 70, 116, 119, 122

Douglass, Frederick, 93, 146–47, 159

Du Bois, Shirley Graham, 179, 185, 188

Du Bois, W. E. B.: on black culture, 56, 93, 110–11; and CAA, 124; and *Freedom*, 138; and Ghana, 168, 191; and Paris Peace Conference, 129–30; passport case, 145, 185; on Robeson, 143; on Robeson's Othello, 91, 189; and Soviet Union, 51, 128; on WWII, 116

Eisenhower, Dwight, 149, 167

Elizabethan era, 7, 12, 29, 45, 61, 73, 99

Emperor Jones, The, 5–6, 35, 50

England. *See* Great Britain

Entertainment Industry Emergency Committee, 3

Espionage Act, 25, 136

Ethiopia, Italian invasion of, 60, 63–66

Fair Employment Practices Committee (FEPC), 116

Fascism: "Ballad for Americans" and, 112; domestic manifestations of, 4, 131, 133; Double Victory campaign against, 64, 70, 116, 122; in Europe in the 1930s, 50, 52, 65, 66, 120; WWII and, 3, 67, 75, 76, 110, 115, 122. *See also* Antifascism

Fast, Howard, 132, 138, 145

Federal Bureau of Investigation (FBI), 96, 112, 136, 144, 155, 158

INDEX

Ferrer, José, 76, 80–81, 84–86, 89, 95–96, 100–1, 103, 105, 126
Freedom, 57, 59, 135, 137–43, 146, 154, 160–61, 164, 168

Garvey, Marcus, 14, 62
Ghana, 148, 167–68, 180, 191
Great Britain: and Africa, 12, 13, 148, 167, 180; Ira Aldridge and, 20, 22; C. L. R. James and, 150, 152; race prejudice in, 32, 77; Robeson and, 8, 26, 55, 137, 145, 152, 157, 164, 168, 169, 170–72, 175, 177, 179, 181, 184–86, 188, 194; Shakespearean performance in, 11, 15, 17, 29, 34, 61, 72; U.S. and, 125

Hagen, Uta, 72, 76, 78, 81, 84–87, 90, 99, 100, 104–5, 177
Haitian revolution, 52, 60–61, 63
Hansberry, Lorraine, 138, 184
Harlem, New York, 3, 5, 21, 36, 56, 87–88, 97, 109, 123, 131, 132, 152
Harlem Renaissance, 55, 57
Here I Stand, 9, 24, 26, 66, 101, 131, 137, 138, 142–46, 149, 151, 165, 192
"Here's My Story," 4, 57, 135, 138–39, 142, 146, 161
House Un-American Activities Committee (HUAC), 136, 158–59, 173; Robeson's testimony, 155, 160, 169, 180; and Jackie Robinson, 122, 131
Hughes, Langston, 51, 97, 99, 110
Hunton, W. Alphaeus, 123, 138–40, 168, 181, 185
Hurston, Zora Neale, 109

Iago (*Othello*), 15–16, 33, 45, 58, 72, 73, 77, 105, 165, 174; Maurice Browne as, 34, 36, 39, 46, 48, 77; José Ferrer as, 76, 80–84, 89, 96, 97, 126; Sam Wanamaker as, 173, 182–83
Independence. *See* Self determination

James, C. L. R.: deportation of, 150–52; on postcolonial Africa, 63–64; on prejudice in London, 32; on Robeson, 55, 62, 99; on Shakespeare, 6, 74–75, 98–99; and *Toussaint Louverture*, 6, 52, 59–65

Kean, Edmund, 12, 14–15, 17, 22, 30
Kennedy, John F., 190, 191
King, Martin Luther, Jr., 140, 141, 167, 168, 190–92
King Lear, 13, 22, 50, 170
Korean War, 136, 139, 141, 193

League of Coloured Peoples, 33, 52, 65
Lee, Canada, 3, 105
L'Ouverture, Toussaint: C. L. R. James's play on, 6, 10, 52, 55, 59–65, 98, 150; Wendell Phillips's oration on, 24
Lynching, campaigns to outlaw, 24, 93, 108, 124–26, 139, 154, 191

Macbeth, 13, 19, 20, 22, 72
March on Washington: A. Philip Randolph's movement, 116–17; march in 1963, 190, 192
Mays, Benjamin, 91, 121, 122
McCarran Act, 136, 139, 140, 155
McKay, Claude, 51, 57
Method acting. *See* Stanislavsky, Constantin

National Association for the Advancement of Colored People (NAACP), 21, 116, 117, 122, 130, 139; Spingarn medal to Robeson, 121
National Negro Congress (NNC), 112, 116, 153
New Africa/Spotlight on Africa (newsletter), 109, 123, 140, 148
New Deal, 19, 51, 96, 119, 158

O'Neill, Eugene, 6, 50
Oratory, 5, 20, 23–25, 47, 58, 101
Othello (*Othello*): final monologue in Robeson's repertoire, 10, 59, 128, 137, 160, 162, 165, 188; Robeson's interpretation of, 7, 10, 26–33; Tommaso Salvini as, 17; Shakespeare

and, 7, 13–16, 41, 58, 74, 89, 91, 92, 94.
  See also Aldridge, Ira; Kean, Edmund
Othello: background on, 7, 11–25;
  Broadway revival of, 69–107; London
  revival of, 26–49; and Robeson's
  passport case, 137, 145–52; Stratford
  revival of, 167–89
Othello Recording Corporation, 143–44

Paris Peace Conference (Congress of the
  World Partisans of Peace), 128–30
Passport case, Robeson's, 10, 114, 136–37,
  139, 142, 145–52, 154–57, 159, 162–64,
  167, 169–72, 175, 177, 180, 186, 188, 191
Patterson, Louise Thompson, 132–33
Patterson, William, 51, 132, 153, 181
Paul Robeson, Negro, 36–38
Peekskill concerts, 131–33
People's Voice newspaper, 4, 88, 103, 104,
  112, 114, 116
Popular Front, 19, 111–12
Powell, Adam Clayton, Jr., 88, 116, 123,
  124, 130

Randolph, A. Philip, 116, 190
Reviews of *Othello* productions:
  Broadway, 82–84, 87–92, 95–101;
  London, 39–49; Stratford, 177–85
Robeson, Eslanda (wife): biography of
  Robeson, 34, 36–38, 101; on Broadway
  Othello, 84; and *Freedom*, 138; on
  London *Othello*, 35, 48–49; press
  releases by, 172, 191; on Stratford
  Othello, 186
Robeson, Paul: on Africa, 33, 53–59, 61,
  64, 101, 126, 136, 139, 146, 148–49,
  151–52, 157, 160, 163–64, 166–67, 181,
  185, 191; on African culture, 53–59; and
  antifascism, 8, 52, 61, 64–67, 71, 105–6,
  108–9, 121, 127, 135, 194; and "Ballad
  for Americans," 112; and Bandung
  conference, 137, 140, 149; in Broadway
  Othello, 69–107; at Carnegie Hall, 26,
  59, 162–63; on colonialism, 60–61,
  64, 67, 75, 128, 135, 145–46, 157, 194;
  and Communist Party in U.S., 62,
  83, 126, 128, 142, 150–51, 159, 160,
  164–65, 168, 184, 192–93; and dignity
  in Othello interpretation, 4, 18, 29,
  38–39, 41, 83, 92, 94–95, 98, 103, 119,
  163, 179–80, 182; in *The Emperor
  Jones*, 5, 6, 35, 50; and FBI, 96, 112,
  136, 144, 155, 158; in *Freedom*, 4, 57,
  135, 138–39, 142, 146, 161; and Great
  Britain, 8, 26, 55, 137, 145, 152, 157, 164,
  168–72, 175, 177, 181, 184–86, 188, 194;
  and *Here I Stand*, 9, 24, 26, 66, 101,
  131, 137–38, 142–46, 149, 151, 165, 192;
  HUAC testimony, 155, 160, 169, 180;
  interpretation of Othello character, 7,
  10, 26–33; in London *Othello*, 26–49;
  and oratory, 5, 20, 23–25, 47, 58, 101;
  and Paris Peace Conference, 128–30;
  and passport case, 137, 145–52; in *Paul
  Robeson, Negro*, 36–38; and Peace
  Arch Park concerts, 157, 160; and
  Peekskill, 131–33; repertoire during
  cold war, 10, 132, 137, 152–66, 189;
  Jackie Robinson on, 117, 122, 131; at
  Rutgers, 5, 24–26, 51, 102, 109, 117; in
  Sanders of the River, 6, 33, 65, 113; on
  self determination for colonies, 8, 10,
  61, 67, 126, 128, 135, 145, 157, 160, 166,
  181, 191, 194; on Shakespeare, 26–33,
  55; in *Show Boat*, 5, 51; on South
  Africa, 146; and Soviet Union, 51, 160,
  164–66; speech at Royal Albert Hall
  1937, 67; in Stratford *Othello*, 167–89;
  in *Tales of Manhattan*, 6, 113–15; and
  theater segregation, 7, 10, 102, 104,
  106, 127, 162; in *Toussaint Louverture*,
  6, 52, 59–65; turned away at Canadian
  border, 155; and Margaret Webster, 49,
  71, 76, 85–86, 100–1; and *We Charge
  Genocide* (CRC petition), 51, 153–54;
  and West African Students Union, 33,
  52. *See also* A.M.E. Zion church; Civil
  Rights Congress; Council on African
  Affairs; Lynching; Method acting;
  Othello Recording Corporation;
  Spirituals
Robeson, Paul, Jr., 36–37, 143
Robeson, William D. (father), 4, 5, 23–25,
  109, 135, 187

Robinson, Jackie, 117, 122, 131
Roosevelt, Franklin D., 96, 116, 119, 120
Royal Shakespeare Company, viii, 22, 170, 178, 182
Rutgers University, 5, 24–26, 51, 102, 109, 117

Sanders of the River, 6, 33, 65, 113
Savoy Theatre (London), 33–35, 38–39, 41, 45–46, 49, 76, 176
Self determination: African colonies and, 148–49, 167, 169, 180–81; Bandung conference and, 149; CAA and, 124, 137, 140; C. L. R. James on, 63–64; *Freedom* on, 138–39; Robeson on, 8, 10, 61, 67, 126, 128, 135, 145, 157, 160, 166, 181, 191, 194; Robeson's passport case and, 136, 146, 148, 151–52, 169
Shakespeare, William: and character of Othello, 7, 13–16, 41, 58, 74, 89, 91, 92, 94; festival in Stratford for, 169–70; and Globe Theatre, 45; C. L. R. James on, 6, 61, 74–75, 99; and language, 45, 57–58, 79, 99, 174; plays in African American community, 20–25; plays in U.S., 18–20; Robeson on, 26–33, 55; and writing of *Othello*, 11–13, 74, 77
Shakespeare Without Tears, 72–73
Show Boat, 5, 51
Shubert Theatre (New York), 3, 87
Slavery/slave trade, 4, 12–15, 20, 23–25, 30, 54, 67, 92–93, 107, 126, 128, 130, 143, 146, 187
Smith Act, 136, 153, 155
South Africa: famine relief in, 110, 123–24, 130, 139; in *Freedom*, 138–39; Robeson on, 146; U.N. votes and, 148
Soviet Union: anticolonialism and, 148–49; critique of U.S. race relations, 154, 165, 190; peace after WWII with, 4, 8, 25, 61, 112, 122–23, 128, 129, 131, 135; Robeson's position on, 160, 164–66; Robeson's Spingarn medal speech on, 122; Robeson's visits to, 51, 164, 165; role in WWII, 122
Spanish civil war, 7, 10, 53, 65. *See also* Abraham Lincoln Brigade

Spirituals, 5, 24, 52, 54–56, 101, 160–61, 164, 187
Spotlight on Africa/New Africa (CAA newsletter), 109, 123, 140, 148
Stanislavsky, Constantin, 17, 69, 86, 101–3
State Department (U.S.), 10, 139, 142, 145–46, 148, 150–52, 157, 162, 169, 170
Subversive Activities Control Board (SACB), 139–40

Tales of Manhattan, 6, 113–15
Theater segregation, 7, 10, 102, 104, 106, 127, 162
Theatre Guild, 77, 84, 87, 90–91, 100
Thorndike, Sybil, 32, 34, 39, 42, 45, 47, 49, 72, 176, 182
Truman, Harry, 96, 120, 122, 125, 126, 136, 160

United Nations (U.N.), 51, 119, 124, 140, 147–48, 153–54

Van Volkenburg, Ellen, 28, 33, 35–36, 43, 45–46, 48–49
Vietnam War, 141, 193

Washington, Fredi, 4
Webster, Margaret: as an actor, 77; background, 71–72; as a director, 19, 72, 73, 77–78, 80, 82, 87, 89, 90, 95–96, 105; letters to parents, 81, 84, 85, 88; on *Othello*, 35, 70, 72–74, 83, 89; and *Othello* cast, 84, 100; and Robeson, 49, 71, 76, 85–86, 100–1
We Charge Genocide (CRC petition), 51, 153–54
West African Students Union, 33, 52
White, Walter, 116, 122, 125, 130
Worker, The. See *Daily Worker*
World War I, 24, 116, 136
World War II, 8, 10, 33, 60, 64, 67, 69, 75, 76, 106, 115, 116, 123, 128, 135

Yergan, Max, 52, 123